Let the Bones Dance

Let the Bones Dance

*Embodiment and the
Body of Christ*

Marcia W. Mount Shoop

WESTMINSTER
JOHN KNOX PRESS
LOUISVILLE · KENTUCKY

First edition
Published by Westminster John Knox Press
Louisville, Kentucky

10 11 12 13 14 15 16 17 18 19—10 9 8 7 6 5 4 3 2 1

Scripture quotations from the New Revised Standard Version of the Bible are copyright © 1989 by the Division of Christian Education of the National Council of the Churches of Christ in the U.S.A. and are used by permission.

"Stabat Mater" in FEMINIST SOCIAL THOUGHT: A READER (PAPER) by Julia Kristeva. Copyright 1997 by TAYLOR & FRANCIS GROUP LLC—BOOKS. Reproduced with permission of TAYLOR & FRANCIS GROUP LLC—BOOKS in the format Other book via Copyright Clearance Center.

"Women" Copyright © 1993 by Adrienne Rich. Copyright © 1969 by W. W. Norton & Company, Inc., from COLLECTED EARLY POEMS: 1950–1970 by Adrienne Rich. Used by permission of the author and W. W. Norton & Company, Inc.

Book design by Sharon Adams
Cover design by Lisa Buckley
Cover art © Magda Indigo/Getty Images

Library of Congress Cataloging-in-Publication Data
Mount Shoop, Marcia W.
    Let the bones dance : embodiment and the body of Christ / Marcia W. Mount Shoop.—1st ed.
        p. cm.—(Emerging theology initiative)
        Revision of the author's thesis (Ph.D.)—Emory University.
        Includes bibliographical references (p.) and index.
        ISBN 978-0-664-23412-6 (alk. paper)
        1. Church. 2. Human body—Religious aspects—Protestant churches.
    3. Experience (Religion) 4. Feminist theology. I. Title.
        BV600.3.M68 2010
        233—dc22

                                                                2010003816

Women

My three sisters are sitting
on rocks of black obsidian.
For the first time, in this light, I can see who they are.

My first sister is sewing her costume for the procession.
She is going as the Transparent Lady
and all her nerves will be visible.

My second sister is also sewing,
at the seam over her heart which has never healed entirely.
At last, she hopes, this tightness in her chest will ease.

My third sister is gazing
at a dark-red crust spreading westward far out on the sea.
Her stockings are torn but she is beautiful.

Adrienne Rich, *Leaflets*

Contents

PART II: THE (EM)BODY(MENT) OF CHRIST

Acknowledgments

Working on this book has spanned life in six different cities stretching across and around this country, the births of two babies and the loss of another to miscarriage, pastorates in two different churches, stints as theologian in residence in two others, as well as the blessing of people I met when lecturing, leading retreats, teaching, preaching, and facilitating in too many churches, conferences, and events to count right now. There is no way to thank everyone or every community that has nurtured me, trusted me, called me, and challenged me since this project first began.

This book is a rewrite of my dissertation. I was fortunate to have a dissertation committee at Emory University (Wendy Farley, Rebecca Chopp, and Elizabeth Bounds) who believe in my ability to do constructive theology, so the core of this project reflects the heart of my dissertation. The rewrite reflects the six years of parish ministry that came after I finished this project and witnessed how this constructive work hit the ground in the church and in the lives of the people I served in those churches.

The intersecting triads that inform this project came into clarity for me while I was pregnant with my son. I was too sick to read, to work, to even move much. All I had was time to think, to pray, and, most importantly, to feel. It was during that time that this project began to flow. Then four years later, my dissertation finished and my Ph.D. earned, I went through another difficult pregnancy, another displacement to a new city, another birth. The heart of this project became even more "live" for me. So I must begin by thanking my son, Sidney Ellis Shoop, and my daughter, Mary Elizabeth Shoop. Their proximity to me these last ten years has inscribed what I express in this book deeply in who I am.

Thanks also to my husband, John Mount Shoop, who has been a source of affirmation, encouragement, and love. His work as a football coach in the

NFL and now in Division I college football takes him away from home way too much, but he consistently finds ways to extend to me steady and heartfelt support for my writing. Having someone who believes what you are doing is worth doing is a great, great gift. I am thankful for his particular kind of "you can do this" in my life.

My parents, Eric and Truly Mount, have read versions of this work with their grammatical eagle eyes. My thanks to them for the way they cleaned up sentence structures and errant commas. Any dangling participles or grammatical hiccups the reader may find are my own doing and must have been added after their last reading! My sisters Diane, Laurie, and Mary Faith are three smart, funny, and intense women who also leave traces of themselves in this work. My oldest sister, Allison, died before the rest of us were born. She is with us still partly as an awareness of tragedy and what Christ's compassion feels like in the lives that fold out of loss and grief. I am ever thankful for the way all of my sisters give me a way to interpret and process life. Each of them brings unique layers to how this project has taken shape.

Thanks are due to Christine Hartman, a poet and my husband's cousin. She lived with us during the early stages of this project. She was a stellar proofreader, and her poetic sensitivities and encouragement helped me step out into new territory in my writing. I know this project is better for her involvement. She also provided the first child care I ever had so I could write.

Wendy Farley, my doctoral advisor and now a dear friend, has walked with me in all the incarnations of this project. She has read chapters, and she has listened to me think aloud. Her most profound gift to me is that she understands. Our common intuitions and experiences make for a relationship that is not only intellectually stimulating, but remarkably edifying spiritually. Without her support in this work, I know I could not have found the courage or the words I needed to see it to this stage of publication. I thank Wendy for her generous spirit, for her healing presence, for her theological imagination, and for her resistance to things that could trivialize what can be.

First Presbyterian Church in Libertyville, IL; Palma Ceia Presbyterian Church in Tampa, FL; First Presbyterian Church in Oakland, CA; and University Presbyterian Church in Chapel Hill, NC, all welcomed me into their communities in a variety of ways as preacher, teacher, and pastor. The wonderful curiosity and earnest questioning of many members of these communities pushed this work along. They helped me find ways to translate difficult concepts into accessible conversations. They were honest with me and they let me into their lives. I also owe Fourth Presbyterian Church in Chicago, IL, my thanks for the good people who took my class in their Lay Academy back when these ideas were just finding expression. And there are many, many others who have come to classes, lectures, workshops, and retreats who have etched themselves into this work all to its betterment. I especially acknowledge all the women who have come to me to tell of their own untold experiences of sexual violence. Thanks be to God for those healing opportunities.

Many colleagues along the way have taken time and expended energy to support this work. I cannot name them all, but a few stand out. Molly Hadley Jensen and her husband, David, are friends and colleagues who have common commitments to embodiment. Late-night conversations in seminary with Molly were full of fine thinking (and hilarity!), and David has been a great advocate of this book in particular. Barbara McClure, also a dear friend and colleague, has been a similar part in clarifying conversation and theological partnership. Members of my writing group here in Chapel Hill (Lyn Hawks, Laurie Maffley-Kipp, Katie Ricks, Beverly Rudolph, and Susan Steinberg) have listened to pieces of this work, read chapters, and blessed it with their affirmations. Their skill at many different kinds of writing from poetry to fiction to sermon to academic has made our collaborations something that particularly helped this book's accessibility.

Others fed this work with the ways they cared for me and taught me about bodies in times of both my own great pain and robust health. Susan Panitch, Rita Jones, Eva Lindsay, Ann Ehringhaus, Stephanie Nussbaum, the Way of Holiness congregation, Seigle Avenue Presbyterian Church choir, along with good doctors, midwives, doulas, and caregivers who have come in and out of my life in all of our moves have shown me "the way" through and into what it means to live in a body.

There are also others who stretch my awareness and take me into places past my own experiences. They are friends who grew up in different cultures than I have, fellow believers who have different views and interpretations of Scripture than I, and family members who need very different things than I do. I am particularly blessed by my godson, Chris Dixon. I thank also the Presbyterian Multicultural Network national board and other friends who have come to me via my work in the multicultural movement in the PC(USA). Our shared vision of the church deeply informs the second half of this book.

I wrote this book because I love the church. That love is in my blood, stretching back into generations in my family of ordained ministers, elders, Sunday school teachers, church builders, and choir members. I am thankful for the ways my grandfathers and grandmothers speak to me from the history of the church. And for the pastoral sensitivities they passed on to me. Their wisdom about how to love people and congregations makes this book not just an academic project but an offering to the church and an act of love and compassion for all believers.

Special thanks to Don McKim, my editor and an author's pastor to be sure. He has been a source of affirmation and direction as well as a valued source of wisdom about what publishing is all about. I appreciate all the ways he takes extra time for conversations and explanations—a gift for a first-time author who doesn't know the ropes! Thanks also to David Dobson, who took time to learn more about this project.

Finally, thanks to my constant companions—the creatures who are always here with me. My dogs Tino (now deceased), Millie, and Buck have walked with me (literally) for countless hours. They sit near me (as did my late cat, Mable) when I write and move through the days with utter attentiveness and expectation. And to my spirited Appaloosa, Zip's Night Traveler, my thanks are due for lessons in intuition and breathing deeply. Horses are not just beautiful; they are conduits of all the layers of experience that we humans tend to ignore. Traveler re-members how deeply we are all connected to everything that is; and an adventuresome dance is always just an open field and a good trail ride away.

Marcia Mount Shoop
Chapel Hill, NC

Foreword

Marcia Mount Shoop takes us into territory mainline Protestants rarely go. She commits many and pronounced violations against Presbyterian propriety. She does not provide a nice, academic feminist critique of theological anthropology. She does not gently suggest we might be somewhat more inclusive in our worship. She uses her formidable academic training to tramp into our heads and hearts to set off one firestorm after another. Both in her theology and in her writing style she engages in guerrilla warfare against the disembodied, intellectualistic, fearful, and homogenizing faith and practice of the Presbyterian Church. Like myself a granddaughter, daughter, and sister of Presbyterian ministers, I read her with amazed and delighted wonder. Calvin himself could hardly have written more passionately or more provocatively as he called the church toward reform.

She writes out of a sublimely deployed frustration that the bodies of women and men and the Body of Christ itself are so thoroughly erased from the theology and practices of the church. For her this forgetfulness is a betrayal of the joyous creation and compassionate redemption the Holy Trinity offers us. To borrow words from Julian of Norwich: God does not despise what God has made. Because we cannot let our faith attend to our embodied existence, we exile most of our real selves from the loving and healing power of the Divine. We wrongly rely exclusively on the language of sin to describe our condition and our relationship to God. We modestly confess our sins while our broken bodies and souls contort themselves into invisibility. She writes: "Church had never been where I could tell the truth that my life did not fit together the way it was supposed to." The sufferings of so many Presbyterians are like bastard children: we are vaguely aware of them but it would be unseemly to acknowledge them in public. But Marcia insists that we are betraying the body of Christ when we let these bastard children wander homeless, unconsoled by a faith community's compassionate care.

Bodies are not only fragile and vulnerable, they are also wildly diverse. With a delicate sense of the absurd beauty of all of God's lovely, wise children, Marcia Mount Shoop displays the variety of bodies that bear Christ's image. She gently reminds us that our anxieties imprison us in a sanitized homogenization. The spirited variations embodied by race, by wandering street people, by energetic styles of music and worship are denigrated or invisible. We betray the body of Christ when our fears defraud us of the adventure of welcoming more of the audacious beauty of Christ's family into our own. We are embodied and our bodies are diverse, imperfect, suffering, interdependent sites of compassion and adventure. Our liturgy and our theology conspire to reinforce our fears that speaking the truth about bodies would be unseemly, inappropriate in God's house. But what if God wishes to meet us precisely as we were created—embodied, suffering, confused, unique? "What if telling the truth really does set us free? What if living a lie really does afflict us?"

Marcia's energy is not primarily critical. She is determined to show us alternative ways of dwelling in our Reformed heritage. Though deeply appreciative of the high value placed on intellectual honesty and education, she shows us that these values need not condemn us to a disembodied, passionless faith. A staunch defender of the principles of social justice that vivify Reformed piety, she unveils a faith that is not only activist but contemplative, not only ethically committed but nurturing and joyous. Like the great nineteenth-century theologian Friedrich Schleiermacher, she insists that piety is not birthed in the intellect or as ethics, though it certainly must be expressed in these places. Piety is deeper than thought and will. It dwells in our bodies, in the preconscious formation of psyche and community. To convey this depth dimension of faith, Marcia borrows from Alfred North Whitehead's analysis of "feeling": not emotion but the precognitive ground from which thought, emotion, memory, intention, commitment emerge. Few Protestant theologians have attempted to seek this precognitive ground of our brokenness and of our healing. If she did nothing else in her book, her ability to provide a language for faith that is not reducible to belief and action, cognition and ethics, would make the book indispensable for rethinking faith.

Because the book is in many ways so radical, it might be easy to miss the conventional structure that animates it. Marcia is a fourth-generation Presbyterian minister. It is as if not only her education and liturgical formation but her cells and DNA bear witness to Reformed sensibilities. It is from thoroughly inside this tradition, by training and disposition and heritage, that she reconstructs it. Delving deeply into the basic structures of Reformed thought, Marcia Mount Shoop refracts a theology of the human condition through bodily wisdom. Systematic theology typically juxtaposes sin and redemption. We look at the human condition once through the distortions of sin, original and actual, and a second time as this condition is transformed by the justification and sanctification of

Christ. Marcia retains this pattern but inflates it quite differently. This double exposure of the human condition by sin and redemption receives its content from a repeating threefold pattern. What Augustine might call "vestiges of the Trinity" structure the deep symbols of fall, redemption, and eschatological community that lurk under the surface of her reembodiment of Protestant faith.

The first trinity is the witness from bodies that have been cut out of the theological conversation. What do bodies contribute to theology's struggle to describe the human condition through the symbols of faith? Marcia chooses three aspects of embodied existence as prisms through which our common condition can be interpreted: tragedy, relationality, and ambiguity. These three aspects of embodiment define and structure our infinitely varied experiences. We suffer in ways that we find unspeakable. We are entwined with the lives of other beings as near to us as our own flesh and blood and as removed from us as butterflies stamping on the other side of the planet. We wish for neat and well-defined situations and values, but much of our experience turns out to be a mixture of good and evil, clarity and confusion, situations that delight and constrain us. These features of our lives are precisely ones that genuinely do shape human lives as deeply as anything possibly can and yet find little or no acknowledgment in churches. The witness of bodies is largely absent from church. The witness of women's bodies is doubly so. To correct this, Marcia chooses to display these features of our lives through analysis of women's embodied experience. Rape becomes the prism through which we recognize the condition of tragedy to which we are subject. Pregnancy becomes the prism through which relationality is explored. Motherhood becomes the prism that exposes the deep ambiguity we so often fear to acknowledge.

Having highlighted for us deep structures of our fate, she turns to Christ to see the pattern redemption writes over these inevitabilities. In the light of Christ, tragedy, relationship, and ambiguity are not erased but they are transformed. Redemption opens tragedy toward a disposition of compassion. Relationship becomes interdependence. Ambiguity is backlit by adventure. It would be typical of a Protestant theologian to leave it at that: sin and salvation described and defined with Christ as the door that opened from one to the other. But here too Marcia takes us in a little different direction. She does not stay with the individualistic frame that is implied in the excruciating concreteness of rape, pregnancy, and motherhood. She moves with great exuberance from individual bodies marked by tragedy, relationship, and ambiguity to the corporate body. Redemption is not individualistic but communal. If it is as individuals that we struggle with the ambiguities of fate and tragedy, it is through community that we find redemption. The healing body is the body of Christ.

A third trinity inspires the last portion of the book. Healing occurs in community and through liturgy. But it is liturgy in particular that presupposes and reinforces the delusion of disembodiment. The compassion, interdependence, and adventure that our bodies and souls crave are only imperfectly captured by the stiff and refined worship of "God's frozen chosen." Marcia reflects on confession, Eucharist, and music as dimensions of worship through which our difficulties might be acknowledged and our healing might be nourished. Confession might be not only acknowledgment of sin but acknowledgment of our pain and difficulty. It might become a way to recognize how our fears block us from a fuller movement into the mercy and joy of God. Eucharist might become a place where Jesus dwells in us, not as perfectible beings but as wounded ones. We put our own bodies and the Body of Christ back together through this eucharistic body. Music might expand, as it does in many churches, to include a variety of forms. Marcia quotes Calvin to remind us that we abuse God's sacred name when our singing does not come from the deepest places of our heart. She imagines communities in which barriers of class, education, race, sexual preference, and aesthetic sensibilities might open up toward a new adventure of faith. She encourages us to drink deeply from our heritage: "this legacy of trusting God's flame in each of us to guide us in a new song."

A few years ago I happened to be visiting my parents a few days after their beloved church had burned down. An electrical failure turned out to be the cause, but at the time there was some suspicion that it was related to the outsized, half-crazy, and decidedly un-Reformed homeless man who had been permitted to use the church facilities during the day. The congregation had just called a new minister who was in transit at the time. A liturgy was quickly constructed by the associate pastor together with a collection of other underemployed women ministers who were part of the congregation. That Sunday we sat on the church grounds facing the burned-out carcass of the beautiful old church. The preacher wept all the way through her sermon, testifying to an unwavering commitment to justice and compassion whatever the cost. The songs and music moved in deep rivers of sorrow and consolation. The youth and children contributed their own expressions of grief and trust. In the midst of their own sorrow, the congregation prayed for injustices that created suffering much worse than their own. The congregation let its own grief flow even as it leaned on the divine mercy in trust and gratitude. I saw grown men—Presbyterian men—cry during the service. I had no idea a Presbyterian worship service could be like that. But it is a testimony to the liturgical and theological resources that ground the Reformed tradition. There is a deep embodied wisdom in the bones of this tradition, and it is glorious to behold when it is given space to spring forward. Marcia's book is both an inspired celebration of this heritage by one of its most dutiful daughters and an impassioned provocation that we live more adventurously, more fearlessly, more lovingly into this heritage.

Wendy Farley
Emory University

Introduction

The hand of the LORD came upon me, and he brought me out by the spirit of the LORD and set me down in the middle of a valley; it was full of bones. He led me all around them; there were very many lying in the valley, and they were very dry. He said to me, "Mortal, can these bones live?" I answered, "O Lord GOD, you know." Then he said to me, "Prophesy to these bones, and say to them: O dry bones, hear the word of the LORD. Thus says the Lord GOD to these bones: I will cause breath to enter you, and you shall live. I will lay sinews on you, and will cause flesh to come upon you, and cover you with skin, and put breath in you, and you shall live; and you shall know that I am the LORD."

So I prophesied as I had been commanded; and as I prophesied, suddenly there was a noise, a rattling, and the bones came together, bone to its bone. I looked, and there were sinews on them, and flesh had come upon them; but there was no breath in them. Then he said to me, "Prophesy to the breath, prophesy, mortal, and say to the breath: Thus says the Lord GOD: Come from the four winds, O breath, and breathe upon these slain that they may live." I prophesied as he commanded me, and the breath came into them, and they lived, and stood on their feet, a vast multitude.

Ezekiel 37:1–10

This is my body, which is given for you. Do this in remembrance of me.

Luke 22:19

THE PROTESTANT PROBLEM

Let sense be dumb, let flesh retire.
    From the hymn, "Dear Lord and Father of Mankind"

It is dangerous to be uncomfortable in your own skin. The sharp edges of self-loathing and debilitating isolation can cut deeply when we are strangers to ourselves. The dangers of that discomfort become more lethal when we believe it is divinely sanctioned. This perilous condition flourishes in much of Protestantism. It forms practitioners of this faith in dis-ease. The body is a liability, a conspirator in our fallenness. Our embodied nature is at times dismissed, at other times distrusted. This suspicion about our flesh-and-blood existence courses through the patterns and paradigms of Protestantism.

My own formation in Protestantism is Presbyterian, a denomination often referred to as the "frozen chosen." Indeed, we reveal this dis-ease of our condition in clear relief. In this Presbyterian presentation of our dis-ease there is a double layer of denial about the true nature of bodies. One layer is a layer of silence; the other layer is a layer of negativity.[1] This silence and negativity form and feed a disembodied ethos that manifests itself theologically, liturgically, and sacramentally. Our dis-ease with the body is palpable—we are uncomfortable in our own skin.

This dis-ease infects many expressions of contemporary Christian life in the church across denominational boundaries. This double layer of denial is apparent with varying levels of acuteness in much of this contemporary Christian landscape. The body is most often ignored in worship in mainline churches.[2] Silence about the body is perhaps most remarkable in how Protestant Christians administer the Lord's Supper. In this sacrament, the meal that is to enflesh the Body of Christ, the experience of the body has been ritually reduced down to a minimum. Re-membering the Body of Christ seems to be close to simple recollection even in denominational settings where that is not the theological grounding beneath the practice. A communal experience in which we face one another, relate to one another, smell, hear, and touch one another is not a part of normal eucharistic practice.

---

1. Although David Tripp argues that "the early exponents of Protestant Christianity reflect a discovery, however inconsistent and uneven, of a sense of body in the person, in the general community, in the church, in the Eucharist," he admits that contemporary Protestants are unknowing heirs to this tradition. Even as Tripp describes the Reformers' rediscovery as an "affirmation of the body as gift and sacrament," contemporary Protestants are hard-pressed to embody such affirmation. See David Tripp, "The Image of the Body in the Protestant Reformation," in *Religion and the Body*, ed. Sarah Coakley (Cambridge: Cambridge University Press, 1997), 147.

2. "Mainline" Protestant is a loaded term to be sure. I use it in a broadly descriptive spirit to point to general habits of thinking and doing apparent in American Christian practices evidenced in many mainline Protestant denominations. It is not the work of this project to parse out who embodies these descriptive tendencies and who does not. The importance of the description is in the spark of recognition it can provide for anyone who has experienced this kind of disembodied ethos.

In many churches, elders stoically pass the plate in an organized alternating pattern while the people in the pews sit quietly, staring straight ahead. There is perhaps quiet background music to reduce the awkward fact that we are not sure exactly what we are supposed to be experiencing in this ritual. Some bow their heads in silent prayer; some examine the wafer or the plastic cup that holds the grape juice. There are scattered glimpses in some congregations of embodied connection and community. Some have those gathered eat the bread and drink the cup in unison. Others share a blessing ("the bread of heaven" or "the cup of salvation") when they serve one another. But even with these glimpses the routine ritual aspects of the sacrament do little to coax us to identify how our bodies are connected, changed, nourished, stretched, healed, even wounded in the reality of being believers in Christ. The ritual of the Lord's Supper seems to dis-member, rather than re-member, the body.

The body is silenced through many other worship practices and patterns. The hegemony of spoken, intellectual, and rational modes of prayer, to the exclusion of other modes of prayer that use the body as helper, such as breathing prayer, silent prayer, walking prayer, and postures of meditation, subtly silences the body. The focus of worship in the Presbyterian tradition, for instance, is usually on the sermon as the proclaiming and hearing of the Word.[3] The sermon is very often left unbalanced by discernible attention to and participation of real, lived bodies. Fasting, prostration, movement, candles, incense, chanting, and other spiritual practices that call on the body to move and sense and act are all conspicuously outside the realm of what one encounters in most mainline Protestant worship. The absence of these practices helps to silence the body's role in worship.[4]

Beyond worship forms, methods of spiritual formation focus more on "knowing and doing"—the ethics of being a Christian—than on the body's spiritual complexity. How the mind and body are integrated is largely left to ethics and morality, as the body falls in line with the mind's ascent to Christian norms and values. Body talk tends to focus mostly on lessons of control and moderation. The connection and complexities of the body as a spiritual entity receive little thematic treatment and even less embodied practice.

3. I believe this focus on the sermon is important for many reasons, including theological ones. I am not suggesting that the sermon should be decreased in importance or decreased in its scriptural and intellectual rigor in Presbyterian worship. The problem is not with the nature of preaching itself, but in the way it is left unbalanced by other spiritual practices and elements of worship that feed the body as it integrates with the intellectual and ethical life of a believer.

4. Music is an interesting area to consider in this ethos of disembodiment. I am careful not to generalize, but I have experienced pockets of both promise and vehement resistance to expanding the musical palate of worshiping communities in the congregations I have served. As evidenced in trends of emerging worship around changing genres of music, there is a desire that many have to experience music in a more embodied way. For instance, there are various examples of the different experiences worshipers have when they sing songs that are easy to memorize and/or are repetitious over and against songs that require our hands to be occupied with a hymnal or music. From gospel music to Taizé to contemporary Christian music there are examples of more embodied participation in worship around music. How a worshiping community engages music in its diversity will be further addressed in chapter 7.

It is a curious fact of life in an incarnational faith that the body is so poorly attended to, or worse yet, even reviled. When silence gives way to negativity this disembodied ethos becomes even more dangerous. Often when there is talk about the body, it boasts a zealous focus on sin and/or encourages an unbalanced intellectualism. This dynamic plays out in the language heard when many Christians worship. Atonement imagery is used liturgically more often than any other traditional christological metaphors. Sin is used more often liturgically to describe the human situation than is suffering—a reality that communicates equally our need for God and our brokenness. Except for sin, there is little to no theological language liturgically accessible during worship for talking about and understanding the body spiritually. This obscuring of suffering and the neglect of the complexity of embodied experience can, at its extreme, fuel an intense focus on purity. When this focus is dangerously coupled with an individualistic, control-oriented approach to living as a body, the body becomes a battleground for moral purity. The rational, faithful self struggles against all the physical urges of the sinful body. This negativity is only enhanced by how the body is subtly communicated to be a distraction in worship. An ignored and insulted body is a dis-membered body.

From suffering to delight, layers upon layers of human embodied experience are rent asunder in this disembodied faith. The body is subdued, buried; its ambiguity is tidied up. Its spiritual capacity is trivialized. Worse yet, the seeds of hatred of the body find fertile ground. If the body is only visible through sin, we are strangers to the whole of who we are and how we were created. Embodied life becomes dis-jointed; believers are dis-abled. Life as a body is ignored, distrusted. This malady is surely an offense in an incarnational faith.

The cost of this disembodied faith is made manifest not only in our practices but in the worshiping communities we tend to create and occupy. A truncated embodied experience feeds the need for safety, homogeneity, and predictability. Welcoming the stranger who is not like us is all the more difficult when we are not acquainted with the stranger in ourselves. Surrendering to change is all the more difficult when we do not practice such surrender in the way we worship. When we are formed in homogeneity it is difficult to know how to stretch into diversity. The unruliness of difference can feel like chaos. The fluidity of change can feel like a loss of control. This disembodied faith is prone to fear, anxiety, and stasis.

In this condition we desperately need to cleave to the Incarnation.[5] We need to explore what it means for us as human bodies. Instead, mainline Protestant Christianity has expended much more liturgical and theological energy on the

---

5. As a theologian, I am well aware of resources in the Protestant theological tradition that have the capacity for correcting or balancing aspects of this problematic ethos. Baptism, redemption, the Incarnation, and conceptions of the Body of Christ all offer clues to more extensive theological understanding of the human body. As an ordained minister of the Word and Sacrament in the Presbyterian Church (U.S.A.), I am also well aware of how entrenched this disembodied ethos is in how many mainline Protestant Christians worship and theologically understand our bodies.

crucifixion as the atoning death of Christ.[6] Compassion, love, and embodied knowing take a back seat to the cycle of judgment, deserved punishment, and forgiveness. The Incarnation is neglected as a light for what it means to have a body. But we need to attend to what we confess: God comes to us enfleshed, as a body. We, as bodies, are loved, fully experienced, and redeemed by God. Christianity is called to embody this good news by attending to the complexity of bodies. Attention to bodies goes beyond the language of sin to a fuller translation of the body's own language. This language is not easily heard, but it cries out for acknowledgment. Tuning into body language means listening to bodies themselves. Indeed, this problem of silence and negativity needs a solution that can truly hear and speak out of embodied experience. My tools for tuning in are varied; all of them serve this exploration through what they help to hear and speak about the nature of bodies.

I describe this ethos, which is informed by a myriad of factors, as a theologian and as a practitioner of this faith tradition. I construct a theology of embodiment in response to this disembodied faith—a condition particularly pronounced in Presbyterianism, but not foreign to many other expressions of the Protestant theological tradition. This embodiment theology is an attempt to expand and to enrich, to deepen and to discern how Christian practice can not only embrace bodies but also stretch into the embrace of difference. The differences to be embraced are not only external to believers, but also interior to our own meandering work to understand ourselves. Our own created nature invites us to integrate and to invite difference into how we occupy this world.

ADDRESSING THE PROBLEM/
EMBODYING THEOLOGY

Like St. Augustine, John Calvin, Friedrich Schleiermacher, and others of my forebears in Reformed theology, I am doing theology formed around a traditional framework. I am describing our human condition under the conditions of sin and then, in turn, exploring what our condition is in light of redemption. This theological anthropology is knit together with the particularity of the stories that many women's bodies have to tell. The interpretive theological tools that I use to describe both our distortions and our promise stretch out both from this Reformed heritage and from the particular kind of attention I pay to women's embodied experiences. I integrate three experiences of some bodies—rape, pregnancy, and motherhood—into more general features of embodied experience for

6. Friedrich Schleiermacher is certainly a strong example of a theologian in the Protestant tradition who made Incarnation central to his theology. His work, however, has not found its way into much clear prominence in the way the Incarnation is addressed in Reformed worship and theology. I have found many of my colleagues in ministry to have, at best, a caricatured understanding of Schleiermacher. Many pigeonhole him as the liberal theologian who distorted the importance of the objective, theocentric thrust of Protestant theology.

all bodies—tragedy, relationality, and ambiguity. These dimensions of embodied experience then expand into a triad of dispositions of redemptive embodied experience—compassion, interdependence, and adventure. These dispositions wear a pathway for exploring what it means to be church when we know these things about ourselves.

I am focused on our embodied condition and a theological interpretation of it. I explore the body itself by way of embodied experience, which is previous to and, many times, resistant to language. Body and embodiment are conflated here and intentionally so. This conflation is a palpable difference in the way I am theorizing body and embodiment from other similar projects. Body is a physical, mental, and spiritual phenomenon. These descriptive areas of experience are not discrete aspects of body, but they are more and more elusive constellations of embodied life. It is well accepted in even the most rigorously Western medical circles, for instance, that things like stress, prayer, laughter, racism, and sleep patterns are all tangled up in how our physical bodies function. These conditions of experience as bodies mean that our embodiment navigates the spectrum of experience and genetics and intangibles that operate underneath/beyond our conscious understanding. The body is not a discrete entity with neat boundaries. It therefore takes careful yet (unavoidably) imprecise work to describe a phenomenon that is this all-encompassing. Body and embodied experience cannot be somehow parsed out from one another. The tangle of it all is the starting place for theological reflection and construction in this project. Unpacking what this conflation means for theology is the flesh and blood of the chapters that follow.

The experiences I explore are the experiences of rape, pregnancy, and motherhood. These are our windows into three common aspects of embodiment: tragedy, relationality, and ambiguity. The experiences I have chosen to explore as theological resources are, notably, all women's experiences.[7] Embodying theology for me is tangled up with these embodied experiences that I have had because I am a woman. They have helped me not just to see but to feel the dismemberment in my faith tradition. These experiences also point to a difficult historical reality in Christianity and to a reality that remains apparent today in some expressions of Christian practice: women's bodies have particularly borne the weight of this disembodied ethos. In between the lines, underneath the text, therefore, are all the women who have suffered and do suffer from the misogyny that found a home in Christianity centuries ago. Woman as temptress, as unclean, as lacking in moral capacity, as irrational, and as inadequate to the task of church leadership are just some of the symptoms of how hatred, distrust, and

---

7. Rape is unique among the three experiences as something that men can experience. I am not sure this fact changes anything about how the reader will encounter this material. I include this note simply to acknowledge the reality of the rape of men. I can only hope the constructive work can be healing for male victims of sexual violence also.

negativity about the body have been particularly heaped onto female bodies.[8] It is as I grieve how women's bodies have been dis-regarded in and even dis-membered from and by the Body of Christ that I seek a new way for women's bodies to be part of the theological conversation. As I honor the theological weight of women's bodies for constructive theological work, I am thankful for all the burdens that have been lifted to allow women's bodies to be "heard" in this way.

STRETCHING INTO A THEOLOGY
OF EMBODIMENT

We are doing something more like yoga than physical therapy in this project. Yoga is a practice that makes assumptions about the deep interconnections in the body and with everything that is. We will not be simply focusing on an injured muscle or a nagging pain. We will be trying to move and breathe and ground ourselves in our bodies in a way that is integrated with countless experiences, perspectives, and possibilities. There is simultaneous simplicity and complexity in the practice of yoga. But it is nothing if it is not integrated.

I invite the reader to stretch into this project with an inquiring spirit and the willingness to suspend constant interrogation concerning ultimate truth. When teaching courses in churches I encourage participants to think of themselves putting those questions of ultimate truth into a drawer for safekeeping. These questions are not discarded, nor are they unimportant or impossible to ask. They are simply not allowed to truncate our exploration. We can focus on the integrity of the experiences and honor their truth-bearing qualities when not constantly burdened by the necessity of their having to yield ultimate truth in order to be legitimate theological resources.[9] This focus means that we will fully examine descriptions and examples for what they offer us.

But theology searches for more than just descriptions. This spirit of inquiry is, indeed, open and adventuresome and interested in better understanding our

8. The complexity of how race, gender, and economics intersect is another layer of this exclusion and dis-memberment that I refer to here. Certainly, the ravages of racism and the diminishing effects of poverty are part and parcel of this problem that I endeavor to describe. I hope that as I explore the promise of attending to redeemed bodies in the context of a vision of multicultural worshiping communities that I will honor some of these dynamics with a more thorough discussion.

9. This mode of inquiry that I invite draws on the spirit of phenomenology as a theological method. The reader need not get bogged down in any technical usage of the phenomenological method or terminology here. Phenomenology does help provide the descriptive capacity that enables me to explore aspects of embodied experience rigorously. It has remarkable descriptive prowess because of its mode of operation in terms of truth and phenomena themselves. I do not employ phenomenology in such a technical way as to argue the subtleties of Husserl's terminology or the accoutrements of his followers' philosophical accounting of "things-in-themselves." My "phenomenological-descriptive" tools free me to use whatever best serves the exploration of the phenomena on which I focus, whether they be history, philosophy, experience, theology, biblical resources, social theory, psychology, medical science, trauma theory, poetry, or statistics.

human condition. There is, to be sure, an irreducible character to located experiences like the ones I am drawing on for this theology. They are what they are. At the same time the human condition is held together by such fabric. That which makes us unique and particular is embodied in a common condition. I am paying attention to both particularity and embodiment. It is in that dual attention that we can all find the "spark of recognition" that may hopefully enlarge our common understanding of our condition.[10] There is freedom, at the very least, in this approach to gain wisdom where we might otherwise shun its worth. This stretching can ground us and expand us. This work is born out of the intersection and integrating of experiences and tradition. It is a theological hybrid—practical, philosophical, constructive, and resourceful. But I believe there is no such thing as theology that does not touch us where we live and practice our faith. This project is no different.

The descriptive fruits of my labor need theological grounding and language for them to translate into embodied theology, not just language or stories about bodies. For this grounding I use the theological category of feeling to reveal aspects of our embodied experience that are difficult to access. This uncommonly used theological category helps me to avoid some of the traps of abstracted concepts such as body and spirit and the subconscious. Chapter 1 delves into feeling in order to describe its nature and function. Feeling is unifying and complex, and it helps to flesh out what rape, pregnancy, and motherhood tell us about our human condition. Feeling also points toward the redemptive possibilities of embodied existence. This category offers a way to intuit a common thread even as it disrupts all attempts to uncover an unchanging human essence. This distinction is both fine and of great importance. Feeling will help us to tune in and listen to the body; feeling will also clear a space for a surrender to that which we cannot readily hear of the body's language. This category is complicated and can be difficult to understand.

My use of this category has been deeply informed by the work of Alfred North Whitehead and Friedrich Schleiermacher. In chapter 1 I describe and interpret this category. My work is enriched by the complexity of Whitehead's and Schleiermacher's usages of feeling, but I hope it is not hindered by it. My own interpretation and usage of feeling strives for accessibility and applicability to the problem of a disembodied faith. This chapter is more intensely philosophical than the others because of all of these factors. The kind of stretching you do in this chapter will serve you well in the chapters that follow. Feeling's character may become more apparent to you as you explore it applied to these specific, embodied experiences.

---

10. Like Wendy Farley's use of this "phenomenological-descriptive" method in her *Tragic Vision and Divine Compassion: A Contemporary Theodicy* (Louisville: Westminster/John Knox, 1990), I endeavor to elicit a "spark of recognition" in the reader.

Three constructive chapters follow the chapter on feeling. In each chapter I attend both to particular, located experiences and to an aspect of our general, embodied human condition. My choice of women's experiences for theological work rests on my assertion that these particularly female experiences have something to tell us about the human condition. Making such a move is, in part, the work of a theologian. At the same time, the validity of such a move is rightly challenged in our current theological landscape with rigorous questions that stem from context and difference. These are questions I myself bring to my own study and to my own work. The claims I make in each chapter are modestly universal. I make such claims because I believe that feeling allows me to recognize general features of the human condition without them becoming static or stifling categories.

In chapter 2 I explore rape at the level of feeling for how it affects the body and for the embodied story it has to tell. Body function, body loss, the limits of consciousness, and contorted subjectivity are four areas of embodied experience that feeling illuminates. The deeply embodied dynamics of traumatic experience and memory weave a story that needs to be told. Feeling expands what this exploration of rape reveals to include the tragic nature of all embodied existence. Tragedy is an important aspect of human experience that allows us to attend to loss and harm in a way that is not focused on blame or even on justice. Feeling helps to tune us into the body's capacity for telling a story, for witnessing to harm, and for holding grief.

Chapter 3 explores pregnancy. When feeling is applied to pregnancy, it reveals the poetic capacity of the body to communicate the relational nature of bodies. This poeisis of pregnancy expresses not only relationship, but the rupture of relationship that harms the body's ability to function to its fullest potential. I explore how feeling helps give voice to the body's figurative language in creativity and creation, in entangled subjectivity, and in the discouragement of body knowledge. Pregnancy offers three models for relationship—the placenta, midwives and doulas, and birth. These three models help fill out the body's need for responsiveness and its capacity for responsibility. Pregnancy, when explored at the level of feeling, gives voice to the body's poetics and offers clues to the relational nature of all embodied existence. We are all tangled with the world the way a pregnant woman is entangled with her baby. This truth is one we ignore at our peril. This interdependence is a cellular phenomenon, not simply an ethical or moral one.

Chapter 4 explores the complexity of motherhood. Motherhood, however, is a distinctively challenging experience to describe and to appropriate theologically. For this reason, the reader will recognize a reversal of form in this chapter. I begin with a discussion of some of the embodied features of ambiguity. I then turn to motherhood for how it illuminates this feature of our condition. Motherhood is less available for the kind of satisfying categorization than are rape and pregnancy because of its amorphous character. This character trait, however, is also what allows motherhood to be theologically productive for this project.

Mothers caring for their children, limited by their children, and expanded by their children are all deeply embodied dynamics. How mothers carry, discipline, and comfort their children are metaphors for embodied ambiguity. I look specifically at the glimpses of the body's ambiguity in motherhood by examining maternal bodies, maternal relationships, and maternal (fragmented) subjectivity. The ambiguity of motherhood awakens us to our own truth. Neat and tidy categories for who we are bleed into other categories and questions more often than not. The embodied truth of motherhood can help us to accept, maybe even to embrace, our own embodied ambiguity.

The second part of this project explores how the tragic, relational, and ambiguous characteristics of embodied existence translate themselves into dispositions of redeemed bodies. Chapter 5 explores these dispositions: compassion, interdependence, and adventure. These dispositions are marks of how redemption works through the body as the sanctifying power that heals and enriches embodied experience. The formation of these dispositions has the potential to support flesh-and-blood bodies who endeavor to re-member the body theologically. These bodies form and give life to on-the-ground worshiping communities, too.

How do our dispositions embody a richer expression of the promises of an incarnational faith? Chapter 6 takes these dispositions into the challenges of ecclesial formation. The Body of Christ is wounded by fear and intellectualization. Compassion, interdependence, and adventure in-form how we encounter the strangers who find their way into our communities. These dispositions of redemption also acquaint us with the stranger in ourselves. The challenges and the promise of churches that do not simply tolerate but seek out difference and diversity on multiple layers of embodied existence can in-form a revitalized Body of Christ.

Chapter 7 suggests how these dispositions can translate into enlivened modes of worship. Remembering Christ's body is more than recollection for Christian communities. It is the heart of Christian identity. We re-member the Body of Christ and therefore re-member our bodies as redeemed by the promise of an incarnate God. Re-membering is reconnecting; it is reintegrating. It is rejoining body parts that have been harmed, severed, maimed, mutilated, or displaced. How can we bring our bodies with us to church and more fully experience our re-membering of the Body of Christ? Confession, the Lord's Supper, and music are three aspects of worship where our bodies can take up more space and revitalize mainline churches.

Tending to feeling bodies can help us to "let the bones live." And the bones may even dance!

Chapter 1

Feeling Our Way

How the past perishes is how the future becomes.
Alfred North Whitehead, *Adventures in Ideas*

How do we translate feeling, a complex and uncommonly used theological category, into language that is accessible and understandable? How do we apply the language of feeling to theological problems that have been long silenced and skewed in Protestant thought? How do we simply talk about feeling, which points toward something that is prior to and beyond language much of the time? These are my challenges. In a quite palpable sense I am trying to give language to something that resists such expression. The urgency of such an unwieldy project is born out of the perils of a disembodied faith. We live in Christian community with only a thin layer of understanding of our own embodied capacity to experience redemption. This trivialized understanding is reflected in the dearth of practices, both liturgical and otherwise, that allow us to live into embodied fullness of life. I use feeling theologically in a unique mode of application. The uniqueness comes not only in my interpretation of this category, but in the problem we are asking feeling to describe and address.

Feeling helps communicate the storyteller, the metaphor, and the poetics of the body. It is the grammar of our body language, and it yields a mixture of language and that which cannot be spoken. It tunes us into the body language, and it clears a space for surrender to that which we cannot understand. Feeling helps

11

give expression to this telling, retelling, and untelling—the flux of silence and speech. The use of language here can be likened to the dynamic and dangerous work of developing language about God. Giving God names and metaphors in order to help our understanding leaves much still that we cannot know, as well as a constant need for disruption. No language tells the whole story, but what it can tell us retains some positive constructive potential. Feeling parallels this linguistic dance of meaning that fills and empties our understanding almost coincidentally.

It is important not to confuse this theological category of feeling with emotion—a common synonym for some uses of the word "feeling." This theological category of feeling is complicated and primal; it is not emotion, not thought, not sensation, but instead the most primary and the most embodied mode through which we navigate all experience, including but not limited to emotion, thought, and sensation. The dimensions of embodied experience that are not expressed with thought, emotion, decision, consciousness, or sensation can be coaxed into some kind of awareness through our attention to feeling.

Feeling is not simply experience; rather it is a physical mode of experience that grounds, conditions, and gives life to all of our experience. Feeling is primal, embodied knowing. Indeed, knowing is an inadequate descriptor for what feeling gives us because knowing suggests consciousness, and feeling only rarely comes into the realm of consciousness. Feeling is both pre- and postconsciousness. It is extra-consciousness—forming and informing our consciousness, but beneath and beyond our consciousness. Feeling is not an inner logic, not a way of grouping or making sense of perception. It is not accurate to equate feeling with intuition or a sixth sense. Feeling is more formal, more basic, more primal, and more all-encompassing. It is the mode in which we process all that intersects with our particularity; indeed, it is the creator of our particularity at the same time that it is the ground of our universality.

Feeling is also the mechanism of our redemption. In a real sense, it is our *imago Dei*. God's image in us is the capacity to be who we are created to be. This *imago Dei* is also a mode of operation that integrates all aspects of embodied existence into wholeness and health. Feeling is a corrective to the negativity of a disembodied faith in that it gives us language with which to speak about the body beyond sinfulness. Feeling has the capacity to disrupt images of the body as a battleground for moral purity by affirming the body as spiritual, vital, and capable of far more than that of which we are conscious.

A BRIEF MAPPING OF FEELING

My usage of this category draws on others who employed this term in their theological constructions, but the description that follows is my own interpretation of the category as it applies to embodiment. Most notably, both Friedrich Schleiermacher and Alfred North Whitehead used feeling (for Schleiermacher,

Gefühl) in their work. Schleiermacher used this category to describe our human condition, our created nature. With it he accomplished a deeply descriptive theological anthropology. Whitehead's usage of this category spun its character into a much broader view of the universe's structure and function. I am indebted to and very much appreciate each of their sensitivities. Indeed, I am profoundly informed by the power of the role of feeling in both Schleiermacher's and Whitehead's theological systems. What I ask from the term is distinctive from both systems and will take feeling beyond what Whitehead's and Schleiermacher's systems have to offer. Even so, a brief appreciation of some of the important wisdom each thinker offers is appropriate for us to discuss. Their wisdom and work will help us at more than a few junctures in this project.

For Schleiermacher, *Gefühl* is the feeling of absolute dependence on God or the God-consciousness that forms the core of the human condition. The more we are in tune with this truth of our created nature the more we are in tune with reality itself. *Gefühl* is the centerpiece of Schleiermacher's theological anthropology.[1] This God-consciousness is the human capacity for God; and it is, for Schleiermacher, what makes us human. Feeling is the element of experience from which piety comes (not from knowing and doing). Piety is connected to knowing and doing; piety stimulates knowing and doing.[2] This feeling of absolute dependence and its coherence with itself is also an important formative element in Schleiermacher's description of redemption. In this created aspect of our nature, we have a given susceptibility to God's love and grace. This susceptibility is blocked in the conditions of sin by our distracted and distorted desire. But even in the conditions of sin and misery, we do not completely lose contact with our God-consciousness. It is simply weakened by the primary illusion or distraction of ego. Sanctified human life is formed in a process that moves us into greater and greater fluidity of God-consciousness. Perfect God-consciousness is a consciousness in which everything mediates God-consciousness, the ego's primacy fades, and we experience the primary truth of interrelatedness with everything.[3]

At the core of Whitehead's description of experience is his technical use of "feeling." It is his attempt to describe the play of feeling that fuels his development of new words (to correct the "fallacy of the Perfect Dictionary"[4]) to name experience, time, subjectivity, and even God. These words serve to name aspects of experience that correspond with common sense as he connects with the most

---

1. *Gefühl* is described most thoroughly in Schleiermacher's two volumes of *The Christian Faith* first published in German in 1821. Its English translation is based on the updated version published in 1830 (ed. H. R. Mackintosh and J. S. Stewart; 2 vols.; repr. New York: Harper & Row, 1963).

2. Ibid., 1:9.

3. See Schleiermacher's "Second Division: The Manner in Which Fellowship with the Perfection and Blessedness of the Redeemer Expresses Itself in the Individual Soul," section 110, "Second Doctrine: Sanctification," in *Christian Faith*, 2:505–10.

4. Alfred North Whitehead, *Modes of Thought* (New York: Free Press, 1938), 173.

basic ways we experience everyday life.[5] This relationality is described in White-head's scheme with his careful use of "feeling." Relationality rather than inde-pendent substance is what gives shape to reality. Process and event rather than materialism and mechanism are the "really Real." For Whitehead these realities are the fingerprints of the primacy of feeling. Feeling is not simply sense experi-ence for Whitehead. The most primal sense reception is not sense perception, not understanding, but it is "immediacy" to all experience.[6] Feeling is the orga-nizing, connective aspect of his organic concept of the universe.

Neither Whitehead nor Schleiermacher presents us with an untroubled or perfectly clear description of feeling. Where I use Whitehead's or Schleier-macher's language, I clearly note it as such. The language that I use should be understood as an effort to explain further and therefore to interpret this category. The discussion of feeling that follows is also not to be mistaken for a complete rendering of feeling itself. Feeling is a phenomenon that calls for constant work at developing an understanding of what it is. This work can never be complete because of the very nature of feeling itself.

UNDERSTANDING FEELING

A twofold functioning of feeling emerges from my study of feeling. Feeling is both the mode of our experience and the mechanism of our redemption.[7] This delineation points to two important facets of how feeling functions in terms of embodied experience. Feeling as a mode of experience places it at the very core of how we live and negotiate ourselves around the world. Feeling as the mechanism of redemption is a function that points us toward our best possibilities and not just our lived realities.

Before examining these two facets of feeling, we need to examine a few quite common words. These words are crucial in understanding feeling, but they threaten our understanding of feeling in the context of accepted habits in West-ern thinking. First, the word "physical" is sometimes important, but quite prob-lematic, in describing feeling. In this conversation the mind and body cannot be understood in a dualistic relationship. Physical and mental facets of experience are all of a piece in giving particular content to all experience. They cannot be disconnected from each other and are constantly conditioning all experience in ways that cannot be cleanly differentiated. Even though there is no strict separa-

5. Whitehead, *Process and Reality: An Essay in Cosmology,* ed. David Ray Griffin and Donald W. Sherburne, corrected ed. (New York: Free Press, 1978), 72. Whitehead describes his "Philosophy of Organism" as an attempt to return to conceptions of the "vulgar," meaning the ability of the human common sense to conceive of this notion of organism and the universe.

6. Ibid., 155.

7. I thank Wendy Farley for helping me gain clarity on this twofold description of feeling both via Schleiermacher's *Gefühl* and in our work together deciphering *Process and Reality.* I particularly thank her for her rich understanding of the redemptive elements of feeling discussed more thoroughly below.

tion between the physical and mental modifications of experience, they do point to unique emphases of experience that are important in understanding feeling as a mode of experience and as a corrective to false consciousness.[8]

When I use the word "physical," I am referring to some modification of experience that is preconscious or unconscious—that is, we are not aware of the experience in a way that would enable us to think about it, analyze it, talk about it, or name it. In this way the word "physical" suggests an aspect of embodiment that points toward the body's capacity to have experiences that are not exhausted by what we know or in what we do. This phenomenon of the body, namely that it is much more than what we know or do, is given flesh in my three constructive chapters. The windows into embodied experience that I use (rape, pregnancy, and motherhood) live out what this aspect of embodiment "looks like." This sensitivity about the body can flow easily from process philosophy, trauma theory, holistic medicine, and even in some Freudian ideas (all of which are appealed to in some form throughout the rest of this project) about how the subconscious informs somatic symptoms. These constructions of the body suggest, as I do here, that the body is a dynamic phenomenon not limited to its outward and/ or visible activities. "Physical," therefore, has the connotation of primacy for our purposes. It is more basic than consciousness. It is even more basic than sense experience. "Physical" points toward one of the great assets of feeling as a descriptive category. There is a brute physicality about the mode of feeling.

At the same time that "physical" is a term I use carefully and deliberately, the term "mental" brings with it its own red flags. When I use terms that suggest some sort of mental or cognitive activity (e.g., consciousness, analysis, awareness), I am not suggesting that there is an inside/outside dichotomy that we can point to in the thinking we do. That is, the "brain," or the mental facet of existence, is not to be equated with essential expressions of us as ourselves. These are modifications of experience that are conditioned and interconnected with all else that is, and they do not give expression to a strict interiority that reveals what we "really" think or know about something. In this way I am suggesting an organic understanding of our cognition. This fluidity or entanglement of our experience is distinguished from a Freudian view of the subconscious.

That said, the term "mental" still points to some important ways in which we make sense of experience that modify it in distinctive ways. While our capacity for thinking and knowing may not reflect a pristine truth about experience, these facets of how we negotiate ourselves around the world are important for

---

8. By "false consciousness" I refer to distortion in how feeling is allowed to flow that results in skewed perceptions and understandings. This concept will become clearer in chapter 2 in relationship to rape and the effects of trauma. Sin can be understood as a kind of false consciousness. For Schleiermacher, for instance, the effects of sin and misery are blocked *Gefühlen* in which we mistake our ego for the primary driving force of reality. Buddhist philosophy has perhaps the clearest and most consistent description of false consciousness in its understanding of conventional and ultimate reality. My usage of the term will focus not on such a sweeping statement about our condition, but more on what such consciousness reveals about the mode of operation of feeling (both as our way of navigating experiences and as the mechanism of our redemption).

how we function and sift through all that is. This terminology that points toward the activities of our mind focuses on a particular level of our cognitively accessible awareness. It points to how we are able to set apart kinds of experience and to reflect on them and then to use those reflections to help shape our perspectives on future experience. Consciousness is not the crown of experience, but it is abundantly powerful in *how* and *what* we experience. "Mental" modifications of experience refer generally to those things that are conscious, analyzable, nameable—those things about which we converse and qualify experience.

"Mental" and "physical" are complicated and interdependent dimensions of how we negotiate ourselves through life. They require each other and condition each other in the context of a complex relationship. This relationship is not a one-way street between nerve endings and brain function. These dimensions operate in a constant, fluid exchange of feeling, which enables feeling to condition physicality and awareness in a complex and ongoing relationship that determines how intensely we are attuned to certain types of experience or how easy it is for us to negate the impact of certain data.[9]

A second point of clarification comes simply in highlighting the fact that feeling does, at its most basic level, point to this mode of experience that is not only prior to consciousness but is even beyond consciousness. That is, some feelings never come into consciousness, but still deeply affect us. Because this extra-consciousness is an important part of what feeling is and how it serves us, it is important to explore what it means. There is an obvious paradox here as "exploration" and "meaning" suggest consciousness and language. This paradox should not, however, induce paralysis or pessimism about the worth of the exploration. This paradox does induce humility. The paradox of "understanding" feeling makes its point in enacting the reality of feeling. The limits of language and consciousness are real—just as real as feeling is, even on levels to which we do not have conscious access. This paradox offers us a way to reclaim the body by tuning us in to its own "language." This kind of body language defies perfect

---

9. The negation of data brings up Whitehead's "negative prehension." He used this term to describe how we get rid of certain feelings that do not gather any steam but simply fizzle in their importance and/or relevance. These feelings have nothing to hook onto to move toward more "importance" (a Whiteheadean term). This sort of negation is important to understand on at least a superficial level for our discussion. See the discussion of feeling and redemption below for more clarifying remarks on negating feeling. Also, n. 12 below contains a definition of prehension that may provide some helpful information. Perhaps a mundane example may help feed a general understanding of the dynamic of feeling's flow into experience. Many may have noticed at various times in their lives that an experience informs them of something new of which they were not conscious prior to this experience. For instance, one could hear a radio news show refer to an obscure island in the South Pacific, and the name of that island is new "data." In the next few days following one's introduction to that island, one sees eight other references to it—suggesting that all of a sudden there is a growing intensity with which one is aware of this island. Without those following eight references perhaps the name of the island would eventually be "forgotten" or negated from one's constellation of experience. Such a negation is, on some level, a negative prehension, although we should be careful not to equate negative prehensions with repressed memory and/or forgetfulness.

translation into our spoken language, but it can still be "heard."[10] The very fact that our experience is operating all the time at this more radical level instructs us about ourselves and our bodies in ways that stretch our ability to think the unthinkable and to live out of the truths of everyday experience.

I negotiate the connection feeling has to other terms Whitehead and Schleiermacher develop in their systems with an eye toward accessibility and clarity for the reader. Because this project is not an exhaustive interpretation of either Whiteheadean metaphysics or Schleiermachean theology, I only highlight the meanings of some of their ideas (or in Whitehead's case, terminology) when such expanded understandings are required for a definition or description in this project. I will largely depend on footnotes, as I have already, to expand on these definitions. It is my hope that with the footnotes the reader will be able to understand the terms enough that the description of feeling is not overly obscure.

Feeling as Mode of Experience

Feeling is how we intersect with everything else—our mode of encountering all that is, our means of negotiating ourselves through life, and the way we incorporate all that we encounter into our "selves." It is how we operate; all that is operates according to this mode of feeling. Feeling defines us, shapes us, and conditions us on every level of experience. Perhaps most importantly, it is the mode of our most primal experience. We are constantly encountering the world around us in this mode. Our bodies gather data that condition us even though we are not necessarily consciously aware of its "content." Feeling is the work of our bodies on a cellular level. This physical aspect of feeling is what conditions the most basic characteristic of human experience—embodiment.[11]

For just how feeling works, Whitehead offers us immense descriptive help with his term "prehension." Prehension is how feelings are experienced or perceived. It is an operation that, in its positive expression, is called a feeling. Every prehension has three factors: the subject that is prehending; the datum that is prehended; and how the subject prehends the datum (Whitehead calls this "subjective form"). There are two species of prehensions—positive or negative. Feelings are positive prehensions. Negative prehensions "eliminate from feeling." Prehension is how we feel; it is how our identity and our particularity are at work in how we feel. The way we feel is conditioned by the unique and particular entity that we are.[12] Whitehead uses "prehension" to complicate Descartes'

10. In the three chapters on embodied experience I will develop what I mean by "body language." Phenomena like bodily memories are an example of body language.

11. Whitehead asserted that Western "philosophers have disdained the information about the universe obtained through their visceral feelings, and have concentrated instead on visual feelings" to their peril (*Process and Reality*, 121).

12. Prehension "reproduces in itself the general characteristics of an actual entity" (ibid., 23). William A. Christian describes prehension as "an operation in which an actual entity 'grasps' some

"cogitations" and Locke's "ideas" even as he claims to be simplifying their language so that it refers to a one-substance cosmology rather than the "two-substance ontology" he sees in their systems.

Prehension takes the mind/body duality out of terms like "comprehension" and brings the physical body out of a subordinate position in how we know. In this way, understanding feeling creates a sense of balance in the way we understand that physical bodies and mental "cogitations" inform our experience.[13] Feeling should be understood in this balanced, nondualistic sense. We prehend feeling. Feeling is constantly becoming part of our inheritance as data that translate into every part of us. It is the fabric, the thread, and the seamstress of who we are. It is the mode of our experience.

The priority of feeling points us to the body's most primal mode of experience. It creates a more complete sensitivity about experience than those that privilege cognition. It helps us to keep in mind that in process metaphysics physical and mental types of experience are not in opposition or cleanly distinct from each other. Rather they are intimately connected and always forming and informing each other. In this sensitivity, knowledge and consciousness are not primary, but they are derivative aspects of experience.[14] Even sense experience is not primary. Whitehead points us toward the "still vague feelings of influence" that have not taken on the character of something we understand, analyze, or of which we are even conscious. The body cannot somehow be abstracted from feeling because neither is what it is without the other. Each conditions the other to be what it is becoming and what it is to others. Every reality promotes feeling. Every reality is felt. Feeling as the mode of our experience tells us some important things about who we are, about our conditions of existence, about how we operate.

As we try to get our minds around the nature and character of feeling as the mode of our experience, we need to remember three things: feeling is not simply emotion or sense perception; feeling shows us the flux of reality; and feeling is radically embodied. First, feeling is not simply emotion, consciousness, sense perception, or "experience." These phenomena are all expressions and manifestations of feeling, but feeling is a much more primary phenomenon. Feeling is immediate; it is prior to anything we call experience. Feeling conditions us to function in terms of experience. It is a physical mode that grounds, conditions, and vivifies every kind of experience that we have.

Feeling is primal and embodied; it is pre- and postconscious. Indeed, feeling is extra-consciousness in the sense that it forms and informs our conscious-

---

other entity and makes that entity an object of experience." He adds that a prehension is "*this* actuality feeling *that* entity." The flow of feeling and negative prehension are intimately connected with the role of intensity and triviality in Whitehead's metaphysics. See Christian, *An Interpretation of Whitehead's Metaphysics* (New Haven: Yale University Press, 1959), 12.

13. Whitehead describes the balance he is trying to strike in a short paragraph in his first chapter in relationship to the work of Descartes and Locke (*Process and Reality*, 19).

14. Whitehead explains, "In feeling, what is felt is not necessarily analyzed; in understanding, what is understood is analyzed, in so far as it is understood" (ibid., 153).

ness, but it is also beneath and beyond our consciousness. Feeling is not a sixth sense. In fact, we are seldom aware of feeling. Only rarely does it bubble up into conscious thought and/or sense experience. Feeling is also not, on its most basic level, a way of grouping or making sense of experience, although feeling does give shape to these cognitive activities. In this sense, feeling is the mode in which we process all that intersects with our particularity. It shapes our fluid and complex sense of self; it courses through our bodies and marks how we become; it translates into our knowing and doing. Feeling is formal, primal, and all-encompassing.

Second, feeling points us toward the fluidity and flux of reality.[15] Changeless and unentangled factuality in a material sense is but a mythic creation.[16] Feeling embodies the permanence of flux. This flux is the play of interconnection, which grounds what is really real and the irreducible nature of particularity. Feeling is the ground of that which is universal at the same time that it is the ground of every particularity. It is that which makes us human, but it is also that which we share with all that is. The universal nature of feeling is palpable only as particularity. All that is feels all else that is, but there is no universal shape or tone or texture to feeling. It can only be expressed or played out or embodied in the particular. Feeling as the mode of our experience tells us about our interdependence, our commonality with all that is in the mode we share. Feeling is the ground of our universality at the same time that it is the creator of our particularity.

Third, feeling is radically embodied. The body negotiates experiences that are not played out in conscious thought. Understanding what exactly is entailed in these primal body feelings is, at bottom, conceptually impossible. In this important and difficult characteristic of feeling Whitehead's description provides a possible glimpse of this radically embodied aspect. He uses the term "antecedent" to point to the body as the most primary point of reception. The antecedent part of the body that has the most primary experience, such as the eye, the finger, the stomach, is the location of the fundamental fact of perception. Only at higher phases of modification of these perceptions do the senses begin to differentiate and transmit to the mind and the nerves a way to define or categorize a feeling. These antecedent parts of the body are constantly gathering in these simple physical feelings, and only a fraction of these feelings ever move into higher kinds of perception or consciousness. But these antecedent bodily experiences have a profound influence on who we are and how we understand experience. I believe bodily memory and hysterical symptoms are two examples of this dynamic of feeling. These experiences will be explored further in the following chapter.

---

15. Whitehead describes this dynamic this way: "There is nothing in the real world which is merely an inert fact. Every reality is there for feeling; it promotes feeling; and it is felt" (Whitehead, *Process and Reality*, 310).

16. Whitehead calls this reality the "fallacy of misplaced concreteness" (*Science and the Modern World* [New York: Free Press, 1925], 51).

Feeling as the Means of Redemption of Bodies

In addition to being our mode of operation, feeling has a restorative capacity. It can reveal at least a glimpse of our best possibilities. It can reveal what is "really real" about the human condition.[17] Feeling has redemptive capacity in the awareness that it enables and in the effects that its healthy flow can produce. It has the capacity to disrupt sin—the destructive habits of living a lie or living by the prompting of a false or partial consciousness.[18] For instance, Schleiermacher's theological anthropology offers a deep description of the blockage that sin creates. *Gefühl* is mediated in all of experience. Sin distorts our ability to live into the truth and the healthy flow of our God-consciousness. The more we evolve into habits that mediate greater and greater kinds of awareness of our God-consciousness, the more we are formed into who we were really created to be. Schleiermacher's system helps us see this corrective capacity that rests in our own created nature.

Both implicit in and beyond this corrective role, I assert that feeling can be specifically redemptive of our bodies. Our bodies are attended to, tuned into, re-membered through feeling. Tuning into feeling itself is like lubricating the connective tissue of who we really are. It facilitates a healthier flow; it enables movement that heals rather than harms. Awareness of feeling empowers an enlivened embodied sensation of divine activity. It can empower us to have the visceral intuition of how the divine intersects in the play of life's constant becoming. Feeling attests to the immediacy of redemptive possibility. It reveals the texture of the fabric of divine participation in existence. In all of these ways and more, feeling has healing, liberating, and truth-giving capacity.

Wendy Farley describes redemption in her book, *Tragic Vision and Divine Compassion: A Contemporary Theodicy*, with great clarity and suggestiveness. She is careful to describe (symbolically) the power of God as the power to redeem—not to control, but to liberate, heal, and restore. Most importantly, she points to the resistance of evil as that which redemption empowers. Redemption is not a clean break from evil, but a power that refuses to let it have the last word. Farley explains that redemption is the power that remains even in the horrible and ongoing suffering of the world to resist, repair, heal, struggle, and even celebrate what is good.[19]

---

17. It is mostly through his critique of the main currents of Western philosophy that one could interpret Whitehead as pointing toward feeling as a means of redemption. He does not use the language of redemption, nor does he focus on how his thinking addresses the problems that we now label as problems of embodiment. For instance, Whitehead spells out this aspect of feeling's redemptive role indirectly in the way feeling functions philosophically as a corrective to the imbalance of authority assigned to the information we gather through conscious thought.

18. Sallie McFague describes sin as "living a lie" in *The Body of God* (Minneapolis: Fortress, 1993) in her chapter 4, "At Home on the Earth," pp. 99–130.

19. Farley, *Tragic Vision*, 132.

Feeling fills out its redemptive capacity in three ways in light of Farley's definition of redemption. First, feeling helps to liberate us from the destructive powers of sin and evil. An analysis by way of feeling can help to liberate us to deeper, more complex awareness that resists triviality. Second, feeling is healing. Feeling is where healing can take root and whence it can usher in more abundant embodied life. Feeling works against suffering, not by justifying it or seeking it out, but by resisting its attempts to have the last word. Feeling heals us from loss, harm, and pain. Feeling does not render scars invisible nor does it restore what is harmed to some prior or pristine state. What this healing looks like becomes real in the genius of the body's survival skills. Third, feeling, by way of theological analysis and by way of embodied experience, is restorative of the worth and promise of the body. In this power to restore, feeling is not simply an example of redemption, but a mechanism of it becoming actual in our lived experience. It is the tool, our *imago Dei*, that allows for redemption to become real. Feeling does not enable the perfection of bodies, nor does it bring us to a somehow untroubled embodied experience. Feeling re-members the body by tuning us in to its complexity, creativity, and possibility. It is the mechanism of our living into the promise of redemption.

Each of the three constructive chapters that follow explores the redemptive capacity of feeling. Three important loci of this redemptive dynamic merit discussion before moving into that constructive work. The direct applications in those chapters will give these loci content. This brief look at these three loci provides us with a framework as we move forward: the construction of subjectivity, the dynamic of simple physical feeling, and the decentering of consciousness.

Constructions of Subjectivity

One can argue that both Whitehead and Schleiermacher contain related critical aspects in their work with feeling. Whitehead's "superject," his "antecedent" bodily feeling, and his critique of the Western privileging of consciousness all certainly inform these areas of my exploration. Likewise, in Schleiermacher's work his premodern sensitivity about human experience is important to my work. He also has elements of how *Gefühl* is informed by habit and practice and formation that suggest the importance of embodied practice. These thinkers are joined by many others who interrogate Western assumptions about certainty, the privileging of cognition, and the dynamics of subjectivity. Much of this movement in contemporary thought is reflected in the work of contemporary social theory (Judith Butler is just one example among many) and in "located" theologies (feminist, womanist, postcolonial theologies, *mujeristas*, etc.).[20]

20. The deep complication of the subject that Whitehead's system provides for the social/biological dichotomies that contribute to how the body is formed and understood is perhaps most closely akin to phenomenologists like Maurice Merleau-Ponty.

For our purposes it is important to keep in mind a few things about subjectivity. In the context of feeling's flow, subjectivity is organic and fluid. It is enmeshed with everything that is and formed in its particularity by the unique constellations of feeling's constant flow. The subject resists the attempt to parse out precisely the effects of biology and the work of social construction on its formation. The subject is not located as an independent entity apart from its entanglement with everything else that is.[21] In this understanding Whitehead explains that the subject (or "superject") "never really is."[22] This "neverness" of the subject also has substantive comparative qualities with the "no-self" of Buddhist thought. Subjectivity is radically relational and constantly in process.

This view of the subject clears a space for the body to show itself as active and ingenious in how subjectivity is formed and forming. Subjects or selves do not operate in isolation. Feelings flow in a complex web of factors. The subject is constantly entangled in the web. Although it is unique in its negotiation of it, it is not extractable from it. In the initial stages there are many feelings, and in subsequent phases complex feelings integrate earlier simpler feelings and move toward "satisfaction," which is one complex unity of feeling.[23] For our purposes, satisfaction suggests expressions of particularity. Satisfaction is, in this way, integral to subjectivity because it is unique and particular. The uniqueness comes in how the inheritance of all that is is felt. This "satisfaction" points toward a dynamic that, like everything else, is fleeting and repetitive. We cannot abstract feeling from that which is entertaining feeling because that which is doing the feeling is what makes the feeling one thing and not many things.[24] What we are and who we are is both a relational and a uniquely particular phenomenon. The

21. For instance, Whitehead believed the basic problem with Western assumptions about the subject to be "the fallacy of simple location," which places the individual separate from the succession of temporal occasions. Whitehead discusses the "fallacy of simple location" in numerous places. He defines it as the "presupposition of individual independence" (*Process and Reality*, 137). In this Western view against which Whitehead constructs his view of the "superject," the subject is seen as a discrete locus of experience and the cognition of the subject was understood as the site of all experience. For more information on how he connects the fallacy with space and time, see Whitehead, *Science and the Modern World*, 49ff. Here he also explains the fallacy of "misplaced concreteness" as the mistaking of the abstract for the concrete.

22. *Science and the Modern World*, 82. Whitehead is echoing the sentiments of Plato's *Timaeus*. Whitehead explains, "This conception of an actual entity in the fluent world is little more than an expansion of a sentence in the *Timaeus*: 'But that which is conceived by opinion with the help of sensation and without reason, is always in a process of becoming and perishing and never really is.'"

23. Satisfaction is a complicated concept in Whitehead's thought, and, like many of his terms, open to some debate as to what it actually describes. Whitehead himself defines satisfaction as the "one felt content" of an actual entity that results from something like choices (he uses "selective concrescence") of which "eternal objects" are used to determine how data are transformed into fact. Here we feel the pull of Whitehead's language world as we feel the need for more and more definition, which in turn brings on more and more terms, which in turn need definition. Satisfaction only instantly moves into the past as the actual entity encounters further data. As Whitehead muses, "Time has stood still—if only it could" (*Process and Reality*, 154).

24. In turn, Whitehead explains, "The feelings are what they are in order that their subject may be what it is" (ibid., 221–22).

body is reclaimed in this description of subjectivity as crucial to the constant creation of how we condition both ourselves and what is around us. We depend on the body for our own formation; and our body, in turn, depends on all that is around it. We are, at bottom, creative and created in a constant sense. Continuity within that creativity is radically embodied.

In our working view of the subject, the body is restored in its value. It is recovered from the diminutive status it holds in a concept of the subject in which we are discrete, isolated, and independent from the flux of the rest of the world, constructing ourselves with our minds, defining the world with how and what we know. The body is no longer the deceiver, the one to overcome, but is an important element in how we live truthfully and well. Because relationality is primary, indeed cellular, sense experience and cognition are fed by a primal physical feeling that, as it plays out in experience, serves to help create the thinker himself or herself. The primacy of feeling and relationship are essentially one and the same. This primal reality creates a rhythmic process of experience in which we move back and forth between what Whitehead calls "publicity and privacy."[25] The subject does not direct this dance, but is directed from the organic publicity of all things toward the immediacy of "who I am." Feeling has the capacity to liberate us from perceived isolation by restoring our awareness of our interdependence on connection and relationship. As water revives a wilting plant, tuning into feeling can help us to tap into the healing and strength-giving power of how we are entangled with all that is. Feeling helps the dry bones to dance like the sinews. Both give us strength, power, and vigor to live a life of zest.

The Dynamic of Simple Physical Feeling

The second redemptive element of feeling for bodies grows out of the nature of our most primary experiences. In human experience the most fundamental reality that feeds our perception is that there is antecedent bodily "prehension."[26] It is only at higher stages of perception that there is the differentiation of what we know as sense experience. When there is a transmission to the mind and then to the nerves, we have sense experience. At still a higher stage we are conscious of the experience and begin to think about it, analyze it, reflect on it, understand it, give voice to it, or even distort it. Because our bodies regulate our cognizance of the world, all that we take in, perceive, and act out of depends on how our bodies are functioning. How we perceive, how we know, how we judge depends on how well our bodies are functioning. Our bodies are not isolated objects but

25. By this movement Whitehead refers to how the subject moves back and forth through the ideal and actual causes of its uniqueness (*Process and Reality*, 151).

26. Rather than reduce all sense experience to the mind or an impression of the mind or as an experience of the mind, Whitehead wanted to highlight the "antecedent" part of the body that has the most primary experience. See the discussion in Whitehead, *Process and Reality,* 117–19. It is here that Whitehead finds resonance in Hume's work, even though many say that Hume was actually talking about the mind instead of the eye. The use of the word "perception" is problematic and one of the reasons why Whitehead coined the term "prehension."

are involved every moment in all else that is. Level of function, therefore, is an organic phenomenon. It is determined by relationship, and it is manifested in every aspect of our bodies. One could liken it to the experience of burning the tongue with a cup of hot tea. One's ability to taste is compromised. One's abilities to judge, describe, and evaluate food are compromised along with one's ability to taste. A similar dynamic plays out with feeling and body function.

Ignoring the importance of the body's functioning translates into ignoring actual harm to our bodies. Harm to bodies has effects much further flung than simple changes, bumps, or bruises. Harm to our bodies has a ripple effect on the entire way our bodies function, all the way up to activities like perception, sensation, reflection, judgment, action, and speaking out of our experience. Harm to our bodies is harm to our very mode of life, to our most basic way of negotiating ourselves around life in the world. Harm to bodies harms our ability to feel. Attending to how feeling is connected to level of bodily function also highlights the body losses, changes, and needs that are ignored if we reduce our experiences to that of which we are conscious.

Body function is related to all the other manifestations of our functioning. Bodies are radically connected to all else that is. These dynamics of who we are reveal how relationships and how they respond to experience can both help and hinder the recovery of body function. This relational aspect of body functioning suggests that all of our bodies are compromised in their function when any body is harmed in its ability to feel. Redemption of bodies then involves attention to the reasons, the responses, and the relationships that are needed in order to address substantially harm and/or changes in bodies. Attention to feeling remembers the body in how it is both harmed and healed. Harm is multilayered and embodied; therefore, healing must be, too.

The Decentering of Consciousness

The third redemptive element of feeling points to how feelings that are not conscious modify the rest of experience. Unlike the illustration of body function in which harm distorts, in this element of feeling well-functioning feeling is indicated by the limits of consciousness. Because of the body's primacy, language and consciousness have limits in their ability to clarify experience. Feeling can help to liberate our bodies from the liabilities of incomplete consciousness. The things that are prominent in our consciousness are many times superficial in the full scope of feeling. What we know comes into prominence because our experience reinforces and develops these feelings into conscious thought.[27] These are simplifications of experience that allow us to name things, to categorize, and to group clusters of events into one constellation of meaning. These qualifications of experience then give shape to how and even what we experience. Conscious-

27. Whitehead uses the term "transmuted feelings" to name the way we become conscious of the world. What is physical may become conceptual in a way that allows it then to be felt as physical again later in an "extended role" (*Process and Reality*, 253).

ness is created out of physical feeling and can actually cycle back into our experience as a felt physical feeling. These layers of feeling shape our awareness. These recycled feelings gather up meaning and content. Their effect goes far beyond themselves as they continue to participate physically in the flow of feeling.

Whitehead explains that there are other elements of experience that are on the "fringe of consciousness," and yet they "massively qualify our experience."[28] Here Whitehead points to the efficacy of feelings that do not ever become conscious experience. Coming into consciousness, therefore, is not necessarily a function of importance.[29] Feelings can have a vast impact even when they remain "under the radar" of conscious thought.[30] The body becomes the central site for how these feelings are expressed and "heard." For instance, "physically unexplainable" somatic symptoms are often the body's communication of an experience that has had an impact and needs some attention. From skin rashes to gastrointestinal distress, the body may "speak" of distress when the consciousness is not privy to the means of expression. The play of feeling in our consciousness, the limited resource that consciousness is, and feeling's intimacy with how the body is functioning all give us a rich sense of how our thoughts are not all we need to make "sense" of experience.

Feeling is redemptive when we take seriously the way it forms us. A simple physical feeling feels another feeling; all relationships are built up of these simple physical feelings. These feelings are constantly giving birth to both the future and the past because they are fleetingly present.[31] Because feelings only sometimes rise to consciousness, when they do it is often after feelings have had time to grow and gather in clarity and distinction. "Thinking" through an issue, therefore, does not exhaust the work our bodies need to be healthy. Embodied practices tune us into the nature of simple physical feeling and how it encourages us to "change" our minds from thinking that consciousness is primary to realizing the way feeling speaks to us in the body. Feeling urges us toward embracing the body's genius for "figurative" communication, its survival skills, and its mystery. Embodied practice can improve our acumen at "hearing" the body's language. Embodied practices that attend to feeling form habits of being alive that make us more at home in our bodies. Habits can develop into *habitus*—a susceptibility, a physical characteristic; embodied practice can actually change the way our bodies function. For example, many different schools of thought, ranging from yoga to meditation to chiropractic theories to some Western medical philosophy, maintain that deep breathing actually improves the functioning capacity of the nervous system. This cycle of increased awareness, deliberate

---

28. Whitehead, *Adventures of Ideas* (New York: Macmillan, 1933), 163–64. Whitehead continues, "it is our consciousness that flickers, and not the facts themselves. They are always securely there, barely discriminated, and yet inescapable."

29. See below, chapter 2, n. 44, for a discussion of "importance."

30. Bodily memory is an illustration of this aspect of feeling.

31. Whitehead uses "conformal" to describe how they conform the immediate present to the past (*Process and Reality*, 238).

practice, and improved body function reveals how redemption works. It is lived out in practice and manifested in our dispositions.

Embodiment is the condition of our existence that renders practice of utmost importance to living honestly and fully. Because of the conditioning power of feelings and the radically relational nature of them, practice is that which urges and coaxes along the continued process of these feelings' integration into who we are always becoming. This capacity of feeling to translate into behaviors and dispositions is apparent in Schleiermacher's focus on formation and the trajectory of redemption in human life. Practice forms feeling into the habitual ways we conform to the past and move into the future. Practice is not to be understood as a mechanistic control or directing of feelings, but as a wearing of a new creek bed in the texture of our particularity so that it is with greater ease that feelings flow in these habits. Practice can condition our consciousness and our attunement to the promise of redeemed bodies. Practice can help us take on certain dispositions that are honest to the ways our bodies function and to the needs our bodies have. Feeling's recovery offers the possibility of the redemption of our knowing and our doing from thinness and triviality toward a zestful, healthy, and robust, albeit more risky, existence.

In the chapters that follow, I take feeling into the embodied experiences of rape, pregnancy, and motherhood and shine a light on three aspects of our embodiment. These three experiences at the level of feeling open into a more complicated and, I hope, more honest way to think about, talk about, and live in our bodies. These explorations are theological, and they search for that something, however modestly universal, that helps us out of the perils of a disembodied faith toward a re-membering of God's embodied hopes for us. The Incarnation tells us that human flourishing is tied to an embodied fullness of life (John 10:10). In a disembodied faith, bodies languish, they are ignored, and they are silenced. As our bodies languish, so suffers everything about us—our spirits, minds, and emotions. In a re-embodied faith, bodies flourish, they are attended to, and they are heard. Feeling trains our ear for stories, poetics, and metaphors of embodied experience.

PART I
FEELING BODIES

The Witness

Plaintive cries for some
      are life's expression
For others there are sweet cadences
      that lift the oppression of pain
      if only for a time.
For them guttural groan comes
      only when death takes a child
      or when companions are lost
      or place destroyed.
Some voices give truth—
      and then the excruciating wait ensues
      flashpoints of being wide open
      then a womb is the one rhythmic haven
      the only place to feel good.
You drink in change
      you know how to be a sieve to fluidity
      and wait for air to open you another day.

Prologue to Part I

"Can I Get a Witness?"

Embodying theology is like writing a poem. In a poem the word on the page is an echo of experience that cannot be fully spoken. The poem allows for suggestion, impression, emotion, and still open space for reception and even for confounding confusion. Embodying theology heightens our awareness of our vulnerability and our potential for wisdom as well as error. The theologian in me asks questions of ultimate meaning. Still I am located and limited. I am vulnerable and well aware of the hazards of a project that means sharing fragments of painful experience as well as glimpses of my own moments of delight. I am a witness, just like you are, to what living as a body feels like. I do this work not to collapse your experience into mine, but to shine some light on our common experiences through the lens of an incarnational faith.

In our current theological landscape, I am both emboldened and chastened in my own act of witnessing. My courage is drawn from centuries of Christian witnessing and, most recently, from the words of women speaking from the margins of the Christian tradition. These women not only have had to work to be heard, they have had to craft new languages with which to speak. They live in the limits and the power of language.[1] Witnessing tells a truth that must function in the flux of lived reality. Its truth is located, but not necessarily distorted, by its particularity. From the words of witnesses recorded in Scripture to the great theologians of the tradition, personal accounts have been shared in the earnest hope that they sound some resonance with the human condition and its relationship to God. Witnessing comes into new relief, for what it both can and cannot communicate about the human condition. Witnessing is not about the last word; it is about a "living word."[2] It functions as a fluid glimpse of reality that vivifies and describes life as it continues in its flux. The manner in which it abides in the everyday is where its power lies. Although its starting place is concrete, its destination is unknown. It is the confidence that grace gives the believer that makes this road less traveled a way through life we can choose to take.

My own witnessing is made both possible and impossible by the complexity of who a witness can be. I live the problematic dynamics of what being a witness entails. Witnessing to personal experience brings with it both authority and irreducible particularity. It is limited, but perhaps also illuminating of something that seeps through the boundaries of its uniqueness. These dynamics can play out in any experience to which one is a witness. The complexity of witnessing takes on another layer of difficulty when trauma is involved. The troubling space that a witness to trauma occupies may mean that telling the story is imperative for any return to well-being, even as it is possessed of the destructive power of the trauma itself. Telling the story is imperative at the same time that the story remains impossible.

My witnessing is born out of varied experiences, some of which intimately inform this project. My role as witness to experiences like pregnancy and motherhood bring with them partiality along with a call I feel to give them prominence in the larger theological conversation. My role as witness to the experience of rape comes with the same partiality, the same offer to theology, but also brings with it all the problems of traumatized memory. Because I bear witness to the trauma of rape, I also bear witness to the importance of witnessing itself. This terrible and liberating gift of finding a way to witness is something I have been able to do only with God's help. God faithfully offers survival and new life into my work. Telling is, in a sense, an offering to God and to all those with whom I share existence. Witnessing sounds the truth of God's sustaining love; it is the hard work of survival, it is an act of thanksgiving, it is the fruit of redemption. Witnessing not only testifies to God's abiding presence, but it is the actuality of God's lure toward greater Beauty and a life of zest.

I grew up a good Presbyterian. My faith and my church provided me with a ground on which to stand, a reason for being, and a way to survive. When my

---

1. Rebecca Chopp points toward this revised mode of witnessing in her call for feminism to "create new ways of dwelling" rather than seeking the "magic city" (*The Power to Speak: Feminism, Language, God* [New York: Crossroad, 1992], 128).

2. Chopp calls on theologians to witness in order to speak a "living Word to and for the World" (ibid., 6). Her invitation points toward the fluidity and the efficacy of located theological work.

life got complicated by sexual violence, I remember my fifteen-year-old self feeling alone, isolated, and ashamed. But I was still breathing, still going to school every day, still making it to track practice, still praying, and still churchgoing. My faith was my ground; it kept me from sinking, it kept me alive. It is only as an adult that I began to take a step back from that ground. I began to dig into it. I began to examine how it was that I survived. I realized that the ground on which I stood to keep me steady all those years might not have been as solid as it had seemed to me at the time. I found quicksand in some places, shifting ground that had sunk me deeper into abusive patterns of relationship. I found some of it dried and cracking, some cold and unforgiving.

Even with its traps, however, this ground remains beneath me. It remains that which keeps me from despair. The texture of my ground has been enriched by my digging, by the painful work of keeping and tilling and turning out and turning over all that composes it. This ground has been irrigated and fertilized by those experiences that have helped me root out its limitations and deficiencies. It is becoming a loamy, rich place that nourishes me as someone who lives into many different modes of relationship, into many different ways of feeling and understanding the world in which I live. It is this ground that enables me to write what follows, to feel seasoned enough to describe a problem in my faith tradition, to feel creative enough to shine a light on the promise of a perspective that is more honest to the realities I have lived and still live. This ground has grown me into a witness to the perils of a disembodied faith and to the promise of tending to feeling bodies.

Being a witness carries a mixture of meanings. There are legal witnesses who have both the authority of presence and the "reliability" of some level of objectivity. They are proximate to, and also somehow removed from, an experience. On the other hand, the history of Christian witnessing calls on entangled and immediate experience. The Christian witness is granted authority because of personal conviction and gives testimony to that experience. Some contemporary theology, for instance, draws on the authority of those who have firsthand experiences of oppression as witnesses. The witnesses are believed to give theological description more accuracy and less obfuscation. In either case, a witness is someone who has a story that needs to be told. This story can manifest itself in many forms: an account of an accident, court testimony, a description of an occurrence, or testimony about a personal experience.

In the intersection of meanings that witnessing carries with it there is a paradox. It can suggest that a bystander, someone watching from the outside, has perhaps the most reliable description of something that happened. At the same time, it can require personal, direct contact of some sort with what is being described. The witness is assumed to possess some knowledge, some understanding, because of his or her proximity to "what happened." This kind of knowledge requires both personal presence and adequate distance. A witness is curiously both participant and observer. "Reliable" witnesses have traditionally been those who have both aspects in their entanglement with experience. With the correct balancing of aspects of involvement the account of a witness is believed to provide proof—confirmation of what "really" happened.

Those who actually experienced something, however, are often not regarded as the most reliable witness as to what "really" happened. Their testimony is that of victim, that of the firsthand account that needs the affirmation of the witness. Who constitutes a reliable witness is weighed down by the kind of witnessing we are able to hear. Indeed, victims of rape are dismissed more times than not because their testimony is "unreliable" due to inconsistencies and confusion even though they are the only ones who actually *had* the experience. Women in labor are often encouraged to take drugs so that the medical staff can tell her what is happening to her body without the interference of the woman's own description of what is happening. Mothers are often dismissed by the more "objective" observers of their children (doctors, psychologists, etc.) in order to diagnose problems more "accurately." Herein lies the bias of objectivity that Western culture has been called to own up to in this postmodern era.

With the fissure in the "truth-telling" of modernity, witnessing has been disrupted along with objectivity. Objectivity has lost its beloved place in "telling the truth," and subjective experience has surfaced with a new kind of authority. Those who have lived, breathed, and died by the experiences that others have tried to describe and interpret for them are telling their own truth now. How this truth is negotiated in the context of larger questions of the human situation is the dance of our day. The dance is delicate, dangerous, and quite demanding in its power to disrupt and deconstruct. There is a space cleared for voices of experience that speak in languages unfamiliar and unknown. With this new space for witnessing comes the troubled truth of witnessing one's own experience, especially when it involves trauma.

The complexity of this troubled truth of witnessing comes into relief in work done about the Holocaust. Dori Laub, in his article "Truth and Testimony," asserts that there are three levels of witnessing as he relates it to the Holocaust. First is the level of being a witness to oneself within the experience. Second is the level of being a witness to the testimonies of others. Third is being a witness to the process of witnessing itself.[3] Laub describes the Holocaust as a "collapse of witnessing"—"the historical imperative to bear witness could not be met during the occurrence" because of the depth of its trauma.[4] Yet those who survived testify to being motivated to live by the need to tell their stories. Laub sees in these survivors the necessity of telling the stories to ensure their survival itself. He sees also the complexity of working within a process in which the horror of the experience has been submerged and requires repeated submergence even as it is revealed and relived. The witnessing out of trauma calls on a different kind of

3. Dori Laub, "Truth and Testimony: The Process and the Struggle," in *Trauma: Explorations in Memory*, ed. Cathy Caruth (Baltimore: Johns Hopkins University Press, 1995), 61.
4. Ibid., 64–65.

listening, a different kind of patience, and the ability to abide by both the return and departure from what happened.[5]

As the Holocaust so horribly substantiates, the need to tell the story of trauma is possessed also of the impossibility of telling it. As Laub explains, therefore, "silence about the truth commonly prevails"; and even for those who "incessantly" tell their story, they feel they have said very little.[6] For those who choose silence, the result is a more grotesque kind of distortion. Not telling the story allows it to infect the survivor's everyday life in distorted form. The longer the story goes untold, the more distorted it becomes, until the survivor doubts that it really happened.[7]

Witnessing to trauma teaches us about witnessing to anything that calls us to realize and live in the limits of language, thought, memory, and analysis. At a time such as ours, witnessing testifies to the constant shifting between listening and speaking. Bearing witness in this embodied context is a new, troubled and troubling, mode of telling and doing and listening and being. It is not the last word, but some word. It is not only words, but silences and bodies and habits and sensitivities. Witnessing conceals even as it reveals; it tells, retells, and untells. It speaks in metaphors. It spins itself out of poetics; it is disorienting with its clarity.[8] Witnesses give flesh to truths untold; they also conjure up the ghosts of what cannot be told.

5. Caruth, "Trauma and Experience: Introduction," in *Trauma*, 10. Caruth discusses knowing how to listen to departure when we take seriously the challenge the trauma brings to how we listen.

6. Laub, "Truth and Testimony," 64.

7. As some Holocaust survivors fall prey to Alzheimer's disease, this delay of trauma and the captivity of memories and experience are set loose to be triggered and experienced in many ways. Many nursing home facilities who are home to some of these survivors have instituted Holocaust awareness training so that they can be more sensitive to how certain words (e.g., "shower") can trigger a reliving of experiences in concentration camps. This reliving in the lives of those whose minds are thrown into dysfunction by Alzheimer's disease certainly illustrates Laub's point in a horribly clear way. See Tom McCann, "Nightmare World: Holocaust Survivors with Alzheimer's can suffer flashbacks of old horrors. Nursing homes are learning how to help them," *Chicago Tribune*, 24 January 2003.

8. This dynamic of revealing meaning so concretely and yet so mysteriously is paralleled provocatively in Jesus' use of parables to describe the kingdom of God.

Chapter 2

Feeling Tragic Bodies

Narratives in the Flesh

Re-collections

Running down the street in small town Kentucky
wet between my legs.
Darkness of night covers red blood.
I resolve between pounding heart and footsteps never to tell.

No way out.

Locked away in my plan for making it all right.
What happened was
my fault, my responsibility.
I could bring order.

My companion—Jesus. My savior—the Christ.
Moral fortitude. Rational control.
Stoic in the face of pain.
Steadfast, unselfish, sufferer.

r-a-p-e . . . something that happened to other people.
I understand though—I mean I understand how it feels,
what it feels like—all of it. Stomach churning. Heart racing.
Face burning. Legs stiff. Arms locked down.
The blood. The secret.

WWJD? Keep quiet, keep believing, make it right. . . .

My body: my problem, my broken part, my damaged goods.
I can control this baggage. . . .
                    No eating for a week.
                    Run on splintering bones.
                    Turn your back, don't listen. . . .
The dull roar of my body's language is background noise
            to his insults and threats—loud and clear.
            WWJD? Love, patience, servitude. . . .

                    One day
            I move outside and say "NO MORE."
    It bubbled up from somewhere deep inside—
            fighting its way up into my throat.
    It was involuntary or unconscious or something
            I didn't think myself into.
    It came out and I heard it for the first time,
                    just like he did.

Then some of his promises came true—knife, speeding car,
            footsteps on my roof.
    Me belly crawling through my dark teenage room
            into my sister's—"help."
                    Lights on.

    He took to the shadows—he still might be there.
I can't remember his face, only his weight bearing down.

            A body remembers.

STORIES TOLD, UNTOLD, RETOLD, UNTELLABLE

Throughout the rape, like so much bad television, like so many bad movies, his words were familiar. . . . Some of what I hate most about what happened to me is the easy accessibility of these words, these images of women. My attacker was able to readily articulate his rage. He had our shared culture to give words to his violence. The injustice in all of this is that now, even months later, I have so few words to speak about my rape from my own perspective. As a woman in this culture I am voiceless.

                                        Laura Levitt

I, like Laura Levitt, struggle for language that articulates my rape. Even with the years that stretch out between me and those lonely days of secret shame, even with new space to say out loud that I have been raped, I live with the jangle of unworded sensation and pain and sadness. I also abide in the patterns and deeply entrenched habits of my body that took hold in me in the unfolding of time. For me, collecting fragments of trauma and tragedy into spoken words is excruciating in its limitation even while this need to find a voice that can speak of it is of chilling necessity. I am not alone in my frustration and in my hard work. I am part of a densely populated cacophony of voices who can speak only in fragments. The words we find and make audible only reflect the edges of the shadows of embodied trauma.

In this chapter I try to give audibility and publicity to the storytelling capacity of the body itself. The body's language is equally partial to the words that we use to describe rape. The body does not render a whole or seamless narrative. But the body tells remarkable and unspoken aspects of what being raped is and what it does and how healing can unfold. And more than that, when we listen to the fragments of the story that the body has to tell around rape, with new clarity we hear of aspects of embodied human existence. In particular we become more aware of the harm of being uncomfortable in our skin. We are confronted with narratives that can help us be more at home with ourselves. We hear and marvel at the genius of our bodies in the wake of trauma.

Entangled in the truth and abiding partiality of words are bodies that need complicated acknowledgment and care. Bodies ignored and left to languish are only more at risk for harm. The church needs to be a place that intentionally addresses bodies in their complicated truth. Remember Christianity is an incarnational faith! The tragic nature of all human bodies and the dynamics of how bodies hold tragedy call out for a new embodied responsiveness from the church. Each of us, as particular bodies, and we, as the gathered Body of Christ, live in need of this new responsiveness. The promise of the Christian life is that we are transformed by God's embodied proximity to us. That transformation re-forms us most deeply when it seeps into the ways we inhabit our own bodies and into the ways we respond to the bodies of others.

All embodied existence entails suffering and so shares in the tragic layers of having a human body. Human bodies are not only steeped in the distortions and deformities of sin, as Reformed theology has described with great acumen. Human bodies are also ravaged by the wounds of tragedy. Suffering is, indeed, entangled with the wages of sin, but suffering is also a fact of human life that is sometimes addressed best outside the framework of sin, guilt, and forgiveness. Sin carries with it moral judgment for suffering; tragedy focuses less on judgment and more on acknowledgment, grief, and compassion. Embodied life inevitably intersects with violence, loss, and victimization in ways that challenge and change us. Some of these changes are permanent scars that deserve recognition and compassion, not blame and shame.

In the larger culture, there are parts of the story of rape that we hear from sources like newspapers and television when a rape manages to register on society's Richter Scale. We hear about weapons; we hear about how perpetrators can force their way into apartments or cars. Most of the story, however, is untold, unheard, and untellable. Even when a rape is reported, the aftershocks that continue to reverberate throughout the life of a survivor of rape go far beyond what we hear about once a news story grows cold. These aftershocks also go beyond what language can tell us.

Before language can articulate an experience, there must be a way for that experience, even in its fragmentation and imperfection, to be acknowledged. Acknowledgment may simply be listening differently or making room in our reality for something that is unfamiliar, troubled, and disorienting—all things at which the ethos of Protestant theology has not excelled. Finding a safe space to speak, finding language to use, and receiving simple acknowledgment are some of the basic needs of victims of rape. All of these basic needs are best offered in a place that is not pushing the rape victim to keep her story straight or convince someone of her legitimacy.

Even with the gift of a place to speak safely, victims still abide in a complicated space where language can be mistaken for the sole goal of healing work. Tragic experiences like rape defy language. Words cannot exhaust or even access all that the body feels and knows. Therefore, the needs of the survivor and the surrounding community go deeper. These embodied needs press upon us theologically and ecclesiologically. A richer, thicker, more enfleshed understanding of the body will not just give us new words, concepts, and approaches to the body, but it will help us to suspend our tendencies to ignore that which cannot be completely understood, that which cannot be drawn into speech. What if we let go of the need to explain away, dismiss, or even despise that which we do not understand? What could it look like for the church to create spaces for body language? Healing from trauma may need a place to garden in a safe courtyard of the church. Acknowledging may mean regular opportunities for healing liturgies that focus not on words but on embodied practices like anointing with oil, laying on of hands, or sacred movement. These embodied practices are of utter necessity since body language does not yield complete comprehension. Embodied healing needs space for its expression even in its mystery.

Feeling does more than give us language for stories to be told and heard with more truth; it offers us a way into the very mode of experiencing, the very body that suffers. Rape at the level of feeling tells the embodied truth of tragedy.[1] All of us live the embodied truth of tragedy. By examining some common themes of tragedy and how they connect with the embodied experience of rape, we can bring to the light aspects of embodiment that we all share. Protestant theology desperately needs to attend to these layers of human experience. When we find language that is honest to these experiences, and when there are dispositions growing out of the truth of embodied life, Protestant theology can live in and live out of the complexity of embodiment with greater integrity.

---

1. All rapes and sexual assaults are not the same; they are as varied as those who have suffered from the experience. There are, however, some common elements that show themselves at least in skeletal form when we look at the phenomenon of rape.

As we explore what we do and do not and cannot know about rape, notice that the church is a conspicuously minor player in the conversation. The layer of silence that quiets talk of the body in Protestant theology can suffocate the voices that cry out from the experiences of rape.[2] When the voices do break through the silence, often they are quickly muffled, if not overpowered, by the church's negativity toward bodies. Even as the pain of sexual violence harms our ability to speak out, Protestant conceptions of the body deal victims another blow, reinforcing the trauma. There is little acknowledgment of the very reality of rape itself. Further, clergy and the church most often address rape within the theological framework of sin and forgiveness. This theological paradigm overlaid on rape often does further harm rather than invite healing.[3] For those in the church trying to deal with rape's aftermath there are remarkably few resources.[4]

When you are sitting in church there may be no visible sign that those around you are suffering. You yourself may be suffering and feel little to no desire or opportunity to give that suffering expression in church. But, whether we acknowledge it or not, all of us bear the marks of suffering and tragedy. Trauma seeps into everything, it affects all that is. Renewal and redemption and

2. My comments here should be understood as a reference to the church as an institution and the silence that has been exercised by that institution. There have been people within the church who have spoken out about and written about rape and sexual abuse. The church as an institution, however, has done little to disrupt the ethos of silence that has enveloped most victims of sexual abuse. At the General Assembly of the Presbyterian Church (U.S.A.) in 2001, one of the working committees took some time at one of their meetings to recognize and hear the stories of some women who had suffered from domestic violence. After they told their stories, many of which included the church being a source of harm rather than help, the moderator of the committee asked for their forgiveness on behalf of the church for how the church had not helped them. It was an emotional moment for all of us who were there in that room. This overture is an important start to the kind of recognition for which I am describing a need in this project. Some examples of important and helpful writing from those who are within the church are: Pamela Cooper-White, *The Cry of Tamar: Violence Against Women and the Church's Response* (Minneapolis: Fortress, 1995); Marie Fortune, *Sexual Violence: The Unmentionable Sin* (New York: Pilgrim, 1983); Toinette M. Eugene, "'Swing Low, Sweet Chariot': A Womanist Response to Sexual Violence and Abuse," *Daughters of Sarah* 20 (Summer 1994): 10–14; Carol J. Adams, "I just raped my wife! What are you going to do about it, Pastor? The Church and Sexual Violence," in *Transforming a Rape Culture*, ed. Emilie Buchwald, Pamela Fletcher, and Martha Roth (Minneapolis: Milkweed, 1993), 59–86; and Kristin J. Leslie, *When Violence Is No Stranger: Pastoral Counseling with Survivors of Acquaintance Rape* (Minneapolis: Fortress, 2003).

3. Later in this chapter I discuss briefly the harm of using forgiveness to respond to those who have been raped. See the introduction for more discussion of how sin is an inadequate theological answer to the complexity of the body. This issue is also touched on at the end of this chapter in the section describing tragedy.

4. Early on in my writing, the Roman Catholic Church came under public scrutiny because of allegations and admissions of sexual abuse in the priesthood. These allegations increasingly revealed the institutional denial of the harm of sexual abuse. The abuse is systemic, not simply the work of a few individuals. Although this painful situation is playing out in a context other than a Protestant one, its dynamics are not foreign to how similar harm is addressed in Protestant churches. This situation, as it has played out in the media, indicates how few resources—from words spoken to actions taken—there are in the church for honestly addressing and authentically healing from experiences of sexual violence.

new life are trivialized when we deny trauma or ignore its effects. Overly intellec-tualized worship forms are dangerously close to being a simple source of sedation to numb us from the permeations of tragedy in our lives. If we stay in our heads and do not feel the losses and the harm that we bear, we are denying the truth of who we are and where we have been, and most importantly, what we need. To be people who know how to thrive and love and heal in God's creation we cannot be afraid to attend more honestly to our own condition.

Survivors of sexual assault bear the truth of our condition in textured relief—some of it seen, some unseen, some palpable, some grotesque, and some hard to access. Post-traumatic stress disorder and rape trauma syndrome, two constella-tions of symptoms associated with rape, may sound like dysfunctions foreign to most people's lives, but their presence is more prevalent than one might assume. Their effects ripple out into relationships, communities, and into one another's bodies with quiet vigor. Examining these symptoms often associated with rape is important because they describe the symptoms that harmed bodies show forth again and again, even when our consciousness and our emotions show no obvi-ous signs of trauma.[5] The pattern and persistence of these symptoms among sexual assault victims show us the persistent and destructive power of harm. We may begin to see how all bodies hold and are marked by what the consciousness refuses to take in.

WHAT WE KNOW ABOUT RAPE

And since [Amnon] was stronger than [Tamar] was, he overpowered her and raped her. . . . She sprinkled ashes on her head, tore her robe, and with her face buried went away crying. When her brother Absalom saw her, he asked, "Has Amnon molested you? Please, sister, don't let it upset you so much. He is your half brother, so don't tell anyone about it." So Tamar lived in Absalom's house, sad and lonely.

2 Samuel 13:14, 19–20

For at least as long as the Bible has been around, rape victims have been told to keep quiet, dismissed even by their own families, and left to mourn alone. Isola-tion, grief, shame, and confusion mark the experience of being raped. The stories of rape survivors often share elements of silence and secrecy, born out of both the trauma of the experience itself and out of the societal response of disbelief. Statistics highlight these patterns of silence—rape is the most underreported crime there is.

---

5. Trauma theory is a growing body of work that will also assist us in our exploration. I do not list it here, however, because it is not accurately cast as a list of symptoms nor is it a diagnostic tool per se. It is, however, quite revealing in the work it includes around memory, physiological changes in the body due to trauma, and much, much more.

Every two minutes someone is sexually assaulted in the United States.[6] In 1999 only 28 percent of rapes were reported—that is fewer than one in three.[7] Now it is estimated that 60 percent of rapes and sexual assaults go unreported.[8] The rates of nonreporting go up the younger the victim. Of sexually abused children who are in grades five through twelve, 48 percent of boys and 29 percent of girls told no one about the abuse.[9] Just a few years ago, most estimates were that one in four women was the victim of an attempted sexual assault. The latest statistics suggest that one in six women is the victim of attempted or completed rape in their lifetime, which means 17.7 million American women have been victims of rape or attempted rape. Among juvenile sexual assaults, 93 percent of those assaulted knew their attacker (almost 59 percent were acquaintances; 34 percent were family members). In 2001 only 11 percent of rapes involved a weapon of any kind; 84 percent report the use of physical force only.

The numbers reveal a systemic culture of abuse even with the gains of the last ten to fifteen years. Through the heroic efforts of various arms of the women's movement, awareness continues to be raised about the prevalence of sexual assault in American society. The most striking area of improvement in the recent past has been in the growing awareness of rape's aftermath in a victim's life. While there are limitations in these developing interpretations, they give important acknowledgment of what many victims of rape experience. These developing interpretations give us a way to talk about this aftermath—even while the language does not exhaustively describe the experiences of rape.[10]

6. The statistics listed here are taken from various studies and compiled on the Web site of the Rape, Abuse, and Incest National Network (www.rainn.org).

7. From the 1999 study of the National Crime Victimization Survey, Bureau of Justice Statistics (RAINN Web site).

8. In criminal justice statistics rape is classified as forced penetration. Sexual assault is a broader term that comprises sexual attacks that do not include penetration.

9. From the Commonwealth Fund Survey of the Health of Adolescent Girls, 1998 (RAINN Web site). While there are many distinctions that I could make between types of sexual abuse and their effects, some that warrant mention here are those that involve children and/or ongoing abuse. These kinds of chronic situations introduce a deeply embodied kind of destructiveness. Ongoing abuse and abuse of children are situations in which the harm takes hold and defines a person with a great deal of tenacity, including but not limited to physiological changes in brain function, hormone production, etc.

10. Laura Levitt clearly describes the limits of these descriptive constellations of symptoms when she explains the betrayal she feels in the assumed understanding of terms like "rape trauma." She says, "I just read Elly Bulkin's *Enter Password: Recovery, Re-enter Password*, a painful but helpful book about recovery from child sexual abuse and the pain of breaking up from a long-term relationship. Yet, even here, I felt my own absence as a survivor of rape. Early on in the text, Bulkin refers to something she calls 'rape trauma' without explanation. She assumes understanding. I cannot. Nor can I let it go because I feel betrayed by such assumptions. I do not know what 'rape trauma' is. Yet, like Bulkin, I too assumed that there was some knowledge out there about rape already and I have been deeply disappointed because I have discovered that there is no such understanding. There is, as of yet, still too little written about what rape has meant for those of us who have survived. Our experiences are still surrounded by silence" (Levitt, "Speaking out of the Silence around Rape: A Personal Account," *Fireweed* 41 [Fall 1993]: 24).

Two constellations of symptoms born out of the guild of psychology have been applied to the experience of rape in helpful ways. These diagnostic tools are being augmented most recently by the revelatory and groundbreaking work of trauma theory, a growing orientation of study that we will explore in the following pages also. We will familiarize ourselves with each of these areas of knowledge so that we can both draw on them as a resource and take our discussion beyond what they provide. We are all affected by the saturation of trauma that runs through everyday life. The church is also affected and infected with trauma's wounds and scars. Understanding the reality and dynamics of rape trauma not only helps us, the church, to deepen our practices of compassion, but also helps us to understand ourselves—our fears, limitations, blind spots, and our own woundedness as the people of an incarnate God. There cannot be authentic revival and renewal of our practices unless we tell the truth about ourselves. In light of trauma's prevalence, the idols of sedate worship forms and intellectualized theology can hide us from the healing power that the church could unleash in a world where violence and harm are not the exception, but that which courses through us like the air we breathe.

Post-Traumatic Stress Disorder

Post-Traumatic Stress Disorder (PTSD) is classified in the guild of psychology as an anxiety disorder, and since 1980 it has been an accepted description of symptoms to assign to victims of rape.[11] The disorder can develop in the wake of any traumatic event, ranging from war, to assault, to catastrophic accidents, to natural disasters. In a given year, over 4 percent of Americans (about ten million) will experience some of the symptoms of PTSD because of a trauma. The disorder is diagnosed when the aftermath of a trauma leads to what the guild calls "life-disrupting" behaviors. "Life disruption" usually indicates that the symptoms last for more than a month and that the person is rendered "dysfunctional" in his/her daily life in some way.[12]

The textbook symptoms of PTSD involve "re-experiencing the traumatic event, avoidance of stimuli associated with the event or numbing of general responsiveness, and increased arousal."[13] The reexperiencing of the event can manifest itself in recurring dreams and/or continuing recollections. In some cases there are even periods of time in which the victim dissociates and reexperiences the event as though it were happening at that very moment. These periods can last seconds, minutes, hours, and even days. Reexperiencing can also occur when the victim is exposed to some reminder of the event; these reminders can

11. It became a clearly thematic phenomenon and loosely used diagnostic tool in the aftermath of World War I. In the last few years PTSD has become a newsworthy topic because of the staggering numbers of soldiers in the Iraq War who suffer from it.

12. Tamar Nordenberg, "Escaping the Prison of a Past Trauma," *FDA Consumer* 34 (May 2000): 21.

13. American Psychiatric Association, *Diagnostic and Statistical Manual of Mental Disorders,* 4th ed. (Washington, DC: American Psychiatric Association, 1994), 247.

range from an anniversary of the event to a sensation that resembles something experienced in the event.

Reexperiencing is often accompanied by patterns of avoidance of anything associated with the event. A person may avoid many different kinds of activities, sights, sounds, smells, and situations only remotely connected to the trauma itself. PTSD sufferers may experience a generalized numbing of emotions and responsiveness, including a lack of conscious memory about the traumatic event. This "psychic numbing" often sets in soon after the event itself.[14] Victims sometimes describe this numbing as feelings of detachment and estrangement. Many people complain of being unable to enjoy activities they used to enjoy, often activities that involve emotions and intimacy.

Along with this numbing often comes a hypervigilance that was not present before the trauma. This "increased arousal" frequently manifests itself in sleep disturbances, difficulty concentrating, and exaggerated startle responses. There may also be an increased level of irritability and aggression, even unpredictable outbursts of anger and aggression coupled with an inability to express the feelings involved in the outburst. PTSD commonly occurs along with various psychiatric problems such as substance abuse, depression, panic disorders, and other anxiety disorders.

In addition to this description of PTSD, the National Center for PTSD describes "Complex PTSD" or "Disorder of Extreme Stress" as the manifestation of PTSD in those who have suffered prolonged trauma (e.g., children who have been repeatedly sexually abused). Research points to the possibility that this kind of abuse can lead to brain and hormonal changes that may contribute to memory, learning, and emotional difficulties. These changes coupled with the effects of an abusive environment can lead to aggression, problems controlling impulses, sexual acting out, eating disorders, substance abuse, emotional regulation problems, and other mental difficulties such as dissociation and amnesia.[15]

Rape-Trauma Syndrome

Rape-Trauma Syndrome (RTS) is a "nursing diagnosis" and is used to describe the results of the experience of being raped.[16] The characteristics of this syndrome are divided into three subcomponents. A rape victim might experience one of these subcomponents: rape trauma, compound reaction, or silent reaction.[17] Rape trauma in its initial or acute stages is characterized by emotional reactions of anger, guilt, embarrassment, fear of violence and death, humiliation, and a desire for revenge. There are also various physical complaints included in

14. Ibid., 248.
15. Fact Sheet from the National Center for PTSD, www.ncptsd.org.
16. "Nursing diagnosis" is defined as "a statement of a health problem or of a potential problem in the client's health status that a nurse is licensed and competent to treat" (*Mosby's Medical Dictionary*, 3rd ed. [St. Louis: Mosby, 1990], 1975).
17. From *Mosby's Medical, Nursing, & Allied Health Dictionary*, ed. Kenneth N. Anderson, 5th ed. (St. Louis: Mosby, 1998), 7656.

the description such as gastrointestinal distress, urinary discomfort, and sleep disturbance. In its long-term manifestation, rape trauma can include changes in normal patterns of daily life, nightmares, and an increased need for support from family and friends.

The compound reaction is characterized by all of these symptoms coupled with substance abuse or with the recurrence of previous conditions such as depression and disordered eating. The silent reaction can occur in place of the rape trauma or compound reaction. This reaction can be characterized by sudden changes in sexual relationships and/or sexual behavior, increased nightmares and/or anxiety, denial of the rape, refusal to discuss the rape, and the development of phobic reactions.

In addition to these subcomponents, descriptions of rape-trauma syndrome delineate three phases of rape trauma experienced by many victims of sexual assault. Those who are raped tend (in the best cases) to move through these phases in the aftermath of the rape. However, survivors do not necessarily move in a seamless, linear trajectory from phase one to phase two to phase three. A survivor may be in multiple phases at once or may not move from one phase to another.

Presenting symptoms also vary. The *crisis phase* is the most immediate reaction to the rape and can manifest in a variety of ways. Some are in shock and are quite calm; others are angry or guilty and very upset. Still others seem oblivious to the magnitude of what has happened to them and seem almost "carefree."[18] Victims may report feeling shock, shame, disbelief, fear, anxiety, and embarrassment.

In the *disorientation phase* the victim may be confused about how to interact with others, about why the rape happened, and about how to act or what to do. They may markedly limit their activities outside their home to avoid any trigger for remembering the rape. They may make other efforts to repress the memory of the rape by curtailing contact with others.

In the *reorientation phase* the victim begins to regain some feelings of control and some understanding of why the rape happened. The rape becomes incorporated into her life in a new, more constructive way as she realizes that her life will never be like it was before her rape. As the literature is careful to explain, not all victims of rape get to this phase. Many remain in the disorientation phase because they have not been able to get the help they need to move out of it.

Trauma Theory

Even as PTSD and RTS may frame and fill out parts of the story that need telling, trauma theory works to challenge the very expectations of a historical understanding of experience and of narrative memory in the aftermath of

---

18. Andrea Parrot, *Coping with Date Rape and Acquaintance Rape*, rev. ed. (New York: Rosen, 1999), 88. Parrot labels this carefree presentation as "inappropriately carefree," thus raising interesting questions about some of the assumptions behind these symptom sets. What is inappropriate about being carefree as opposed to shock, guilt, anger, etc.? I do not use the word "inappropriate" in my description for just this reason.

trauma.[19] Trauma theory is a growing body of knowledge most recently renewed in its developmental trajectory by the aftermath of the Vietnam War. This body of knowledge encompasses the work of many different fields—including, but not limited to, psychiatry, neurobiology, literature, social theory, philosophy, and historical studies. Trauma theory points toward the complicated and often ambiguous reality of trauma and its treatment.

I see in trauma theory a desire to describe and understand more of the nature of trauma and its effects. Because of the intense suffering of trauma victims and the nature of trauma itself, this endeavor to "understand" trauma introduces unique difficulties. Surviving trauma is part of trauma itself: it is often the remembering and the reliving that render the impact of the event rather than the event itself. Trauma theory attends to this apparent paradox in the experience of trauma—the unruly patterns of delay, return, and retreat.

Trauma theory disrupts our accepted notions of experience by finding a way to point to the gaps introduced by trauma. At the core of trauma is an "incompletion of knowing."[20] Trauma denies us neat and tidy understandings of memory, history, sensation, subconsciousness, and truth. It even disrupts our accepted concepts of pathology and abnormal behavior because of the inherent delay that comes with traumatic experience.[21] Trauma theory challenges the assumption that "good mental health" in the wake of traumatic experience necessarily involves being able to narrate history as a straightforward, linear, even perspectival set of descriptions and ideas. Indeed, trauma theory invites a modified understanding of mental health itself.[22] As Cathy Caruth explains, "Trauma . . . does not simply serve as record of the past but precisely registers the force of an

19. By "historical understanding of experience" I refer to the expectation that what has "happened" can be placed neatly into the past and described as such. This conventional understanding of history assumes a linear flow of events that come and go in completion. In using the term "narrative memory" I assume that it can be understood in a general way as the act of being able to tell the story of what happened, or even to tell a particular version of what happened. Pierre Janet's more technical understanding of narrative memory describes it as the series of mental constructs that people use to make sense of experience. See Bessel A. van der Kolk and Onno van der Hart, "The Intrusive Past: The Flexibility of Memory and the Engraving of Trauma," in *Trauma: Explorations of Memory*, ed. Cathy Caruth (Baltimore: Johns Hopkins University Press, 1995), 160. Clearly, the disruption of these two categories brings with it the larger question of the nature of truth itself.

20. Caruth, "Trauma and Experience: Introduction," in *Trauma*, 5.

21. "Pathology" and "abnormal behavior" are clinical terms that describe a deviation from that which is classified as normal and healthy. Trauma theory works to develop the ways in which trauma disrupts the way these categories are used. For instance, Laura Brown argues that the definition of a traumatic event as something "outside the range of human experience" is problematic from a feminist perspective because abuse is within the "normal" range of experience for many women. See Laura S. Brown, "Not Outside the Range: One Feminist Perspective on Psychic Trauma," in *Trauma*, ed. Caruth, 100–112. I want to push this idea even further with my suggestion that typical responses to trauma are actually the body's genius at work, through feeling, both protecting and ascertaining the impact of trauma in the same moment.

22. This statement of mental health is not intended to suggest that trauma theory espouses the idea that good mental health is reversed in its very nature. Rather, the critique that trauma theory poses to some conventional notions of mental health is around the assumption that good mental health is always indicated by the capacity to put traumatic experience into narrative historical form. The body's survival skills can actually steal the experience from consciousness to maintain health.

experience that is not yet fully owned."[23] Trauma theory tells us that memory is a troubled phenomenon. Indeed, neurobiological findings indicate that trauma elides the "normal" encoding of memory. Trauma is characterized by a "lack of integration into consciousness."[24] It needs to be integrated in some way, but the dynamics of trauma disrupt the very possibility of historical understanding. A person can experience a delay of comprehension, and the trauma may integrate into behavior and consciousness in ways without narrative consistency or the ability for the brain to classify it as memory. Indeed, the "memory" of the experience may lose precision when it becomes conscious and is assigned language.[25]

Trauma takes possession of those who experience it. It is uniquely lived out in belated, repeated, fragmented expressions and experiences. As Caruth describes, the refusal of trauma simply to be located turns us away from viewing trauma as a neurotic distortion.[26] The patterns of trauma indicate the complicated ability of the body to comprehend harm immediately and, at the same time, to protect us from its full destructive capacity.

Post-Traumatic Stress Disorder and Rape Trauma Syndrome are often used to describe and diagnose the behavior of rape victims. They are helpful in their descriptive power and in their acknowledgment of the potency of the experiences these descriptions include. Their increasing acceptance in medical and counseling fields legitimize aspects of experience for those who seek help in the aftermath of sexual assault. Trauma theory is a growing influence in treatment, although the systems of treatment are not necessarily well suited for what it tells us. In fact, some methods of treatment are disrupted by what trauma theory reveals.

Underneath these helpful descriptive constellations are bodies that have found a way to communicate rape's horror by surfacing these symptoms. Feeling deepens the embodied content of what these symptoms and theories can tell.

23. Caruth, "Recapturing the Past: Introduction," in *Trauma,* 151.
24. Ibid., 152–53. Pierre Janet's distinction between narrative memory and traumatic memory grew out of this difficulty of trauma to be accommodated by the schemes of meaning existing in the mind already. Janet believed that such "subconscious fixed ideas" influence "perception, states, and behavior" and "emotionally constrict" those whom they inhabit. Janet's understanding of the normal flow of memory integration involved understanding the workings of memory as the "central organizing apparatus of the mind." It is composed of meaning schemes into which experiences are placed in order to make sense of it. New experiences are automatically plugged into existing schemes of meaning. They are synthesized and adapted to those meaning schemes in order to make them "fit" into the more general orientation to create a healthy and unified operation of the memory system itself. See van der Kolk and van der Hart, "Intrusive Past," in *Trauma,* ed. Caruth, 159.
25. Ibid., 163. Van der Kolk and van der Hart (ibid., 158–82) describe the interesting way in which Freud borrowed from the clinical work of the lesser known Pierre Janet on trauma and the subconscious (a term actually coined by Janet). An important discussion related to my work is how Freud chose to focus on repression (a "vertically layered model of mind") rather than dissociation (a "horizontally layered model of mind") as Janet did. The change in emphasis shaped a great deal of the orientation of the Western psychological guild toward trauma.
26. Caruth, *Trauma,* 10. Caruth explains, "By turning away . . . from the notion of traumatic experience as neurotic distortion . . . [we are brought] back continually to the ever-surprising fact that trauma is not experienced as a mere repression or defense, but as a temporal delay that carries the individual beyond the shock of the first moment. The trauma is a repeated suffering of the event, but it is also a continual leaving of its site."

Rape and Feeling

A body lives, breathes, feels . . .
trusts, hopes . . .
wonders, worries, feels . . .
Another body intersects, interjects, penetrates, jars.
Feelings like a tidal wave, bombarding, racing—chaotic, uninvited.
Full throttle, full feeling is too much.

Escape,

e s c

a p e

Foggy unmodified unconsciousness.
Feeling meanders tenaciously and ingathers truths.
If it is safe, when it is safe it may unfold itself,
nursed to stretch out,
to entangle with expression and boldness
when it meets tenderness, perhaps correlation.
With some world at its side,
with a world on its side.

Sexual assault harms everything that is. It penetrates us on a cellular level, seeping into every facet of who we are—into how we think, know, dream, eat, sleep, love. It seeps into how we are embodied—into the crevices of the way our body functions, into how our organs work together, into how our systems flow, into how our synapses fire. Harm is expansive and persistent. And even though the harm of sexual trauma is ever-changing, developing, ebbing and flowing, it is also permanent. Rape ripples out from the tissues and spirits that it tears apart to condition the fabric of life.

Sleep disturbances, nightmares, exaggerated startle responses, weight loss and/or weight gain, chest pains, abdominal pain, sexual detachment, depression, fatigue, anxiety attacks, mineral deficiencies, hormonal imbalances, and other physiological and psychological symptoms can last for days, months, even years. For many, these symptoms last for a lifetime. Most rape survivors find themselves living out behavioral changes all along the continuum between risky sexual behaviors and detachment from others. Many times we limit our interactions in order to avoid thinking about the rape and in an effort to try and bury its memory. Survivors can even be confused about whether the rape "really" happened, and even more often we fear that any activity could trigger our memory. This confusion and fear isolate us and thin out our relationships with others in ways that challenge and diminish us.

Miscarriage, vaginal dryness, abnormal pap smears, and sexual dysfunction are also some of the body's storytellers. These stories are not often an accepted part of the psychological and medical narratives of rape's aftermath, but they are the recurring chapters simply told among those who have been there. No matter who legitimizes the whence of a body's trials, all of these "symptoms" of rape's aftermath raise questions of how the body is changed, what is lost, and how our very existential roots languish as trauma finds a home in us. How do we listen to the body and the stories it tells? How tenaciously are we tuned out to our own body language? What do we stand to gain should we open ourselves up to these layers of embodied truth?

In an incarnational faith, the promise is both that bodies matter and that bodies can be redeemed. Giving flesh to those promises is the work of Christian communities and the theology that grounds our life together. Feeling gives us a way to entangle ourselves to both truth and promise. Feeling tunes us in and re-members bodies.

Re-membering is not simple recollection or memory; re-membering is reconnecting body parts that have been severed, blocked, trivialized, compromised. When we re-member we do not only access the narratives that define us or simply finally find publicity for some hidden pain that we have experienced. When we re-member we begin to integrate the threads of the untellable into the narrative of who we are and where we have been and how we live with truth and with authenticity. Re-membering does more than recollect; re-membering re-collects bodies and their broken, ingenious, tenacious parts into the sphere of how we pay attention.

Re-membering is a radically embodied epistemological orientation that begins with discrete bodies—with feeling bodies. The radicality of this kind of know-how is that we will have to operate outside and in between the common filing systems of our experience. Feeling creates a more unruly, although beautifully entangled, mode of listening and being and accepting and honoring. I describe four strands of this entangled mode of operation in the sections that follow. I call them the limits of consciousness, body loss, body function, and contorted subjectivity. These four threads of stories in the flesh help us to re-member.

The Limits of Consciousness

Dreams . . . many common elements—always no one hears me.
Their backs are to me and they won't turn around. He is there doing what he did—he's hurting me, threatening me, touching me, he's doing it all. They won't turn around—none of them, my dad is there most of the time. Sometimes my husband. Sometimes friends. They don't hear me, they don't see. He is so brazen—he knows they won't turn around. It doesn't faze him a bit that they are right there, because he knows they won't turn around.

My rape counselor told me to wake up and finish the dreams how I want them to finish. Why can't I do that? It's like my mind won't do it. Every time I close my eyes I'm back to what is going on—like I have no say about it. It helps every once in a while if I can say it out loud to someone, if I can talk about how I want the dream to end. I wish there were some way to move, to actually physically do it and know what it would feel like. I feel like that's the gap that I need to bridge. . . . My body just goes limp.

Journal entry

The expression "you'll feel better in the morning" does not ring true for many survivors of rape. Unlike the mysterious efficacy of most dream sleep that helps us work out things from our waking life, the dreams of trauma function in a far less edifying pattern. Sleep is often an unwelcome portal to trauma without the healing benefits. Even Sigmund Freud was baffled by the phenomenon of the recurring dreams of trauma survivors. He could not explain them away as repressed wishes or desires of the subconscious. These dreams are instead the involuntary remembering and painful reliving of a traumatic experience. Many other contemporary dream analysts agree that these dreams are usually, on some level, quite literal—resisting the curative effect of working through the symbolic content of most other dreams.[27]

Reliving trauma is not symbolic, but enfleshed for the survivor. The body, on some level, experiences the trauma itself in these horrible moments of return— moments of truth, moments that seem to demand repetition. The existence of these dreams offers us a foggy glimpse into the complicated and highly developed activity of the body that falls outside our understanding of conscious thought and physical experience. The body feels and is constantly processing experience in ways we cannot begin to characterize as extensions of rational thought. Our consciousness is often not the focal point of this processing of pain.

Feeling affirms the limits of consciousness in all experience—why should sexual assault be any different? Remember that feeling is the fabric of who we are, and feeling only sometimes bubbles up into conscious thoughts. Trauma theory extends what feeling highlights about the limits of consciousness. Feeling is what goes on in most of who we are, since consciousness is not privy to the bulk of our experience.[28] Consciousness is composed of what are many times quite superficial elements of the full scope of our experience.

The quite minimal role of consciousness in everyday functioning is attested to in process philosophy, Eastern philosophies and practices, and even in growing trends in Western biological science. Rape brings the limits of consciousness into chilling and clear relief. With a trauma like rape, the event itself is characterized by a lack of integration into the consciousness. In trauma there exists a complex

27. Ibid., 5.
28. Christiane Northrup explains that 90 percent of what we do every day is unconscious. "Remember always that 90 percent of your bodily functions take place without your conscious input. Who keeps your heart beating? Who metabolizes your food? Who tells you when you need to replenish your fluid intake by drinking water? Who heals your skin when you cut yourself? Who tells your ears to listen to beautiful music? Who tells your eyes to see beautiful sunsets?" (*Women's Bodies, Women's Wisdom: Creating Physical and Emotional Health and Healing*, rev. ed. [New York: Bantam, 1998], 607).

relationship between knowing and not knowing. This complexity is the "new ignorance that trauma introduces among us."[29] At trauma's core is a delay or incomplete knowing because of the "overwhelming immediacy" of the access to the experience. This depth of proximity creates an uncertainty that is not a displacement of meaning or falsity, but a challenge to "history itself."[30] Trauma is, in an embodied sense, this incapacity to witness fully the event as it occurs.

Rape sets into motion the same mechanisms that are at work daily in our bodies. This flow of feeling in the face of trauma shifts into a mode that protects us. The lack of memory or consciousness of an event, feeling confirms, is not an indication of a lack of impact of an event. To the contrary, that event can massively shape us without our being conscious of its full impact. It is perhaps the immediacy of the event at such a deeply embodied level that makes the limitation of consciousness kick in with such rigor. The fact that feeling has pointed us toward the limitation of consciousness even in normal functioning challenges us to rethink how we characterize the body's reaction to trauma. Incomplete knowing is not an abnormality, but it is an aspect of the wonder of the body's complexity. This incompletion is also a testament to the strength of a body's competency for survival.

Consciousness is not the crown of experience, and trauma can make it even more difficult for consciousness to synthesize an experience. Because these two facts are true of all of us, then we need to approach healing work differently. We do not simply hear words, but we cradle the body in its time of pain and disorientation. "Remembering" shifts to "re-membering." This re-membering requires, first and foremost, attention to what feeling tells us about ourselves. Re-membering is a level of healing and embodied awareness that resists the modifications of consciousness and so invites practices that let our bodies take the lead.

"Bodily memory" is a suggestive aspect of the body's storytelling. The language of bodily memory speaks directly to the phenomenon that re-membering entails. This phenomenon is also called tissue memory, cellular memory, or somatic memory.[31] While there is no consensus definition of what many call "bodily memory," several researchers have connected the workings of the memory to the body and not simply to the working of the mind. As Saul Schanberg, professor of biological psychiatry at Duke Medical Center, explains, "Memory resides nowhere, and in every cell. . . . It's about two thousand times more complicated than we ever imagined."[32] Most of these researchers are, in some manner, pointing toward how the body itself holds memory in its cells, how it is encoded in everything from tactile sensation to muscle spasm to smell and light intake. As Christiane Northrup explains, "Much of the information we need to heal is locked in our muscles and other body parts."[33]

29. Caruth, *Trauma*, ix, 4.
30. Ibid., 5.
31. Miraka Knaster, *Discovering the Body's Wisdom* (New York: Bantam, 1996), 123.
32. Ibid., 124.
33. Northrup, *Women's Bodies*, 628.

Aside from the relatively recent work of Western medical science that attempts to account for the bodily nature of memory, practitioners of various kinds of bodywork can testify with great regularity on the experiences of their clients of massage, body movement therapies, and other kinds of "energy work."[34] These practitioners steward along the reconnecting and renewal of feeling's flow through touch, postures, and other practices that are often grounded in Eastern ways of understanding the body's functioning. These accounts are supported by the stories of many survivors of sexual abuse who find a particularly efficacious healing effect in various kinds of bodywork. This healing is not the same as recovered memory; it reawakens the body in ways that are not always describable, although quite discernible.[35] These bodywork practices are not simply good for trauma survivors; they can create health and wellness for all of us.

Bodily memory is not necessarily about unlocking a narrative that needs to take the form of conscious memory. Bodily memory is also not necessarily about releasing something that has been repressed or forgotten. Bodily memory remembers as it reintegrates the body with restorative connection of feeling. These spaces of bodily memory may not ever be connected to trauma on a conscious or historical/narrative level. The healing effect, however, remains remarkably efficacious. Many rape survivors reach a new level of healing and well-being with sustained attention to massage, yoga, and other embodied practices. These practices can, over time, begin to coax feeling into stretching out and flowing more freely. These practices tap into the body's story and they invite the body into a place where it re-members, integrates, rejuvenates.

Embodied healing work embraces the body's wisdom and follows its lead. The intricacy and genius of our body's survival skills and our body's potential for healing work rests in how feeling is honored and given space to flow not simply in the quiet of one's pain, but in the contexts of our communities. If our church communities ignore or even deny the body's wisdom in healing work, then we have only served to further entrench patterns of harm and even illness. The limit of our consciousness is a fact of embodied life. Rape shines a light on just how real and formative this fact is.

34. There are too many different kinds of bodywork to name and describe here. Some are more widely accepted than others. They range from more conventional Western massage methods to practices like Reiki and myofascial release. The best encyclopedic collection of these methods I have found is Knaster, *Discovering the Body's Wisdom*. While many of the methods have their origins in Eastern conceptions of the body and mind as a unified system, some come out of a more Western, and therefore, more dualistic, understanding of the body. In general, however, these methods are built on some understanding, however weakly construed, that the body and mind are of a piece.

35. The phenomenon of "recovered memories" has been a contentious subject for some time now. For a well-informed accounting of this phenomenon and of the backlash of so-called false memory accusations, see Ellen Bass and Laura Davis, *The Courage to Heal: A Guide for Women Survivors of Child Sexual Abuse*, rev. ed. (London: Vermilion, 1990).

Body Loss

Even while clothed I am naked, even in family I am alone, even speaking I am silenced and even living I am dying.
          Ruth Schmidt, a survivor, "After the Fact: To Speak of Rape"

Being alone. . . . Do other people have this feeling, this sensation, what can I call it? It's just this pungent thing, this unbelievably real sensation or feeling or something like that. It happens sometimes and it just takes me over—I feel alone and I realize I am alone and I realize what that means. It is strangely comforting in its truth, but blood-chilling for the same reason. Is it true? I know I've felt it for so many years—just in glimpses, just in little moments of clarity—is it clarity? Sometimes it's when I'm not really awake all the way—like I can know things differently in that state—I'll start to feel my brain sorting through this idea, this existential something, and then I get to it—you are alone—there is no one that understands, no one that really cares in a way that would make a dent in what you're feeling. And my life is full of people who love me. Rape does that—it sets you apart from everyone, sometimes the isolation is minuscule—but it never goes away. It's always there—like a poet, removed but more involved, more immersed in something that's real about life than other people. It can be too much to take—I can see that—I can't stay there for long.
          Journal entry

The limits of consciousness point us to how the body holds trauma. The flow of feeling helps us understand and honor the body's wisdom. The intricacy of the body's holding of trauma does not simply point us to the heft of traumatic experience itself, but it also points us toward places of loss. The "antecedent" bodily experience that Whitehead describes tells us that the body, as a collection of cells, tissues, and organs, is "marked" in a primary sense in all experience. Antecedent body parts experience a simple physical feeling; consciousness is not involved. The body "knows" through the simple physical feeling. This feeling is more basic, more primary, than even sense perception. There is no cognitive, thematic way in which to talk about what is entailed in such an experience. The nature of feeling, however, tells us that these simple physical feelings are constantly conditioning us. The efficacy of bodywork, as discussed in the previous section, speaks to the power of simple physical feeling to condition us.

The body is constantly in the process of changing because of the inheritance these antecedent experiences relentlessly give to our particular and collective bodies. While we cannot descriptively uncover the most primal physical inheritance of rape, we can notice traces of loss that are written on the body. These traces of loss are another way to address how the body holds trauma and heals from it. Trauma makes its mark on the body when the body puts up defenses to protect itself from more pain. We can see the effects of loss when victims of sexual violence, even unconsciously, avoid places, activities, thoughts, and people who somehow relate to or remind them of the trauma. The body's loss also manifests itself in how victims close themselves off from connection through an intense hypervigilance and through a sensitivity to certain things manifesting in overactive startle reflexes, sleep disturbances, and irritability. This hypervigilance can exaggerate the emotional detachment experienced by many survivors. Some begin to live on automatic pilot. These embodied losses take survivors out of full engagement with basic parts of who we are, cut off from relationship with ourselves and with others.

Avoidance, hypervigilance, and isolation result from a body change, a body loss. Emotions dulled, experiences avoided, and stimulus feared are traces of an antecedent bodily experience, one in which a wound was inflicted. Swelling, bruising, sometimes tearing and cuts point us to evidence of harm. When a wound is inflicted there is a change, a loss. Never again will the body be the same; there is no chance to return it to its prewounded state. Instead, the body continues into the future with a new texture to its inheritance, a new experience conditioning the particularity of feeling. The body has lost a certain openness and receptivity. The loss is permanent. Even with deep healing, the embodied losses are irreplaceable, and the truncation of feeling's reach is not easily repaired. The body cannot help but be different, changed, and even deficient in some way. There are things that the body will never be because of sexual assault; there are experiences it can never have. The body has no choice but to act out of these changes and loss.

The body's loss means that there is a loss of connection, a loss of vitality, a loss of possibility, a loss of receptivity—a newly embodied intuition of death and isolation. Feeling helps us to read parts of stories that are written on the body; these are narratives of expansive loss. This loss ripples out from the simple, physical feelings and conditions all that is and all that can be. How this kind of loss is read and heard is crucial to what the future holds for victims of sexual assault. Feeling helps us to hear these stories by tuning us in to our body's language.

Just as the limits of consciousness alert us to the importance of embodied healing, body loss points us to the importance of bodywork for grieving. It is crucial that the body be addressed at its most basic point of intake in order for it to grieve. Even touch, smell, and sound take us ahead of ourselves in the places where the body cries out and many times languishes unheard. Massage, energy work, and body movement methods can address body loss where it is felt with the most force—in the fibers and flow of the body. Attention to body loss enriches other more conventional modes of grieving with attention to the whole body. Body prayers like walking a labyrinth or the Hesychast prayer stance also invite the body to feel its grief.[36] Kneeling, lying prostrate, lying in the

---

36. The Hesychast method is something some parishioners in different churches I have served have embraced even after some resistance to it. Its stance is something like the crash position that we would assume on an airplane. On a low stool or step one leans over the knees with arms down. Breathing deeply is traditionally coupled with the Jesus Prayer ("Lord Jesus Christ, Son of God, have mercy on me"). This stance can be used with any breath prayer.

fetal position, and taking on these postures in sacred spaces like sanctuaries and chapels can provide a way for our bodies to grieve. Something as simple as a garden for survivors to tend also creates such space. A garden brings us close to the rhythms of birth, life, and death. For me, intentional spaces for my body's losses to find expression have been the lifeblood of healing. I have longed for the church to provide some of those spaces with compassion and integrity. This kind of space is unknown ground for many mainline churches. Grief's expression is given full flower in our salvation legacy, and embodying our heritage is a promising possibility for our future.

Body Function

He was six-two and very muscular. His legs were like tree trunks, and his arms could probably crush me if he held me too hard . . . I was barely five feet and very petite. My whole hand could almost fit in his palm. . . .

*   Of course, I trusted him. He loved me. He would never hurt me. He would not make me do anything I didn't want to. How could I refuse him? If I did, that would signal that something was wrong. My mind couldn't handle that. . . . It was as horrible as the first time, but I blocked it out. That was all I could do, and I had to repress it to keep my sanity. It was to be three years before I could accept the true meaning of what happened that night.*

Rita, a survivor, quoted in Andrea Parrot,
Coping with Date Rape

After he left, I stayed alone huddled in the corner of my bedroom with a blanket over me. I felt paralyzed. I couldn't move. I was afraid he'd come after me again. I must have stayed this way for two days. I lost track of time.

A survivor, quoted in Lee Madigan and
Nancy Gamble, The Second Rape

Rape trauma takes us out of time, out of ourselves, and into a slowed-down mode of operation on many layers of who we are. Embodied loss goes far beyond a need to grieve. A close look at body function takes us deeper into how trauma ripples through the entire body. Body function is compromised, changed, and its effects have consequences that seem strange and counterintuitive for those watching from the outside. For both survivors in the narratives above, the truth was too much; the trauma took them out of the experience to a place in which they could survive. Both women describe a compromise in functioning—one more subtle than the other. Both, however, are just as powerful an arrest of the body's ability to comprehend the full extent of the situation, while at the same time they are a testament to the body's remarkable way of comprehending the full force of what is happening. The wonder of feeling is how quickly and competently it takes in experience, and then how it takes care of the whole entity's needs. Clearly, the idea that the body and the emotions can be treated separately is troubled by these reactions.

In conventional treatment for victims of rape, the "bodily" aspects of the problem are remedied with a medical exam and the appropriate follow-up procedures (such as an AIDS test, a pregnancy test, or treatment for sexually transmitted diseases). The emotional aspects are often addressed with talk and/or group therapy, possibly medication, and an effort to continue with or return to "normal" life. If law enforcement is informed, they expect a clear narrative account of what happened, which is ironically precisely what trauma interrupts or may render impossible. Our system of justice expects that the victim will also be able to endure all that ensues if the story becomes public.

While all of these aspects of response may, for some, prove important for the healing of victims of rape, they are built on some dangerously truncated conceptions of the nature of the body's functioning. The nature of feeling highlights this truncated conception of body function in terms of all bodies. Trauma theory further radicalizes the impossibility of "normalcy" after rape. Feeling and trauma theory together point us toward the compromise experienced in the body's very ability to function in the aftermath of rape. These lenses of experiences into the body also give us a glimpse of the body's genius in the face of trauma. The body is actually working overtime to sort through the experience in a way that enables survival.

The nature of this compromise in function is what I call a survival shift—a shift from the capacity to narrate and analyze a direct physical experience to a survival mode in which the experience is held in the tissues of the body with an increased tenacity. Experiences are always held in our tissues and cells even as we can talk about them, analyze them, describe them, and even try to duplicate them. But in the traumatic experience the subterranean bodily memory must hold the lion's share of the experience. Expression, analysis, description, processing become different work than simple narration. The survival shift slows down the flow of feeling so that conscious thought has only bits and pieces in the interest of continuing life. This shift changes the expectations and perceptions of the traumatized body. Current trauma theories assert that there is actually an inherent latency in the experience of trauma—that is, that the immediacy of the experience is belated; amazingly only in an initial "forgetting" is the trauma experienced at all.[37] Survival itself is traumatic because it is only in and after this delay that trauma is experienced. A trauma like rape is an ongoing way of living that takes hold of the body.

The level of our body's functioning (via feeling) determines how and what we perceive. In the survival shift that it elicits, rape dulls feeling by muffling the body's ability to let feeling flow in its fullest creativity. The experience sends the

37. Caruth, *Trauma*, 10.

body's ability to feel into dormancy in order for it to survive, to function even on a lower level in order for it to keep breathing. Rape brings the functioning of the body down at the feeling level so that all that flows from it. Sensation, cognition, and judgment are not nourished with the same potency of feeling that a fully functioning body enjoys. Rape trauma flips a slowdown switch that enables the vital organs to keep going, but zestful life to be put on hold. This compromised level of functioning takes us out of full relationship with ourselves and with others. Feeling writes the story of the body's survival. To continue to live, one must remain only partly alive.

If we take in the full force of this survival shift, we begin to see that many of the ways rape victims are "helped" ignore the body's needs. The demand for the "whole story," for proof, and for consistent memory asks those who are raped to do things their bodies cannot do. These expectations and the failure of many rape victims to meet them remove the blame from the perpetrator and point it toward the victim. The burden of proof is on the one who was rendered unable to tell the story in the ways that satisfy society's standards. It is sad that, because of their own woundedness, rape survivors are often held accountable for failures of justice. These misguided expectations of our systems of justice diminish the body's remarkable ability to react to rape and the survivor's valiant efforts at survival.

Body functioning is relational; the social nature of this survival shift is a pivotal factor in how survivors live into the rest of their lives. Tragically, the social aftermath of rape only does more to compromise function and to damage the ability of the body to feel. The body's best gift for survival becomes its most tragic trap for falling prey to continued harm. These sharp double edges of body function manifest in societal reactions, conditions not conducive to healing, and in a remarkably entrenched self-loathing in the inner life of survivors. These conditions make the sin-guilt-forgiveness theologies of mainline Protestantism especially dangerous as a means of healing.

Contorted Subjectivity

> To speak out is, at least for me, a cry for acknowledgment. I want to be seen in my multiple identities. I am all of these things as a survivor: frightened, angry, strong, vulnerable, and brave. Sometimes when we are strong this seems to cancel out the fact that we are also terribly frightened. . . . What I want is a clear sense of my own complexity. I am afraid of having to be OK too soon. I want my friends and family to know that I hurt and that despite my strength, I am very tired.
>
> Laura Levitt

Laura Levitt's description of her complicated sense of self is familiar to all of us. Each of us has this complex of strength, vulnerability, resolve, and fatigue. Her yearning for that to be recognized and affirmed is answered in the very good news that Jesus brings to us. We are known in all of our truth, in our light and in our shadows. And we are loved, accepted, and embraced by the One who knows us that well. Redemption is a beautiful thing! This sense of self that incorporates dissonance is directly correlated in many theological anthropologies of Reformed theology. "We are sinners and we are children of God" is a simple expression of one layer of this concept of self. Reformed practices tend to do more to describe our sinful condition than they do to find language and expression for our redemption. The complexity of who we are is often reduced down to the polarities of good and bad. These are the orienting markers of self-discovery—how we sin and how we are in total need of God's grace. Laura Levitt is asking for her sense of self to be recognized with much more texture and complication than that. All of us need it. Rape survivors embody the harm embedded in not telling the truth about all of who we are. The space in a community for different fragments of subjectivity directly feeds the room there is for churches to be places of healing rather than more harm.

Guilt and denial are all too common "holy habits" for many mainline Protestant churches. Our formation tends to embed us in a privileged self-denial. In order to avoid what we perceive as self-absorption and selfishness, we reject our own complexity and along with that our own embodied dissonance. This culture of guilt and denial can create a communal tentativeness around personal brokenness and undeserved suffering. This dis-ease with vulnerability and expressions of pain severely compromises the spaces available for embodied truth to trauma survivors in many mainline churches.

When we pay attention to how feeling works we see the diminishing effects of these conditions of guilt and denial even more clearly. Feeling provides a frame for interpreting how we are constantly being created and creating out of all that is. For feeling to flow and flourish it needs a place to go, a way to continue to grow and to sharpen its modification, its definition. If feeling finds nothing to join in, nothing to add to, nothing to modify, it begins to fade and eventually will be negated or atrophy. Subjectivity is both a socially constructed and a uniquely particular phenomenon because of the nature of feeling. Our bodies are an integral part in this ongoing construction of subjectivity as they depend on and condition all else that is. The self (and its particular body) are not isolated or independent from the flux of all else that is; the self is constantly constructing and being constructed out of this flux.

With this dynamic and open rendering of subjectivity, it may be difficult to imagine how such an indeterminate phenomenon can be "contorted" since there is a given fluidity to it. By "contorted" I mean a loss of keenness with which feeling is able to participate in and condition all that goes into the creative process of subjectivity. Subjectivity becomes contorted because that particular constellation of feeling loses its potency; its ability to translate itself into consistent and clearly discernible patterns of identity has been compromised. Contorted subjectivity is the result of the extreme and irreplaceable loss that the body suffers with rape. This loss of potency in these constellations of feeling plays out in the same way as a recipe suffers if an ingredient like baking soda is no longer active when it is added to the mix. Its important role in eliciting certain responses from the other ingredients as they react to certain temperatures is missing or compromised. The result may be bread that does not rise, has an undesirable consistency, or does not taste as good. When the connections are made and the reactions are not firing, then the coming together of these ingredients yields something less robust than what could have been.

This lack of potency is not an isolated factor in how subjectivity is contorted by rape. Because of rape, feeling is weakened. Feeling then continues into the flow of all that is and tries to find a home, a road toward clarity or satisfaction.[38] How society reacts to those who are raped is part of what conditions the simple physical feelings of rape. These responses are often not hospitable to the building of importance for the primal experiences of rape.[39] Collections of feeling already languishing in their ability to be modified and to come into clarity are further compromised. Their ability to integrate fully experiences of violence in healthy ways is diminished by the reactions they meet in the larger society.

Feeling in the aftermath of trauma many times takes hold as contortion because of the way society responds to those who are raped. Feeling is deeply relational. Experience needs the reinforcement of intersubjectivity for it to be clarified, affirmed, and processed. In the experience of rape, those reinforcements are dissonant with the experience itself. The distortions of the experience of rape that are prominent in our culture—doubts about its veracity, blaming the victim, ignoring its harm, belittling its effects—take hold of feeling in its weakened state and contort the ongoing construction of subjectivity. The feelings that find a home are not those of the primal loss, the embodied loss of function; the feelings that find a home are generally those of self-blame, disbelief, silence, continued harm, and a retrenched denial of the body. These are the feelings that find the referential strength they need to take hold in the construction of the self. The others languish from lack of relationship; they grope in the dark alone.

Uncovering pieces of these responses that are evident in our culture can bring this contortion into clearer focus. For those few women who make their way into the halls of hospitals or police departments after their rape, there are often not correlating constellations of feeling to touch them where they have been harmed. Emilie Buchwald and others describe American culture as a "rape cul-

---

38. See the definition of satisfaction in chapter 1, n. 23.

39. Whitehead uses the term "importance" in *Process and Reality* and in other writings to indicate the gathering of, for lack of a better term, heft (Whitehead uses "massiveness" in a related sense) to feelings, experiences, etc. "Importance" indicates that a constellation of feeling has taken on a degree of being "felt" that makes it a player of interest, of impact in the way the past, present, and future take shape and are understood. He describes importance most clearly perhaps in *Symbolism: Its Meaning and Effect* (New York: Fordham, 1927), in which he spins out the dynamics of how a symbol is enjoyed. A particularly illustrative section on this topic is entitled "The Contrast Between Accurate Definition and Importance" (pp. 56–59).

ture."[40] This cultural identity is formed both out of the patterns of reaction to rape and out of the conditions that make American society conducive to rape. The culture of rape helps to make it the most underreported crime there is. And when a rape is reported, it is common for rape victims to be cast as habitual liars, vengeful, and sexually deviant in the courtroom. Lee Madigan and Nancy Gamble call the acts of "violation, alienation, and disparagement" a rape victim receives when she seeks help "the second rape." They describe a pattern of dismissal, rage, denial, and condemnation in reactions to those who are raped displayed in everyone from friends, family, and police to doctors, pastors, and the courts.[41]

Any confusion about what happened is often used to prove the falsity of her accusations. Often even before a rape case gets to the courts, those who are seen by the victim as helpers, like police, build on her confusion by further distorting her perspective.[42] If police feel a victim does not have a good chance of winning a court case, they will not encourage the victim to press charges.[43] For instance, Madigan describes how one police officer (a female) assessed whether a rape victim should prosecute. A credible witness in the courtroom had to be able to remember and articulate what happened before, during, and after the rape. The police officer explained, "If there are contradictions and inconsistencies in her story, the defense attorney will rip her apart on the stand."[44] This kind of narration of the event is precisely what trauma theory indicates is impossible. Madigan adds that if alcohol or drugs were included in the assault, then the woman is immediately suspect, and more likely to be held responsible for what happened to her, even if she has a firm story with no "loopholes."[45] The issue becomes the victim's character, appearance, occupation, social status, decision-making, and behavior rather than what happened and the actions of the perpetrator. It is clear how this kind of response from those who are seen as helpers and protectors reinforces the victim's self-blame, rather than helps to empower feelings of loss, grief, or indignity.

40. Buchwald et al., eds., *Transforming a Rape Culture*, 7–10. The conditions that compose a rape culture include everything from misogynist speech to pornography to the depiction of women in advertising to assumptions about women's roles in the family. Buchwald et al. use statistics about rape, prosecution, conviction, and punishment to illustrate how pervasive rape is in American life. Their collection includes articles about pornography, the church, fraternities, language, celebrity rapists, parenting of boys and girls, politics, statecraft, sexual harassment, the commodification of women, the military, and violence. All of these things and more contribute to the assertion of American culture being a "rape culture." Women are often blamed for "bringing it on" themselves through dress, demeanor, or activity. We live in a society ripe for rape to flourish.

41. Madigan and Gamble, *Second Rape*, 7. Madigan and Gamble gathered information from statistics and from rape survivors themselves. For the few who actually report their rape (about one in ten), only 20 percent of the perpetrators are convicted. Madigan and Gamble report that 98 percent of all rapists go free.

42. Ibid., 20.

43. Given legal realities, this lack of encouragement can be an expression of compassion.

44. Madigan and Gamble, *Second Rape*, 73.

45. Ibid.

The intrusive nature of post-rape medical examinations coupled with the fact that many victims report not being told what was being done to them during these exams signal another loss of control for women. Having this passivity and submission expected and encouraged from someone who has been raped further entrenches the feelings of helplessness and loss of control that characterize the experience of rape.[46] It is yet another violation and objectification of our intimacy and vulnerability.

At the same time that the medical aftermath expects passivity and submission, the law-enforcement response scrutinizes the victim for how strongly (read: convincingly) she resisted her attacker. One detective put it this way: "No longer does a victim have to use force [to prove that rape has occurred], but she must communicate that she was not willing to go along with the sexual acts."[47] When asked to give examples, she suggested "squirming, struggling, and screaming." The trends of conviction for rapists suggest that many people assume that a victim who does not fight back with all the force at her disposal is not really a victim. This bias shows itself again in how conviction rates decrease for those who had any delay in response and/or did not immediately report the attack.[48] One police officer said, "There's no excuse for not reporting immediately any longer. She can always report it to a hotline now."[49] The truth of the attack for many people rests in an immediate and unambiguous response to what was happening.

Even those victims who choose not to report their crime to authorities find responses from family, friends, and pastors to be equally, or perhaps even more, harmful. We need only to look back at the rape of Tamar for an example. According to the study conducted by Madigan and Gamble, one-half to two-thirds of all intimate male-female relationships end after a rape is revealed by the female.[50] Indeed, they report that "husbands or partners may reject their wives and accuse them of having enjoyed the sexual contact."[51] Many women who keep their rape from law-enforcement officials, family, and friends often confide in their pastors. Sadly, many times pastors fail to correctly name what has happened to the victim and only encourage more silence and denial.[52] Many pastors ignore all the indicators of sexual abuse and miss the chance to help the victim sort out what happened. Even when they acknowledge what happened, many pastors encourage the victim to forgive their attacker in order to be faithful to their religious

---

46. Ibid., 84–85.
47. Ibid., 76.
48. This information is important for how the change in body function and the limits of consciousness are used against those who are raped. To be expected to have an unconfused narration of what happened denies the very nature of what rape does.
49. Ibid., 79.
50. Ibid., 6.
51. Ibid., 15.
52. Adams, "I just raped my wife," 60.

convictions.[53] Women have been told over and over again to let go of their anger before the wrong done to them is even minimally acknowledged.

And what about the fact that much sexual violence comes at the hands of someone known, familiar, even a loved one? About 73 percent of female rape victims knew their attacker: 38 percent of victims are raped by a friend or an acquaintance, 28 percent by an intimate, and 7 percent by a relative.[54] Madigan and Gamble report that the closer the victim is to the assailant, the less likely a jury is to believe the accusation. In the context of an ongoing relationship, women will often not describe a sexual assault as "rape" when asked, but will answer yes when asked if their partner has ever forced them to have sex when they did not want to.[55] Acquaintance rape is most often coupled with feelings of responsibility on the part of the victim. As Madigan and Gamble explain, "The victim becomes convinced that he or she is an accomplice to the crime and takes on deep feelings of guilt and shame."[56]

The low level of functioning that rape hastens is used against those who are raped. The worst of rape's aftermath is reinforced by society as the true nature of the harm is disregarded in the expectations placed on the victim. Contortion is disabling, and it shows itself in how rape survivors make decisions and engage in relationships. It is hard for survivors and those around them to discern what real choices are. Risky sexual behavior, disordered eating, silence, and lack of relationship seem like control in the context of contorted subjectivity to a survivor. These same behaviors look like pathology to those who claim to know her. These actions are often the body's continued effort to tell a story of harm and violation that words cannot voice. The body's language of being harmed often underlines harm over and over again through repetition. The repetition of harm is written on the body as self-destruction. The body remembers the pain by revisiting it, perhaps hoping that in repetition its pain will be heard.

Even in its most zestful incarnation, feeling complicates any untroubled, unchanging conception of self. Its contorted status muddies the waters in another way. Subjectivity becomes contorted and distorted not by the fact that there is constant flux, but by the lack of referential feeling with which the self can create itself out of what it experienced. Contortion is a result of lack of relationship; it is the picture of groping in the dark alone. Contorted subjectivity feeds on itself until its dis-eased relationships are regenerated by recognition of the embodied truth of rape.

53. Adams discusses the destructive use of forgiveness among clergy when it is encouraged with women who have been abused by their spouses or significant others. Adams points out how forgiveness requires attention to justice. I examine this issue of what I call "demonic forgiveness" in my unpublished paper, "Indignant Suffering: Toward a Christian Practice of Forgiveness."

54. From 2005 NCVS statistics (RAINN Web site).

55. Madigan and Gamble, *Second Rape*, 17.

56. Ibid., 19.

Feeling Bodies/Tragic Bodies

The limits of consciousness, body loss, body function, and contorted subjectivity are fragments of re-membering bodies. These fragments tell us pieces of stories that need to be told. These narratives are from those who live out of traumatic experience; these stories are our own. The complexity and permanence of rape tell of the nature of all embodied experience. Tragedy and the suffering, pain, and loss that come with it condition all of us and the way we live as bodies in this world. The way that the body holds and is marked by harm is not unique to the experience of rape, but it is the nature of the body itself. We, as bodies, are conditioned on a cellular level by experience. Experiences that harm have particular power to affect our embodied life. Tragic experiences are those of unrecoverable loss and intense suffering that are part of all human experience.

There is no loss or reduction of particularity in the fact of this general truth. It is only a marker, a pattern of how bodies themselves create certain conditions for the lives of those who cannot help but live through them. Rape allows us a view of the inescapably tragic nature of bodies. There are many other traumatic experiences that could show us more about the tragic nature of embodied existence. Rape is particularly helpful because of the depth of the harm and because of the societal dynamic it brings into relief. Illness and affliction, for instance, involve undeserved suffering but do not necessarily elicit that same complex of relational harm, although they all too often do. Feeling helps us to understand what this dynamic of embodied experience means for us in our human condition. Tragedy stretches what rape points us toward to encompass a common part of human existence—an aspect of our condition that none of us can avoid.

Tragedy

> Each tragedy is the disclosure of an ideal:—What might have been, and was not: What can be.
> > Alfred North Whitehead, Adventures of Ideas

> Tragedy presses upon us a dark vision of reality, but it is in turn transcended by the apprehension of ultimate goodness. Its appeal to justice and its evocation of compassion are traces of an ethical order that is frustrated but not destroyed by unjust suffering.
> > Wendy Farley, Tragic Vision and Divine Compassion

Tragedy means that what could have been will never be, what will be is forever shaped by what was lost. Tragedy involves loss that is permanent and that conditions all that is. While tragedy is a painfully honest testimony of reality, it offers us an authentic ray of hope in its resistance to the ultimate triumph of suffering. Tragedy signals a depth of loss and the body's refusal to surrender to suffering. These two aspects of tragedy are highlighted by the way feeling works. Feeling tells us that loss is written on our bodies in permanent ink—what could have been will never be. At the same time that the loss is permanent, there is fluidity to how it can move into the present and future. Feeling has the capacity to keep the body alive with a remarkable efficiency and consistency, and it has the capacity to pave the way for renewed life and zest. Feeling is the mechanism of our survival as well as the mechanism of redemption. Feeling habituates harm by writing it on our bodies, by making it heard in the language of our bodies. Feeling is also the location of where deep healing can occur, where the resistance to suffering can take hold at a place deeper than consciousness and emotion and translate itself into new, fuller, more zestful existence.

Tragedy brings with it a theological resource that Protestant theology needs to offset the inadequacy of sin's capacity to address the kind of harm that bodies often suffer. Tragedy highlights the fact that bodies can suffer not because of the fault of those who suffer but because of the vagaries of violence, illness, and harm in human life. The strong Reformed theological attention to systemic sin is a helpful framework for aspects of this dynamic, but it remains a paradigm in the extreme. It is left unbalanced by a tragic sensitivity as it still builds itself on culpability. It needs the nuance of suffering as a fact that does not radiate around blame. Tragedy stops us from emptying all human experience into sin by making us sit with the suffering itself, especially with the undeserved suffering of victims.

Wendy Farley uses the term "radical suffering" to describe the kind of suffering that renders obvious the limitations of traditional theodicies and the "problematic of sin."[57] Radical suffering is defined by Farley as destructive to the human spirit and resistant to being understood as deserved. Farley explains how "radical suffering" renders meaningless the descriptive power of traditional theodicies such as punishment for sin, which is left as an offense to any sense of morality by the reality of radical suffering. Similarly the traditional argument of plenitude is also rendered impotent by radical suffering, which cannot be rendered invisible by looking at the larger whole. As Farley explains, there is no justice that can justify itself on the torture of innocents. The pedagogical argument is equally delegitimized by radical suffering, which does not make its victims stronger, but instead destroys them. Finally, the prediction of an eschatological solution is no comfort, explains Farley, because we live in history.[58] Farley asserts that tragedy comes in the gap between suffering and a "longing for justice." Tragedy, unlike traditional theodicies, does not try to justify suffering. Instead it acknowledges the reality of suffering and the understanding that some suffering is irredeemable and unjustified.

Farley offers four "regular themes" that she finds associated with tragedy in her work. First, tragedy is characterized by an attentiveness to suffering—suffering that cannot be reduced to fault and that has a distinctive destructive power.

---

57. Ibid., 19–39. Here Farley provides a substantive description of tragedy and her "tragic vision." I will not cover all of the important ways she uses tragedy to answer the deficiencies of sin in its ability to respond to undeserved suffering. I will, however, use some of the themes of her tragic vision to fill out how tragedy can be applied categorically to embodied experience.

58. Ibid., 21–22.

Second, tragedy holds within it the dynamic of freedom and responsibility characteristic of human life. People are not passive, but human action is constantly "constrained" within the situation, by ignorance and by conflict. Farley calls this recognition of the complexity of responsibility the "genius of tragedy." Third, tragedy brings clarity to the fact that the way the world is distorts freedom and includes tragic suffering.[59] Fourth, tragedy includes defiance—resistance to tragic suffering. Even in the face of destruction, tragedy keeps some aspect of human dignity, worth, and goodness intact. Farley explains that it is this tragic knowledge that contains the "final release from tragedy."[60] Farley's description of tragedy tells us, therefore, that tragedy faces the truth, the tragic truth that plays out every day in history that life involves suffering that is located in the very nature of human life. Tragedy provides us with a way to be brutally honest at the same time that it affirms the worth of survival and compassion in the midst of suffering.

Tragedy gives us a way to respond to what happens to us with recognition of its truth and its sadness. It offers an understanding of the complexity of suffering without diminishing its reality and its destructive power. It does not explain suffering away; tragedy acknowledges suffering by attesting to its inexplicable presence and possibility in all life. Where sin focuses on blame for what befalls human life, tragedy opens up a space for compassion, indignation, and grief. Our bodies are harmed sometimes by no fault of our own, and tragedy gives us a way to say out loud that "something better could have happened and it did not and what could have been will never be." Tragedy sits with the body's loss; it allows for how it changes us.

Tragedy acknowledges the kind of loss that the body suffers and invites the kind of healing that re-members the body. Indignant suffering helps it to translate the body's story of trauma into theological language. Embodied life entails harm that is grossly destructive, and it entails a remarkable capacity for survival, both aspects of experience that feeling fashions in all particularity.

If rape tells us anything it is that our bodies re-member with great tenacity and promise.

59. Farley has a quite important and helpful discussion here about how tragedy questions the very existence of a moral order. She uses Prometheus and Antigone to illustrate how the virtuous are the most vulnerable. See Farley, *Tragic Vision*, 26.

60. Ibid., 27.

Chapter 3

Feeling Relational Bodies

Cellular Poetics

New Life/New Death

There was an opening—
        a way in, but not all the way.
It was all so natural. I knew. I knew.
Confirmation. Heart beating. Elation.
Each morning I woke enchanted by my body/proud/beautiful.
I was the pregnant runner—full of life, not missing a beat, the picture of health.
That's when it happened, running.
        A dissonant flow; red blood.

"You should come in and get it checked out." I knew. I knew.

I dreamed of a little brown-haired boy.
Perfect, but nothing else was right in the dream. I knew. I knew.

"The pregnancy is not in the uterus. . . . Your baby is not viable. . . . This will just prick you for a minute. . . . You may have a lot of bleeding."

Isolation. Sickness. Sadness. . . . Tears to fill the sea. Where is my baby?

More death.
"You may need surgery/ Blockage/ Dangerous/ Risky/ Wait/ Have you ever been sexually abused?" I knew. . . .
Then there was only time—days and days of it.
Staring vacantly at our beige walls, wood floors. Waiting for the door to open. . . .

There was nothing there—a quiet chasm, a space ravaged.

Perhaps something had died in me long ago in that basement under the weight of the man who raped me. I knew. . . .

The blood I lost then was the same bright red—new, unused, wasted, lost. . . .

Then in a moment of hopefulness . . . life, slowly growing, powerful, assertive.

It was all my body could do to form this life.

It was more than that little life, it was my own.

    Everything in slow motion,

                everything for him,

                        my second son.

Sixty-one hours of labor, then two hours pushing through that tightening, that immense cramping down deep in my abdomen. I felt it all, thank God—I needed to. I screamed, I cried, I breathed, I did it with my sister gripping my hand, her tears falling on my arm, with my husband in emotional abandon holding me, watching, speaking through his tears "you can do it." And I did—I did it. I birthed a child—a beautiful, alive, amazing spirit of a person so familiar, so new. It left me new, too, tapped into myself in a way that had been gone for years. I stayed awake that first night even after three days of labor with no sleep.

I was electric with our new life. I felt re-membered.

INTRODUCTION

What if bodies refused to be invisible? Pregnant bodies take up space. They expand into our line of vision. They are beautifully creative, even spiritually provocative. They reacquaint the alienated. In their fullest expression pregnant bodies revel in connection. Pregnancy is intricately ordered and audaciously unruly.[1] Divine mystery and earthy groundedness swirl about, creating new life that is knit together with the pieces of what already is. Pregnant bodies carry theological weight.

Pregnancy tempers the loss of tragic bodies with the gift of life even as it encompasses tragedy in the risk it embodies. Pregnancy also points toward the ambiguity of bodies (as highlighted in motherhood) with the mystery and promise of what it brings forth. Pregnancy complicates with its entangled reality. Lines between biology and culture, between the self and others, between body and mind are not simply blurred, but revealed as chimerical. Pregnancy reveals most remarkably the relational nature of bodies as it reflects the fullness of life that is born out of connection and its creative power.

---

1. As one of my doctors, Dr. Martin Weiner, used to tell me often during my pregnancy when I would ask why I was having certain symptoms, "The baby didn't read the book."

This hefty and promising embodied experience is full of theological possibility. Why isn't there more space for it in the ways we worship, in the ways we form sacred communities, or in the ways we talk about and understand the Christian faith? Just as is apparent with a tragic embodied experience like rape, pregnancy wants for language and theological content. The church and its theological ethos have been largely silent on what this life-creating process means for believers. This silence is intensely curious in a faith that boasts God's embodied entry in the world through a woman's womb and a childbirth as natural as they come—in a barn in Bethlehem. This strange silence leaves a formidable gap in how pregnant women are supported and encouraged to understand themselves spiritually during this powerful experience. This gap is filled most often in American culture with the information and understanding that medical science and technology provide. The spiritual nature of birth suffers under this lack of theological attention. As sociologist Robbie Pfeufer Kahn explains, "The social context created by obstetrics denudes childbirth of the sacred."[2] As the spiritual and sacred layers of birth are unaffirmed with language and practice, pregnancy is thinned out in its ability to mediate embodied truth to us. The body falls further off the theological radar screen.

But the theological weight of pregnant bodies has exceptional truth to tell. Pregnancy embodies wakefulness and attunement to relationship not simply for those who experience it directly, but for all of us as children of God's creative birthing. New life and new death are immediate in pregnancy more than in any other facet of embodiment. All embodied creatures live in this entanglement with new life and new death; pregnancy simply expands it into our visual, palpable, and conscious awareness with unique concreteness.

My own pregnancies were not blissful experiences. Intense and prolonged nausea and vomiting for most of the months of pregnancy made enjoying the experience difficult. Even with the hard daily realities of what pregnancy was like for me, these stretches of time to be simply and intensely in my body reawakened me to what and who we are as embodied creatures. It was not through delight in the unfolding of pregnancy, but in the unfiltered nature of the experience that I woke up to my own body's desire to integrate and reconnect. It is in this utter proximity to our relatedness that pregnancy re-members us.

Pregnancy re-members us with layers of experience that we may find a way to ignore in the rest of life. It puts the body back together by awakening us to the characteristics of our own embodied nature. It insists on recognition of our interdependence and our creative capacity. Pregnancy can grow our capacity to be re-membered. It tunes us in to our deep need for responsiveness—to be responded to and to be response-able. This need for response is not simply an ethical or moral desire to care for others and to be cared for. Responsiveness is cellular and existential; it is a gauge of feeling's well-being. "Response-ability" is a deep, embodied capacity for responsiveness. It is the embodied capacity to

2. As quoted by Sheila Kitzinger, *Rediscovering Birth* (New York: Pocket, 2000), 93.

respond to all those with whom we are connected. These connections are already in place, extended beyond our awareness, and entangled in the cells of our bodies. Response-ability is the potency of the fabric of all life; it is the efficacy of entanglement. Response-ability draws us inside and out—into the divine connective tissue that breeds and breathes new life in us all.

PREGNANCY: PROSE AND POIESIS

Now why do you cry aloud?
Is there no king in you?
Has your counselor perished,
that pangs have seized you like a woman in labor?
Writhe and groan, O daughter Zion,
like a woman in labor;
for now you shall go forth from the city
and camp in the open country;
you shall go to Babylon.
There you shall be rescued,
there the LORD *will redeem you*
from the hands of your enemies.

Micah 4:9–10

Organogenesis is the formation of body parts. It takes place in the month between weeks six and ten. . . . By the time it is over, the embryo is the length of a paper clip, and, by definition, all the organs and structures of the body are present in "a grossly recognizable form." . . .

Of all the biological processes I've ever studied—from photosynthesis to echolocation—organogenesis is, hands down, the most fantastical. Sometimes it seems like a magic show. At other times it's like origami, the formation of elegant structures from the folding of flat sheets. It also involves cellular wanderings worthy of Odysseus. No single metaphor can describe it.

Sandra Steingraber, Having Faith

While I was writing an early version of this book, a family member who is a poet was living with us. Perhaps this fact is one reason why I came to see pregnancy's body language as *poiesis*—the art of poetic composition, a making. A pregnant woman, like a poetic artisan, embodies the capacity to elevate the way we think about, talk about, write about life itself. Pregnancy stretches the imagination on many levels, holding within it something we all can understand. At the same time it leaves us with an overwhelming sense of the limits of the ways we express ourselves with language. This stretching reveals the potency of our embodied nature, its creativity, its delicacy, its entanglement. The pregnant body reveals material reality and the mystery of life. It is the place where life unfolds as flesh, cells, and some spark, some connection and redemptive possibility of more abundance than we have known.

Poetry uses language both as its way to take flight and as the limit beyond which it pushes us. Our resident poet once told me that the struggle of poetry is to say the most you possibly can with as few words as possible. In addition to this economy of poetry, there is massiveness of meaning that can be contained in the way words are chosen, placed on the page, read, spoken, or heard.[3] Poetry is fluid and formative in this way, and pregnancy mirrors that tensive and beautiful mix of form and openness, of structure and mystery. Pregnancy, like poetry, brings forth something altogether new, embodying so much indeterminacy even within the bounds of its stark, hard-won body. Poetry and pregnancy create meaning figuratively.

Pregnancy's embodied poiesis shows itself in what I describe as a heightened attunement. For instance, many women report that their dreams during pregnancy sometimes provide them with accurate information like the sex of the baby, when their labor is going to begin, or, sadly, the coming of a miscarriage. Women who are pregnant generally have a keener sense of smell and sound, and they are often affected in clear ways by things like the weather and the cycles of the moon. It is as if pregnancy makes the body a more immediate presentation of the interconnection of all that is. Awareness flowers as an embodied reality. The mystery and solidity of this kind of embodied "knowing" are the poiesis of pregnancy; this heightened attunement is part of its figurative language.

In the poiesis of pregnancy lies its spiritual and theological weight. Pregnancy cannot escape its figurative nature. Its fullness holds within it life and death, both offered up as its unflappable truth. It is the recapitulation of the enfleshed, yet-to-be-seen-ness, of life. It is generous in its handing out of massive experience, not without cruelty in its inescapable trials. In its straightforward and mysterious nature, pregnancy is the flesh of our connections to all that is. In its uniquely demonstrative way, pregnancy re-members us. How it re-members is an embodied dynamic we will explore through its poiesis and through the prose of scientific narrative. Together prose and poiesis communicate how pregnancy is an exemplar of embodied connection, relation, and redemption.

The biological prose that tells of pregnancy provides an amazing story of determination and precision beginning before conception occurs. The egg works to make itself available to the strongest and most viable sperm. Once they meet they begin to travel together, moved by the pulsing of the fallopian tubes, into the uterus. There they find a home. As the now-fertilized egg works to become

3. An exceptional example of the poetic and pregnancy can be found in a collection of poems by Toi Derricotte, *Natural Birth* (Trumansburg, NY: Crossing Press, 1983). Also, soon after writing this chapter I read some of Luce Irigaray's discussion on "bodily poetics" or *poétique du corps* in *This Sex Which Is Not One*, trans. Catherine Porter (Ithaca, NY: Cornell University Press, 1985). I appreciate the way her use of poiesis speaks to the fluidity of meaning located in the body that gives birth. See also the discussion of Irigaray's body poetics in Michelle Boulous Walker, *Philosophy and the Maternal Body: Reading Silence* (New York: Routledge, 1998), 153–58.

comfortable, a newly pregnant body is working to send the necessary information to the rest of her. Hormone production shifts, and the whole body begins
to focus on the new task at hand. Slowly, indications begin to present themselves
as conscious confirmation that the pregnancy is under way. Breasts are tender,
fatigue, maybe the beginnings of nausea, a missed period, a different tonality to
things. Some women claim to "just know," even in the context of unplanned
and surprise pregnancies. The body delivers the news of pregnancy to a woman
although some women report not feeling "officially" pregnant until they go to
the doctor and get confirmation.

As the consciousness becomes privy to this new state of affairs, the embodied
system of creativity is already hard at work securing the early construction of
what will soon be a fully formed fetus, wanting only for size and developmental
progress. As the furious pace of life taking shape continues—interrupted only by
complications or interventions—a woman's body only slowly begins to morph
into someone who "looks" pregnant. Hormones facilitate everything from the
formation of the placenta to the bonding that occurs between a mother and
child after birth. The body's accommodation of new life is the story of relationship and connection.

The prose of medical science narrates the remarkable story of how the systems of the body work together to form life and then direct the body on how
to give birth and feed this new life. Even with all we do know, however, there
remains much that is beyond scientific knowledge. The poiesis of pregnancy is
not separate from this prosaic tale, but an important enhancement to how we
understand the experience and its theological meaning. Sinking too deeply into
biology can create a distorted sense of pregnancy's predictability. Its revelations
are not mechanical, but abundantly multifarious. Social, cultural, economic,
spiritual, and any other conditions of one's existence deeply affect how a woman
experiences pregnancy and affect even how the cellular activity of pregnancy
takes shape.[4] Not only do women in different cultures vary, according to their
cultural context, in their descriptions of how labor and delivery feel, but so does
the actual manner in which their bodies function in labor.[5] Pregnancy, just as
with everything else, is an experience shaped by all else that is and is irreducible
in its particularity. Pregnancy clearly embodies the dance of feeling's universality
and particularity. Feeling is the ground of our connection with everything that
is, and it is the seat of all particularity. Pregnancy is an apex of this truth. The
biological processes follow a pattern—so intricate, so common. The result is
something new that is composed of all that is.

In this project as a whole, I seek to encounter the complexity of the body and
construct theology that helps us live into that complexity with greater integrity

---

4. In light of all of this diversity in the very way pregnancy is experienced, I use great care in
critiquing different methods of addressing pregnancy and childbirth. There is no unproblematic
"method" that could possibly address women in all of their diversity of needs and circumstances.
There is also no method that can have stripped itself of societal standards and contextual assumptions.

5. See Kitzinger, *Rediscovering Birth*, 93.

and zest. In this particular chapter, I am focusing on how this complexity owes itself to relationality, the dance of all that is. We encounter and experience multiple layers of embodied experience. Pregnancy helps frame our response-ability to relationality. Pregnancy can liberate the body from theological invisibility and hostility.[6] Pregnancy can do even more than liberate; feeling helps us to glimpse the character of our own redemption in the cellular poetics of pregnancy. The immediacy of connection, the blurring of boundaries, and the attunement to embodied capacity in the experience of pregnancy tell us who we are and who we can be. Feeling is the mechanism of our redemption in this way.

Even with the concreteness of pregnancy's embodied poetics, it can be hard for us to recognize and embrace its redemptive promise. Our receptivity is obscured by many patterns of modern Western culture. These patterns distort and displace pregnancy's figurative relationality. These patterns can also block the redemptive power of feeling and its capacity to reawaken us to who we are and can be. Pregnancy in Western culture is, therefore, also a window into how we often ignore the reality of relationship to our peril. It is a window into how estranged we are from who God made us to be and how God calls us to live.

An overly medicalized view of pregnancy, for example, can make it seem like the body's creation forms itself in mechanical, unentangled steps. The work of pregnancy may seem to go on in a mode that requires very little willfulness or conscious effort. Abigail Lewis, a woman pregnant in the late 1950s in this country, remarked:

> Were I to lose consciousness for a month, I could still tell that an appreciable amount of time had passed by the increased size of the fetus within me. There is constant sense of growth, of progress, of time which, while it may be wasted for you personally, is still being used, so that even if you were to do nothing at all during those nine months, something would nevertheless be accomplished and a climax reached.[7]

---

6. Carol Bigwood wrote her article, "Renaturalizing the Body," while she was pregnant. Perhaps it is no coincidence that she was able to theorize about the need to rethink the body "releasing it from a dichotomized nature and culture" with such clarity while she was pregnant (Bigwood, in *Body and Flesh: A Philosophical Reader*, ed. Donn Welton [Oxford: Blackwell, 1996], 103). This nature/culture intersection is a common trope in much of the feminist/poststructuralist discussion about embodiment. This characterization has given way to some important conversations about the body. Some examples are: Judith Butler, *Gender Trouble: Feminism and the Subversion of Identity* (New York: Routledge, 1990); Butler, *The Psychic Life of Power: Theories in Subjection* (Stanford: Stanford University Press, 1997); Butler, *Bodies That Matter* (New York: Routledge, 1993); Susan Bordo, *Unbearable Weight: Feminism, Western Culture, and the Body* (Berkeley: University of California Press, 1993); and Moira Gatens, *Imaginary Bodies: Ethics, Power, and Corporeality* (London: Routledge, 1996). Bigwood works to develop a model of bodies as "incarnate" and "indeterminate." She uses Merleau-Ponty's "sentience" (*sens*) to correct some of the problems of the nature/culture duality. This "third term" holds within it the noncognitive, nonlinguistic modes of the body. This *sens* is not unlike feeling in the way it functions in theorizing embodiment. Along with Bigwood, I endeavor to think about the lived complexity of the body. Both feeling and *sens* complicate false dichotomies that are imposed on the body (Bigwood, "Renaturalizing the Body," 106).

7. Abigail Lewis, *An Interesting Condition: The Diary of a Pregnant Woman* (Garden City, NY: Doubleday, 1950), 78.

Pregnancy is, indeed, a purely embodied experience. The monumental feat that results from pregnancy leaves a woman hard-pressed not to somehow gain a new appreciation for her body's ability. But far from revealing this kind of experience as utterly passive, pregnancy communicates the subtlety of activity and passivity in embodied life. In fact, these terms are troubled by the poiesis of pregnancy. Everything from stress to relaxation, from toxins to nutrition, travels through the umbilical cord and affects how we breathe, how we eat, how we move, how we feel, and how we encounter the fetus. Even though it seems beyond our control, it is deeply affected by us.

This interconnection, this relationality, points us toward the importance of responsiveness in order for feeling to flower fully in its creative capacity. We need this full-bodied responsiveness to be response-able. To create and to nourish full life requires this response-ability. This ability is the capacity to let ourselves, as bodies, function well as we tend to what our bodies need to function well. The figurative language of pregnancy provides models of these kinds of embodied relationships. Pregnancy models both response-able relationships and relationships that are wounded or distorted in their capacity for responsiveness. These models inform our human condition and our theological imagination. They challenge our communal practices, and they stretch our sense of interdependence with those outside our familiar contexts. How we worship, how we understand the sacraments, and how we honor and embrace the body in who we are as church are touched by what these models show us. There are three features of embodied relationality for us to explore: our relationship to creation and creativity, our entangled subjectivity, and our relational body knowledge. These three features of embodied relationality are models of relationship and of relationship's rupture.

PREGNANCY'S PROMISE AND PROBLEMATIC: RELATIONSHIP AND RUPTURE

Has anybody ever thought about Mary having contractions?
Yes, she had contractions.
but there is just that one line, something like . . .
"and then the time came that she should be delivered" or whatever.
She had Jesus in a barn, for Christ's sake.
She had to let out at least a few shrieks along the way.

Has anybody ever acknowledged that Mary had a cervix,
much less that it dilated and was all stretched and bloody?
What was that like for her?
What was it all like for her?
Breathing, sweating,

gripping whatever was closest to her determined hand. . . .
What was it like to labor with God that way?

Pregnancy gives us that space for laboring with life, life force, life's boundaries, life's potential. It is the intersection of God's promise for abundant life and the risks of our own finitude. Just as Mary labored with God, we labor with the embodied promises and perils of life. Pregnancy can delight us with the miracle of new life; pregnancy can devastate us with its proximity to death. We dance in this mystery of creation with sometimes strange rhythms of self-assertion and surrender. We are caught in life's web at the same time that we help create it.

As if the mystery of this dance were not baffling enough, we are also deeply formed by the distortions of our illusions and idols. Pregnancy shows us what life really is: creative, relational, interconnected, and interdependent. These cellular connections define the nature of our human condition. But we live as if we know better. We live as if we occupy space that is only our own, as if we can claim separate cosmic property in the grand scheme of things. We fashion our individuality with rugged determination. Although we are as connected with everything that is as a mother is to her fetus, we live as if our actions and conditions are only our own.

These distortions create the conditions that rupture our relationality. With "rupture" I refer to a fissure, a fracture, a wound that renders feeling unable to flow freely. A rupture does not destroy relationship, but it can disfigure it. It can render a relationship different in its shape. It can alter the ways it can interact with all that comes after it. Rupture can compromise a relationship's ability to connect. A rupture creates a gap or a place that may trap within it feelings that were needed for the healthiest possible inheritance. Ruptures can be so deep that feeling trapped there is left to languish, never realizing the connections for which it was so desperately needed. A rupture is a disruption of responsible relationship, of the body's response-ability. Relationship's rupture comes when relationality is ignored or denied. The experience of pregnancy in the United States gives us clear examples of these ruptures.

Three features of relationality are given flesh by the poetics of pregnancy: creativity, subjectivity, and body knowledge. Within each of these features of relationality, pregnancy provides a model of relationship and a figurative image of the rupture of relationship. Within the feature of creativity, pregnancy provides the placenta as a model of relationship. Within this same feature, an image of rupture is evident in the effects of environmental toxins on the fetus. Within the feature of subjectivity, pregnancy offers a model of relationship through the effects of midwives. The image of rupture within this feature of relationality comes from the effects of interventions that take a woman out of relationship during pregnancy and birth. Finally, within the feature of body knowledge, pregnancy provides the power of birth as a model of relationship. This model of body knowledge provides a way for us to see also relationship's rupture when excessive technology truncates the body's capacity for knowing.

Feature One: Creativity and Creation

For all eternity, God lies on a birthing bed, giving birth. The essence of God is Birthing.

Meister Eckhart

The theological weight of pregnancy brings with it hefty claims about the most primal facts of our existence. If God created us, then who does that say that we are? What is it about God's creative activity in the world that weaves its way through us? Creativity is not simply how we were made, it points to the nature of who we are made to be. God's nature is creative. God's nature is active through the play of feeling, which is our mode of existence. We are, therefore, creative at our most basic, functional level. Feeling as our mode of creativity is the spark of divinity that continually fires in us. Feeling's link to creativity reveals this mode of our existence as the image of God in us, our *imago Dei*. We are created through and for creativity, and feeling is the mode that enables our creativity.

The way feelings encounter and interact with other feelings can be described as "creativity." For Whitehead, creativity is the defining characteristic of the universe. It is forever the novel expression of entities and relations arising from the flow of events. He describes God as the primordial instance of creativity. God is the "formative element in the flux."[8] Creativity is the "factor of activity" that is the reason for the existence of a particular "occasion of experience."[9] An experience or actual occasion does not come out of a passive collection of data. Our experiences are not a reaction to static factors of existence. On the contrary, everything that forms our experience is characterized by the activity of creativity. Creativity signals the novel nature of all that proceeds from the past we inherit.[10]

Because of its capacity for response, feeling is the conduit of all creativity. Creativity, therefore, is involved in all responsiveness and relatedness.[11] Creation is both the activity and the seat of existence. It is what we do and where we live. The body is the nexus, the locus, the focal point for how creativity functions and takes shape in human life. Feeling is how we create, and it is what we create. Feeling is how we are connected to God's constant creative power and how we grow out of that power. Our embrace and our resistance of creativity have a direct impact on how feeling functions.

---

8. See John B. Cobb Jr. and David Ray Griffin, *Process Theology: An Introductory Exposition* (Philadelphia: Westminster, 1976), 141. I will not go into great depth about Whitehead's doctrine of God. See *Process and Reality*, part 5, chapter 2 (pp. 342–51), for his most complete description of God's primordial and consequent natures.

9. Whitehead, *Adventures of Ideas*, 179.

10. According to Whitehead (ibid., 236): "Creativity . . . expresses the notion that each event is a process issuing in novelty."

11. Cobb and Griffin discuss this as "creative transformation" and in relationship to Christ (*Process Theology*, 100).

Pregnancy exposes how feeling and creativity are inexorably linked. The dynamic creative capacity of the placenta is a model of relationship that captures the cooperative and mysterious aspect of creation's processes. The placenta shows us the ways interconnection and interdependence weave together all of life. This "organ," which is our first home as we develop in the womb, nourishes us in the complexity of our relationship with everything that exists. It is our most primal environment. It embodies a figurative model of our human condition; it reveals a poetics of embodied creativity.

The Placental Model

> A placenta is an intertwining of mother and child in the closest kind of embrace biologically possible. . . . The placenta is a biological mystery. It is an evolutionary shape-shifter. It dodges the mother's immune system while immunologically guarding the fetus. It is the flat cake that feeds us all. It is another brain that is slowly overriding my own. It is a blood-drenched forest. It is the sapwood of pregnancy.
>
> Sandra Steingraber, Having Faith

The ability of the placenta to mediate and protect mother and fetus is unrivaled in biology. It is not a passive sieve for blood and nutrients. On the contrary, it is an active, even ingenious, partner in the processes of pregnancy. The placenta takes from the mother's blood what is needed for fetal development. In many cases it even deconstructs certain materials in order for them to pass to the fetus in their appropriate form.

Some proteins are "disassembled and carried over brick by amino-acid brick."[12] The proteins are then rebuilt specifically according to what the fetus needs. The placenta is one of three parts of the human body that possesses the ability to block the entry of harmful substances into a certain area. These barriers are all "functional rather than anatomical."[13] There is no wall, but they use some kind of cell membrane equipped with what Steingraber calls "subcellular gadgets" to control what molecules in maternal blood pass through. Bacteria that get in are diverted to the Hofbauer cells, which are special immune agents. Unnecessary adrenal hormones are taken care of by enzymes in the placenta that render them deactivated. The placenta enjoys the immediacy of knowing how to attend to mother and fetus at the same time; it is thoroughly response-able.

The placenta is an active and creative participant in pregnancy, drawing from the resources and needs of both mother and fetus to encourage growth and well-being. It seems to be able to read situations and then to respond while considering the intimate connection, and the important particularity, of both mother and fetus. In Luce Irigaray's interview with Helene Rouch, they discuss

12. Sandra Steingraber, *Having Faith: An Ecologist's Journey to Motherhood* (Cambridge, MA: Perseus, 2001), 31.
13. Ibid., 14.

the "placental economy."[14] Rouch describes the placenta as a "tissue, formed by the embryo, which, while closely imbricated with the uterine mucosa remains separate from it."[15] Irigaray and Rouch use the nature of the placenta as a model for relationship—it creates and enables independence and interdependence. The placenta does not fuse mother and fetus; on the contrary, the placenta mediates all exchanges between the mother and fetus.

While its strength is how it operates out of interdependence, the fragility of the placenta shows through because of this same feature. In the case of some toxins, like mercury, the placenta mysteriously magnifies their effect, putting the fetus at a higher level of risk. Some chemicals, like nicotine, pose a risk to the fetus by harming the placenta itself rather than by crossing through it. Steingraber explains that nicotine damages the placenta's amino acid transport system used to take proteins from the maternal blood to the baby's. Also, polychlorinated biphenyls (PCBs) alter placental blood vessels, reducing their flow. Car exhaust, which contains the heavy metal nickel, compromises the placenta's ability to make and release hormones.[16] The strength and the fragility of the placenta are both functions of the immediacy of its interdependence with all that is. The potency of its response-ability also makes it deeply susceptible to the destructive power of toxins. We, too, are so interdependent that such fragility is a fact of our lives.

Rupture and Creation

In keeping with the tragic nature of bodies, some of the only moments of clarity for Western culture about the body's interdependence come from disease and malformation. Steingraber calls us to admit that sad fact of our Western habits of thinking.[17] Steingraber, an ecologist, examines how diseases, drugs, and environmental toxins affect the unborn and how these dangers have been culturally ignored and exacerbated by the refusal to acknowledge the connections. The placenta's potent interconnections show us the harm of the rupture to responseable relationship. The rupture of the delicate relationship between humanity and all that is comes into focus in how pregnancy incorporates environmental toxins.

Mercury poisoning is a particularly telling example of relationship's rupture. Pregnant women have been increasingly warned to avoid eating certain kinds of fish before, during, and after pregnancy. The Food and Drug Administration's (FDA) 2004 guidelines recommend that pregnant and nursing women

14. Luce Irigaray, *Je, tu, nous: Toward a Culture of Difference*, trans. Alison Martin (New York: Routledge, 1993), 37–44.

15. Ibid., 38.

16. Steingraber, *Having Faith*, 34.

17. Steingraber (ibid., e.g., 36–55) looks at four lessons of the twentieth century alone that should have rendered this myth dead: rubella, thalidomide, Minamata, and diesthylstilbestrol (DES), and wonders how so many environmental hazards to unborn children can continue to be unregulated and plentiful in the air, water, and food that goes into our bodies. She says, "The womb is a wondrous and mysterious threshold. It should not enter our awareness only when poisons flow through it" (ibid., 55).

and women who may become pregnant should avoid eating shark, swordfish, king mackerel, and tilefish. In fact, the latest warning by the Environmental Working Group warns that women of childbearing age who might ever have children should avoid eating many other kinds of fish in addition to those in the FDA's guidelines at any time—including tuna fish, Gulf Coast oysters, sea bass, halibut, marlin, pike, and white croaker. The Environmental Working Group's report also warns that canned tuna, mahi-mahi, cod, and pollack should not be eaten more than once a month.[18]

The biggest contributor to the growing amount of mercury contamination in the environment is coal-burning power plants.[19] The amount of mercury released from these plants is fast approaching 100,000 pounds each year.[20] Science confirms that mercury damages brain and motor development. Methylmercury binds directly to chromosomes, therefore interfering with their ability to replicate themselves. This glomming on of mercury to chromosomes stops the all-important process of cell division in fetal brain development. This same strand of mercury inhibits the movement of brain cells in the important stages of development that involve muscle control and development.[21]

Perhaps the most sinister and tragic part of the equation is that when mercury is pumped through the placenta its impact is magnified. Study after study

18. The Environmental Working Group's article entitled "FDA's Midnight Mischief Heightens Mercury Risk to Pregnant Women, Infants" can be found at www.ewg.org. This article was written in December of 2008. Additional information about the Environmental Working Group's report was found in a CNN report found on the Internet at the following Web site address: http://www.cnn.com/2001/HEALTH/parenting/04/12/fish.pregnant/story6.pregnant.fish.jpg. In 2002 an article appeared in the *Chicago Tribune* that instructed women of childbearing age and children under the age of fifteen not to eat fish if they believe it was caught in a body of water in Illinois because of high levels of methyl mercury caused by coal burning plants. "Women warned to limit fish: State concerned about mercury," *Chicago Tribune,* 2 April 2002.

19. Steingraber, *Having Faith,* 121.

20. Ibid., 122. There are many other sources of mercury contamination—mercury-containing products in landfills (thermometers, fluorescent lights, and electrical switches to name a few), chlorine production plants, and crematoriums from burning dental fillings. Since Steingraber wrote her book the EPA has come out with new regulations and statements about mercury from coal-burning plants. The following quote describes the Clean Air Mercury Rule: "On March 15, 2005, EPA issued the first-ever federal rule to permanently cap and reduce mercury emissions from coal-fired power plants. The Clean Air Mercury Rule will build on EPA's Clean Air Interstate Rule (CAIR) to significantly reduce emissions from coal-fired power plants—the largest remaining sources of mercury emissions in the country. When fully implemented, these rules will reduce utility emissions of mercury from 48 tons a year to 15 tons, a reduction of nearly 70 percent. The Clean Air Mercury Rule establishes 'standards of performance' limiting mercury emissions from new and existing coal-fired power plants and creates a market-based cap-and-trade program that will reduce nationwide utility emissions of mercury in two distinct phases. The first phase cap is 38 tons and emissions will be reduced by taking advantage of 'co-benefit' reductions—that is, mercury reductions achieved by reducing sulfur dioxide (SO_2) and nitrogen oxides (NOx) emissions under CAIR. In the second phase, due in 2018, coal-fired power plants will be subject to a second cap, which will reduce emissions to 15 tons upon full implementation." From www.epa.gov/air/mercuryrule/basic.

21. Although Steingraber does not discuss the threats of mercury poisoning to those other than the unborn, the dangers are proven and documented in other places. For references see www.mercurypolicy.org.

confirms that mercury levels in newborn infants is higher than those found in their mothers. Many of these studies also confirm that the more fish a woman eats, the higher levels of mercury there are found in the blood of the umbilical cord. Steingraber explains that the arguments are not whether there is mercury contamination in babies whose mothers ate fish; rather, the arguments center around how much is too much.[22]

The danger is there; much damage has already been done. The National Academy of Sciences reported in July 2000 that some sixty thousand children are born each year at risk for developmental problems due to prenatal exposure to mercury.[23] In 2001 a study by the Centers for Disease Control that directly measured the mercury levels in the blood and hair of one thousand women and children in the United States reported that one in ten women of childbearing age has mercury levels in her body that are close to those that heighten her risk of having children with neurological deficiencies.[24]

In the example of mercury contamination, we see clearly how both creativity and creation are violated. There is a rupture in relationship because there is a denial of relationship. This rupture is cellular; it runs through our oceans, through the bodies of fish, into our bodies, and into the developing minds of our unborn. The myth of placental impermeability, the fallacy of environmental compartmentalization, the vicious cycle of imposing more and more dietary abstinence on pregnant women while dismissing the root causes of the problem all deny the cellular way we are related to all that is. We cannot fathom a more intimate connection than that which shapes the very way our cells divide and are constructed. In our denial of our interdependence at a cellular (even molecular) level, there is structural damage that prevents creativity from reaching its highest levels of promise. When water is poisoned, fish are poisoned. When fish are poisoned, those who eat them are poisoned. When we are poisoned, our unborn children bear the poison's heaviest weight.

Feature Two: Entangled Subjectivity

> *The first movements of the fetus produce this sense of the splitting subject; the fetus's movements are wholly mine, completely within me, conditioning my experience and space. Only I have access to these movements from their origin.* . . . *I have a privileged relation to this other life.* . . .

---

22. Steingraber, *Having Faith*, 126. These differences in opinion are entangled in the same web that lead poisoning was mired in for years in the United States. Steingraber tells us, "When I look into the history of mercury regulation, it very quickly sounds like the story of lead all over again: Industry groups working to downplay the dangers. Regulatory agencies intimidated. Public health initiatives thwarted. Scientists ignored. Calls for action drowned out by calls for more research. A public confused. It's the same plot, but with a different cast of characters, set fifty years later."

23. Ibid., 125.

24. Ibid., 126. Steingraber warns that this study's findings "indicated that exposure to mercury is not just limited to large consumers of fish. They indicate that the margin of safety for at least six million women of childbearing age—and their children—is razor thin."

Pregnancy challenges the integration of my body experience by rendering
fluid the boundary between what is within, myself, and what is outside,
separate. I experience my insides as the space of another, yet my own body.
                                    Iris Marion Young, "Pregnant Embodiment"

More than one heart beats in the confines of a pregnant woman's body; they share so much, yet each creates its own particular take on experience. Pregnancy, in the brute facts of its function, shows us the truth of entangled selves. Unlike the loss and contorted subjectivity that rape brings, pregnancy brings with it the possibility of new life, not out of harm but out of health and well-being. Within this positive possibility lies the inherent risk of loss and death just as any potent possibility for good does. Unlike contorted subjectivity, entangled subjectivity has the capacity to hold within it the full flowering of feeling as well as those things that can hinder its good growth.

Iris Marion Young describes the "splitting" or the "doubling" of the subject and the loss of the subject in pregnancy.[25] The quickening of the baby illustrates this splitting, this doubling of the self. A pregnant woman embodies connection and particularity. The baby in the womb is an active subject, as is the mother. The baby contributes to how the pregnancy and birth proceed in ways we cannot totally enumerate. The baby's subjectivity is so entangled with the mother's that we cannot always discern where they are differentiated from one another. Young is pointing toward this blurring of boundaries in her language of "splitting" and "doubling" of the self. The self is so entangled with another self that the very fact of some internal, discrete self is exploded by the disappearance of even the perceived barrier of the physical body.

We all live in this entangled subjectivity; feeling tells us that. This tangled-up fact of our relationality is figuratively modeled in the poetics of how support affects the character of birth experiences. The way in which a woman's experience of birth dramatically changes when she is surrounded by the kind of support she needs models entangled subjectivity. Webs of relationships shape our perspectives and experiences. Relationality's power to transform is especially clear in the way midwives and doulas have proven their worth in the processes of birth.

---

25. Iris Marion Young, "Pregnant Embodiment: Subjectivity and Alienation," repr. in *On Female Body Experience: "Throwing Like a Girl" and Other Essays* (New York: Oxford University Press, 2005), 46–61. Young uses pregnancy to both fill out and critique the phenomenologies of the body found in many existential philosophers such as Erwin Straus and Maurice Merleau-Ponty. She describes her project as the continuation of their undermining of Descartes and a challenge to their retention of assumptions of a unified subject. She is careful to qualify that her analysis takes into account pregnancy in Western, technologically advanced cultures, which, she asserts, largely involves women who choose pregnancies. Young borrows from the work of Julia Kristeva, who describes the experience of pregnancy as the "splitting of the subject." Kristeva is using this description from a psychoanalytic standpoint; Young applies it outside that framework to what she calls a decentering, "myself in the mode of not being myself." See Young, "Pregnant Embodiment," 46, 47, 49, 50, 52, 54.

The Midwife Model

> *Where water is available, midwives often use it to ease pain . . . to offer*
> *a laboring woman a powerful visual image of the uninterrupted flow of*
> *liquid. . . . In Greece, the midwife may pour water through the sleeve of the*
> *husband's shirt or down the chimney. In Jamaica, the nana soaks a cloth in*
> *hot water and cocoons the mother within it.*
>
> *Sheila Kitzinger,* Rediscovering Birth

A midwife is "with a woman: not just comforting, not just near, but in contact."[26] Midwives use their hands to communicate with women. Sheila Kitzinger
says, "[The midwife] receives information through the sensitivity of her touch,
and gives comfort, confidence and courage by touch. A good midwife knows
exactly how and when to touch, just as she also knows when to be hands off."[27]
The language of touch, figurative and unspoken, is an acknowledgment of relationship. It is artful in the way it coheres with the poiesis of pregnancy, attentive
and responsive to how the needs of a pregnant woman are embodied, unable to
be parsed out as "mental" or "physical."

Just any kind of touching does not achieve the same result as the knowing
and supportive touch of a midwife. For some women the way they are touched
during pregnancy, labor, and delivery by the doctors and nurses who attend
them can be traumatic and painful.[28] A midwife's touch is not a touch that is
meant to manipulate, control, or even always to diagnose, as many times a doctor's touch may be (e.g., attempts at manual dilation, routine premature rupture
of the membranes, repeated vaginal exams). Midwives use touch to gather information about the pregnancy and birth, but most of the touching a midwife does,
particularly in labor and delivery, is for comfort, support, and pain relief. This
kind of touching includes massaging during contractions, using pressure points,
holding a woman in a position that is comfortable, and massaging the perineum.

A good midwife knows when she needs the help of technology for a healthy
pregnancy and birth because she pays close attention and knows the warning signs of complications.[29] Because she pays attention, she can respond to

---

26. Kitzinger, *Rediscovering Birth*, 200.

27. Ibid.

28. Kitzinger explains that "some women use the language of rape when they describe how they
were touched. They feel 'victimised', 'invaded', 'violated' or 'abused'" (ibid., 213).

29. Suzanne Arms describes the good midwife's formula for success as follows: "(1) keep a
woman's spirits up; (2) maintain her privacy and dignity; (3) don't intervene in the process when it is
working; (4) do as little as is necessary to right things when they go wrong." Still within the spirit of
this formula, many midwives today are also trained as nurses because this kind of training is required
by many hospitals and licensing regulations in order for midwives to practice legally. Because of this
training, midwifery does not have to be cast as a decision against technology. See Suzanne Arms,
Immaculate Deception II: Myth, Magic, and Birth (Berkeley: Celestial Arts, 1994), 44.

real problems. Many doctors and nurses use many interventions "just in case" because they do not have the time to monitor closely all of their patients.[30] Nurse-midwives have a cesarean rate between 5 and 10 percent while the overall national rate is now at 30 percent.[31]

Doulas are also trained to support pregnant women before, during, and after labor and delivery. A doula is literally "a female servant." Her role is to give continuous support to a laboring woman. This kind of support is something that nurses on busy maternity wards do not often have the opportunity to give due to understaffing and all of the other duties they are expected to perform. A study of the use of doulas in over two thousand births showed that having this kind of companion shortened labor, decreased the cesarean rate by 50 percent, and reduced the need for pain medication.[32] With this presence of support and encouragement, women are able to live in the intensity of pregnancy without a lot of drug or technological intervention. This enabling shows the power of relationship to shape a woman's self-concept. What others believe she can do is directly correlated to what she is able to do.

Research not only reflects how doulas and midwives help improve a woman's chances of a vaginal delivery with a lower rate of interventions, but it confirms that having these supportive relationships translates into a more positive interpretation of the birth experience. Women assisted by midwives and doulas describe their experiences, their abilities, and the birth in positive terms. They use words like "spiritual," "dream state," "restorative," and "powerful."[33] The relationships of midwives and doulas with the pregnant women they serve honor the dynamic of entangled subjectivity rather than try to bypass it or erase it. These relationships are responsive, and they feed our capacity for responsiveness to ourselves, to our bodies, and to others. They re-member the body's response-ability.

30. Both Arms and Susan Diamond describe this "just in case" approach. See Susan R. Diamond, *Hard Labor* (New York: Tom Doherty, 1996).

31. Sandra Jacobs and the American College of Nurse Midwives in *Having Your Baby with a Nurse-Midwife* (New York: Hyperion, 1993), 90, put the percentage at 25 percent. More recent statistics put the figure at 30.2 percent as indicated by the Centers for Disease Control 2005 statistics on cesarean births. They explain the 46 percent rise in the cesarean rate as follows: "Preliminary data for 2005 indicate that 30.2 percent of all live births in the United States were cesarean deliveries, marking the highest U.S. total cesarean rate ever reported. Since 1996, the total cesarean rate has increased by 46 percent, driven by both an increase in the percentage of all women having a first cesarean and a decline in the percentage of women delivering vaginally after a previous cesarean. Cesarean rates vary considerably among states but tend to be lower in the western mountain states and upper Midwest region and higher in the Southeast and East regions." From www.cdc.gov.

32. Catherine M. Poole and Elizabeth A. Parr, *Choosing a Nurse-Midwife* (New York: John Wiley and Sons, 1994), 76. Suzanne Arms also describes a similar study of doulas in *Immaculate Deception II*, 162.

33. Examples of women who use much of this language can be found in some of the interviews in Arms, *Immaculate Deception*.

Rupture and Subjectivity

Just as supportive relationships enhance the experience of pregnancy and actually improve a woman's capacity to function well in pregnancy, those relationships that frustrate the healthy flow of feeling have equally discernible effects. Susan R. Diamond, a registered nurse who worked for years in labor and delivery in multiple hospitals, describes that the ways doctors talk to pregnant women often seems to accuse women of being inadequate for the task of labor and delivery. "Without consciously realizing it, doctors grow adept at expressing their frustration and hostility toward the patient by couching their words in an accusatory manner . . . [such as] 'you're not contracting efficiently' or 'you're not pushing hard enough.'. . . I have repeatedly seen women apologize to doctors for the failure of their bodies."[34] Accusatory language taps into a pregnant woman's fears of inadequacy and creates a situation in which she needs to be rescued from the situation. The use of technology and medicine fits all too easily into this perceived need to be saved from the inadequacy of one's own body.[35] Drugs numb the pain. Technology gives "reliable" information. In these kinds of situations, women use language like "weak," "near death," and "bloody mess" to describe themselves.[36]

It is not simply the norms of many hospital environments that starve the full flowering of feeling for many women during pregnancy. Our cultural context and discourse about pregnancy also poorly nourish a woman's sense of power and possibility. Young describes how discourse about pregnancy erases the subjectivity of women. The language of "expecting," she asserts, is a clear example of how the subjectivity of the pregnant woman is omitted. "Expecting" suggests that the woman is only waiting, watching, passive, detached from the development of the new life.[37] In our cultural context, a pregnant woman's sense of herself is shaped by the way women are sometimes erased from the equation in common discourse about pregnancy. This cultural construction of meaning and selfhood is yet another layer of entangled subjectivity.

The kind of imposed invisibility that Young sees in the language of expecting is only exacerbated in what she labels the "medicalization" of birth. Here the female subject is alienated from herself as medical models of pregnancy and birth cast the experience as a disordered one and then use instruments and technology to control and interpret the course of the experience.[38] Doctors in the West

34. Diamond, *Hard Labor*, 119, 322.
35. Both Arms and Northup use the language of "rescue" in their descriptions of the role the doctor plays in relationship to a pregnant woman's fears.
36. Arms, *Immaculate Deception II*, 243.
37. Young, "Pregnant Embodiment," 54.
38. Ibid., 55–56.

are traditionally trained to treat complications. Because doctors many times are working in the context of liability restrictions and experiences of life-threatening complications, they may not approach pregnant women in ways that encourage their confidence in their own bodies. The things doctors say during prenatal treatment may instead build on the fears of inadequacy and dysfunction that are a normal part of pregnancy. Northrup asserts that "women have learned collectively, though not necessarily consciously, to fear the birth experience."[39]

Those relationships that do not nurture a woman's connection to her body, her connection to her baby, and her connection to others deny the importance of interconnection. This denial points us to the rupture of the healthy flow of feeling. How a woman feels is entangled with what others tell her she can do and what they enable her to do. These relationships deeply affect the capacity for the body to function well. A woman is particularly vulnerable during this experience; and, as Northrup asserts, "She can be talked into almost anything."[40]

Feature Three: Body Knowledge/Body Function

Fear did not dominate my pregnancy or my labor. I had looked at every possibility: having to have a cesarean, the baby not getting enough oxygen in labor, even the baby dying or me dying. What finally came loud and clear was my commitment to taking responsibility for this baby's birth, its life, everything. After that it really became an honor to give birth. I looked forward to it and I surrendered to the whole process.

Diane, a new mother

A woman is called on in pregnancy to listen to her body in ways she may never have in other circumstances. And, in a culture that is not known for its nurturing of body knowledge, this call in pregnancy to pay attention to the body is all the more challenging. The information gathering, the building of knowledge, is an important part of growing into a pregnancy and into the challenge of labor and delivery. Pregnancy can be a remarkable opportunity to learn to listen to the body because of its uniquely figurative body language. Without circles of support and influence that encourage such attentiveness, however, the opportunity can be lost. The danger in this loss is that all life is trivialized. We all lose layers of zest and wisdom when we deny the embodied knowledge that we have.

Pregnancy's lesson is in the skill of listening to the body not because of illness or dysfunction, but because of the very way the body is made to be. Young contrasts this experience of embodied awareness in pregnancy with the way existential phenomenologists cast awareness of the body. For them such awareness of the body for its own sake is a sign of fatigue or illness, a breakdown of

39. Northrup, *Women's Bodies*, 493.
40. Ibid., 466.

its normal instrumental relation to life.[41] In pregnancy, however, this kind of awareness is not due to self-absorption or illness, it is not from estrangement or obsession, but it is because of the new capability the body is showing forth. A pregnant body is one that increasingly demands recognition and that collapses the distinction between awareness of the body and the "accomplishment of my aims."[42] In other words, body awareness is not a sign of loss of function, but a signal of healthier life.

Body function is tied to our capacity for response-able relationships. Birth uniquely instructs us on how knowledge of the body is directly connected to healthy functioning of the body. The body's knowledge comes through loud and clear in the awe-inspiring experience of birth when its responsiveness is honored. It is the dance of power and passivity. How and why the body functions in the way it does during pregnancy in all its variation and in all of its predictability is not something science can completely explain.[43] Medical interventions have the potential to help to enhance a body's knowledge when they assist the body in its efforts to function well. When they are used to replace and reject body knowledge, they instead harm our ability to function well. Birth's poetry tells us just that.

The Birth Model

> *Where did you go during your contractions?*
>
> *Well, you know when you are in the ocean, in a heavy surf, if you stay on the surface you will get thrown about against the reefs and the rocks, and you get a lot of water in your nose and mouth and feel like you're drowning. But if you dive down and hold on to something and let the wave pass over you, you can come up in between and feel just fine. Well, that's what I did during labor. When the contractions came, I dived down and let them pass over me.*
>
> Conversation in Northrup, Women's Bodies

Birth is the poetic embodiment of self-assertion and surrender. It is the dance of power and passivity. Passivity can come out of fear, or out of power. When

---

41. Young quotes Hans Plugge as follows: "The transformation into the bodily as physical always means discomfort and malaise. The character of husk, which our live bodiness here increasingly assumes, shows itself in its onerousness, bringing heaviness, burden, weight" (Young, "Pregnant Embodiment," 50–51).

42. Ibid., 51. This loss of distinction between awareness and the ability to accomplish aims is also a reaction to the existential phenomenologists' take on body awareness.

43. For instance, Margie Profet, an evolutionary biologist, argues that pregnancy ("morning") sickness is the body's knowledge creating the best chance for good nutrition and low intake of toxins for the important early developmental weeks of pregnancy. Her argument, while not necessarily one of the leading arguments for the causes of pregnancy sickness, is an example of how the body's knowledge about what is needed during pregnancy directly reflects itself in the way the body functions. See Margie Profet, *Protecting Your Baby-to-Be: Preventing Birth Defects in the First Trimester* (Reading, MA: Addison-Wesley, 1995).

passivity comes out of fear, it is the submission to a power that looms over, apart from, outside one's ability to impact a situation. This kind of pacification subdues women and overpowers their need for one-on-one, labor-intensive care. Women are then more easily controlled and more readily made to adhere to timetables and instructions.

When passivity comes out of power, it is a surrender to a power in which one shares. This kind of passivity is responsive, responsible, response-able. When a woman gives into the power of her own body, she embraces the passivity that allows her body to do the work it knows how to do. The power of birth is about surrender, and therefore about passivity, not to those things that quiet the body's ways of knowing and doing, but to the things that accentuate these things. Surrender lets go of the need to control with our rationality or consciousness. The pain of birth becomes a way to listen and react, a way to know when to relax and when to move. Passivity becomes a way to be responsive. This knowledge translates in birth with utter immediacy. It is this immediacy that makes it such a life-giving experience. The power and passivity of birth are figurative models of responsive relationship for us all.

"Birth is movement."[44] Breathing, rocking, walking, kneeling, squatting, and floating are what many women desire to do when given the freedom to choose. The "birth dances" of many different cultures show the commonality of these urges to move and position oneself in various ways.[45] Women who are free to do as they please desire to move with their contractions. They desire to use breathing and assume different stances while they are pushing. The movement of labor and delivery itself gives a woman a chance to settle into what makes her best able to relax and allow her body to do its work with the most efficiency. Early labor gives a woman a chance to become acquainted with what contractions feel like and to practice relaxation and breathing. This settling in can be difficult because of the discomfort of contractions and because it can last for a prolonged period.

Women who are able to relax and work with their contractions in the early stages with breathing are the most successful working with the more intense contractions of active labor. In active labor the contractions become stronger and longer as they more effectively open the cervix. As the cervix nears complete dilation, the contractions become particularly intense in their strength and frequency. During this time, women often want to float in water, take a shower, lean against someone, stand upright, or get on their hands and knees.

In the transition of labor to full dilation many women feel an overwhelming urge to push. Contractions at this stage will often space themselves apart, although their intensity remains high. This spacing often allows the laboring woman to rest between pushes. Some women even fall asleep during these rest periods. During this time many woman desire a place to squat or sit, like a toilet or a birth stool. As the baby crowns, the perineum bulges to accommodate the

44. Kitzinger, *Rediscovering Birth*, 180.
45. Ibid., 168–97.

baby's emerging head and body. The baby's entry into the world is best when it is patiently helped along with perineal massage. Once the baby is born, the uterus continues to contract in order to expel the placenta. New life is born out of power and passivity, surrender and self-assertion. New life is an act of responsiveness replete with relationship.

Rupture and the Body's Wisdom

The body's wisdom is often discouraged rather than empowered in cultures that place a premium on medical procedures. There are many resources that provide clear arguments for how drug and technological interventions during pregnancy, labor, and delivery are often unnecessary and not without risks.[46] These procedures and approaches are, however, generally presented to women as risk free, even normal parts of the birth process today. For instance, about 80 percent of women who give birth in hospitals receive an epidural.[47] The birth classes offered at most hospitals present this option for pain relief as an expected part of the birth experience. These classes often incorporate some information about breathing techniques, but the deep embodied preparation and practice it takes to ready oneself for the rigors of birth are not the focus. Only women who look for "alternative" information may find extensive information about the risks involved in receiving an epidural as well as the dangers involved in the overuse of many other technological devices.[48]

The unsettling fact is that the natural processes of pregnancy, labor, and delivery have become discounted, feared, and even loathed parts of being a woman. In fact these experiences offer women unique opportunities for living in the immediacy of their bodies' wisdom and power. Medical interventions have come to replace the power and possibility available to women in birth. These interventions have become a block to the responsiveness of feeling. Interventions have enabled fear to block the healthy flow of feeling.[49] Fear and feeling have been used against one another, fear being that which has been helped to flourish, feeling as that which has been left to languish.[50]

46. See discussion on these risks in Arms, Bradley, Northrup, Korte, and Jacobs as well as their references to other resources of information.

47. "Childbirth Trend: Blend the Bliss with Some Relief from Labor Pain," *Chicago Tribune*, 3 March 2002.

48. There are references for dangers of epidurals in Northrup, Arms, Bradley, and Jacobs.

49. Fear can also hinder the body's own ability to alleviate pain during labor and delivery with hormonal pain relievers. See Jacobs, *Having Your Baby*, 45. This issue is also addressed in Lucia Capacchione and Sandra Bardsley, *Creating a Joyful Birth Experience* (New York: Simon & Schuster, 1994).

50. By making this distinction between fear and feeling I am suggesting that fear is something that can modify feeling and its ability to flow freely. Feeling is not to be equated with emotion; fear, while often classified as a feeling, is not to be equated with "feeling" as it is being used here. Fear is an emotional reaction that grows out of and then in turn helps to shape feeling (just as everything does). Fear is an emotional reaction that we should pay attention to as it does arise out of what information feeling gives us.

Fear is not a problem in and of itself. How it affects our ability to be receptive to feeling is the critical edge of its effectiveness and destructiveness in our embodied lives. The harmful capacity of fear lies in its ability to take over our ability to attend to feeling. When fear moves us toward the kind of existential slowdown that was discussed in the previous chapter, it can harm us.[51] Most women feel some fear during their pregnancy—it is to be expected given what is at stake and the challenges of labor and delivery. Feeling's good health depends on how fear is acknowledged and addressed.

In the challenges of pregnancy and birth, fear can make us lose touch with our own body's knowledge. As midwife Nancy McNeese describes it, "the fear-tension-pain cycle" is hard to interrupt in labor in women who have not addressed what they fear.[52] The feelings that find a home in our interactions with others are those that will follow through and most powerfully affect our decisions. We see the power of such body knowledge in the description of birth. Body knowledge is integrated, responsive, response-able. Such responsiveness, such capacity for response, is made of feeling and can be shut down when fear cuts off feeling.

Every part of the way labor feels is there for a reason because the process of labor and delivery is relational—a process of relationships that feed on and grow out of each other. Feeling's flow is severely compromised in any circumstance when drugs are used whose purpose is to dull the body's response-ability.[53] Feeling is left to make countless futile attempts to do its job when drugs render our nerve endings impotent. The need for relationship during labor and delivery is more deeply seated than at any other time in our lives—relationship with the baby, relationship with those who support and encourage us, and relationships with our own bodies. In many births in this country, relationships have been replaced by numbness. Feeling is left to sputter, at loose ends on many fronts. Its connections are distorted by interventions that deaden our response-ability.

Some of the most common interventions in the United States today have the potential to help alleviate fears as well as to give in to the debilitating power of fear.[54] Epidurals are sometimes overused because they make labor and delivery more manageable for doctors and nurses. They can also tap into the fears of many women about what the pain of birth feels like, how they will or will not be able to handle it. Pain in many circumstances is an unwelcomed example of the body's limitation—something from which we seek relief and escape. In this

51. See sections on trauma theory, body loss, and body function in chapter 2 above.
52. Jacobs, *Having Your Baby*, 45.
53. I am working under the assumption that pregnancy and childbirth cannot be equated with other circumstances that mercifully include the opportunity for drug-induced pain relief like surgery, an abscessed tooth, or a broken leg. Pregnancy and childbirth are not diseases or dysfunctions of the body. This is not to say that pain relief is an inappropriate part of pregnancy and childbirth. On the contrary, they are quite appropriate; the nature of the pain relief has unique implications, however, in the context of pregnancy and birth.
54. Northrup describes the overuse of epidurals as a symptom of the mind/body split at work in Western culture. Women want to be present with the intellect, but not with the body for the experience of birth. See Northrup, *Women's Bodies*, 464.

culture pain is often viewed as a sign of a problem, whether disease or injury.[55] Pain is indeed often a symptom of a problem, and it can mercifully be decreased in many health challenges.[56] The uniquely powerful pain of childbirth, however, is not a signal of the body's limits, but of its creativity and knowledge. It is an ally in the process. The sensations of birth are the body's knowledge working to facilitate the body's function.[57] With drugs come risks and a kind of imposed passivity in a process that calls for the mother to be able to actively assert and pacify herself.[58] The poiesis of the way a woman feels and moves during birth— with her motion, her sounds, her silence, her power—is often forbidden in the way many interventions dictate that she be positioned. The prevention of movement and the pacification of a woman's capacity to respond to her laboring body are ruptures of the body's wisdom.

FEELING BODIES/RELATIONAL BODIES

> Jesus gave living water
>   To a woman others called unclean, incapable.
> He gave her living water
>   healing, comforting, patient, wise,
>   washed with power.
> Like wombs, flowing rivers, pulsing oceans,
>   and even tears
>   washing through
>   rushing
>   renewing.
>   Replete in relation.

55. See Korte, 224ff., for a discussion of pain in birth.

56. Northrup asserts that "modern anesthesia is a godsend in many instances, but in labor it is used far too often" (*Women's Bodies,* 469). There are some cases when epidurals in birth are quite important and appropriate. See Jacobs, *Having Your Baby,* 88.

57. Fetal monitoring is another example of an overused intervention that characterizes "normal" hospital births today. Studies show that fetal monitoring may actually increase c-section rates, rather than markedly improve birth outcomes in comparison to a nurse listening to a heart rate periodically. Constant monitoring feeds fears that the baby is not doing well, that birth is a crisis situation, that there is reason for alarm. There are normal variations, jumps and dips of the baby's heart rate during labor and delivery. Constant monitoring can have the tendency to use these normal variations as a signal of a problem. Periodic monitoring, however, has the capacity to pick up on problems as well as the ability to give affirmation to a laboring woman that all is well. The overuse of episiotomies is another disturbing indicator that women's bodies are not trusted or allowed to move at their own pace. Northrup cites the overuse of episiotomies as an example of how such mistrust even overrides overwhelming statistics that support not doing an episiotomy. (A 1992 study of episiotomies confirmed the long-held belief by midwives that episiotomies should be performed only when there is evidence of fetal distress. Even with strong evidence such as this, over 80 percent of women still receive them. See Poole and Parr, *Choosing a Nurse-Midwife,* 77.) See Northrup, *Women's Bodies,* 469.

58. Northrup explains that the risks of epidurals include "arrest of the first and second stages of labor, fever, increased forceps use, pelvic floor damage, and fetal distress, with a subsequent increase in cesarean section rates" (*Women's Bodies,* 469).

What do placentas, midwives, and birth stories have to do with the church and with the people who populate them? These embodied models of response-ability carry immense theological weight. Mainstream Protestants have not been a particularly attentive crowd to the wonder of birth. Certainly we have paid even less attention to the intricacies of placental interdependence and to who surrounds women when they work to birth their babies. These models of relationality and the figurative icons of relationship's rupture that each provides are theological poetry that we can discover, savor, and ponder. How can we live into our own *imago Dei* when we attend to these embodied truths?

Relationality

Before it is baby pee, amniotic fluid is water. I drink water, and it becomes blood plasma, which suffuses through the amniotic sac and surrounds the baby—who also drinks it. And what is it before that? Before it is drinking water, amniotic fluid is the creeks and rivers that fill reservoirs. It is the underground water that fills wells. And before it is creeks and rivers and groundwater, amniotic fluid is rain. When I hold in my hands a tube of my own amniotic fluid, I am holding a tube full of raindrops. Amniotic fluid is also the juice of oranges that I had for breakfast, and the milk that I poured over my cereal, and the honey I stirred into my tea. It is inside the green cells of spinach leaves and the damp flesh of apples. It is the yolk of an egg. When I look at amniotic fluid, I am looking at rain falling on orange groves. I am looking at melon fields, potatoes in wet earth, frost on pasture grasses. The blood of cows and chickens is in this tube. The nectar gathered by bees and hummingbirds is in the tube. Whatever is inside hummingbird eggs is also inside my womb. Whatever is in the world's water is here in my hands.

Sandra Steingraber, Having Faith

Feeling binds us together with all that is and with God. Feeling is our *imago Dei*, the creativity of God that works through us. Feeling gives life to God's sustaining work in all of life; it is the mechanism of God's redemptive work. Creativity, relationship, zest, and Beauty are the handiwork of God's responsiveness. Our human condition is infused with connections that offer abundant life; human life is pregnant with possibilities for new life and new creation. Pregnancy shows us this poetry of how we are made. We are response-able and responsible to our created nature. We are always gestating, always being born, always entangled in the web of life.

We live in a shared world, and our cells are knit together with universal threads. Our universality is our relationality. So it is not static stuff that we share. Our shared world is like a pregnant woman—swollen with expanding, entangled life. Whitehead eschewed essences with his concept of the "extensive continuum."[59] The extensive continuum is the "relational element in experience" rather than the "stuff" of which all things are made.[60] It is solidarity, not undifferentiated attributes that are unaltered in the vagaries of individuals. It is the birthplace of feeling's particularity and the legacy of a shared world.

In our shared world God extends throughout with poetic potency.[61] God is the goad toward creativity and newness. God is the muscle of all movement. The shared nature of feeling gives shape to God's responsiveness. God holds the immediacy of all possibility and the reality of all loss. These are the conditions for novelty, indeterminacy, and freedom. There is always the yet-to-be seen and what is hoped for. We are formed in and by these conditions; we condition the conditions.[62] Particularity makes freedom not grossly unique. Freedom is novel in the way it creates, but not chaotic. This constant process includes the self.[63] The particular way we inherit the past and contribute to the future forms us; this particularity is always already building perspective and relationship out of uniqueness. The uniqueness is not static; it too is relational in how it grows into each new moment.

Relationality is the poetics of our cellular heritage. We are interconnected with all that is; we are entangled. In a shared world we measure our embodied health by gauging our responsiveness. The body is the focal point of our receptivity and our connection to all that is. Care of bodies is care of others; care of creation is care of ourselves, just as pregnancy communicates. Living responsively and responsibly is a mandate for all bodies, and the figurative poetics of pregnant bodies asks us to wake up to our human condition. Taking responsibility is nurturing our body's response-ability. The interdependence of the placenta, the interconnection of midwives, and the embodied wisdom of birth are figurative icons of response-able relationships.

These enfleshed icons of our cellular response-ability deepen the ethical mandates of Christian community (as the Body of Christ) to incorporate our feeling bodies into who we are becoming. These icons of interconnection show us the wounds of our alienation from our bodies. These wounds infect all of creation and truncate our relationship to God. We can renew our sense of interconnection to our bodies, to one another, and to God not just on the surface but in the

---

59. This continuum "expresses the solidarity of all possible standpoints throughout the whole process of the world." The extensive continuum is the way all actual entities are related. It is present in all actual entities just as all actual entities "pervade" the continuum. See Whitehead, *Process and Reality*, 66, 67.

60. Ibid., 72.

61. Whitehead calls God the "poet of the world" (ibid., 346).

62. Part of novelty is that it is conditioned by the texture of each "subjective aim." Whitehead describes the subjective aim as "the subject itself determining its own self-creation as one creature" (ibid., 69).

63. Marjorie Hewitt Suchocki describes the "continuity of the self" as "in the successiveness of instances" (*God, Christ, Church: A Practical Guide to Process Theology*, rev. ed. [New York: Crossroad, 1995], 10).

cells of our bodies. Being numb to our flesh is no way for a people of an incar-national faith to live. Response-ability does not simply enhance human health, it is our conduit to God's presence and power in this world. What can church look like when we are response-able to ourselves and to God? What if mainline Christianity says no to the numbing effects of overintellectualized worship and we settle into the labor pains of new ways to be church? What if we let go of fear and surrendered to the power in which we all share? Pregnancy wakes up our deep need for such response-ability.

Chapter 4

Feeling Ambiguous Bodies

Manifesting Metaphors

What is the best I can hope for for my child?

I think it is that he'll love life, or maybe not always love it, but that he'll never not want to live. I realized that as I helped him learn to nurse in the first few days after his birth. He worked so vigorously to get what he needed to thrive. I knew then that my sadness as a mother would be at its height if he ever lost that desire to survive. I never want him to reject life.

What does my mother want from me?

Self-sufficiency, happiness, for everything to be ok? She hopes for strength—lots to smile about. I guess she's entitled because she's had to watch a child die—only fourteen months into her life out of the womb. My mother had to let her go.

I have this glimmer of understanding about how society created a distance between us—institutions and expectations, how-to books, and all the walls and sacrifices that closed her in. And then there was her resistance to some of it that took her away. Somehow it kept her near me, too.

What do I want from my mother?

Something like understanding, something like connection. I love my mother.

She fades in and out. That voice that is music, such comfort. That voice grows faint. But sometimes I hear her, feel her more than I ever have. Sometimes rocking my child I feel her holding me.

What's the best I can hope for?

Nobody has ever done motherhood "right."
It's about something I can't quite name—an ambiguous something.
Not polarities, not ambivalence, not chaos, not nothingness.
Open spaces—not empty. Availability, responsiveness maybe.

A space ripe for flowering and for fire, or for maybe just the wind . . .
Journal entry

INTRODUCTION

Mothers mold and mark us, hold and release us, birth and differentiate us. The ghosts of our mothers swirl around us and course through our veins no matter our proximity to the geography they inhabit. We are mothered in multifarious ways by layers of people and modes and experience. When I moved into the realm of being a mother myself, I felt the immediacy of how it is simultaneously like vapor and like concrete. It manifests metaphors of an almost infinite array of tendencies, habits, hopes, and fears. Its embodied character is both obvious and elusive. This complicated snarl of experience is why motherhood as embodied experience is such fertile ground for theological reflection. All of theology is metaphor, and motherhood embodies this characteristic of theology irreducibly. Motherhood embodies ambiguity with all of its promise and peril. But what is the theological value of such deep and abiding ambiguity?

Ambiguity is usually something we would rather avoid than embrace. It smacks of chaos, anarchy, and the dreaded unknown. The theological worth of this aspect of human existence may be, for some, simply summed up in how to eliminate it. Knowing the enemy, in other words, has its purpose. I am suggesting something far different than a way around or past ambiguity. I submit that motherhood's embodied metaphors of ambiguity are lifelines for churches and for believers. Not only can we not avoid ambiguity in human embodied existence, but the sooner we become better acquainted with this aspect of who we are, the richer our believing communities and our lives as believers will be. Indeed, motherhood is a source of life reinvigorated because, at our best, our lives resemble its powerful possibilities.

Pregnant with meaning as well as power, motherhood gives birth to and rears much more than the children it bears. Motherhood, for me, suggests embodied styles of existence—not a static essence or ideal, or a certain set of practices.[1] These "styles" of existence are fashioned by the distinctive and embodied characteristics of ambiguity. Motherhood is held together by internal inconsistency, flux, and blurred boundaries, although it rests in spaces not without structures, boundaries, and immense concreteness. Motherhood brings with it a dizzying kind of immediacy to life's movement, change, and power. It invites a vulnerability to what life has to give that nurtures attunement and availability. Motherhood points to the multilayered experiences, institutions, practices, and ideologies that intersect in being a mother.

Because of the distinctively amorphous character of motherhood, this experience does not lend itself to the same precision of description that rape and pregnancy were able to offer in the previous two chapters. Motherhood is remarkable in its richness, but elusive in its character. For this reason, this chapter will take a different form than the previous two constructive chapters. With rape and pregnancy I began with these particular experiences and moved to the more general embodied experiences of tragedy and relationality. With motherhood, I start with embodied ambiguity in general and then move to the particular ways that motherhood fleshes out this ambiguity. Then I reflect on ambiguity theologically. To flesh out our discussion of ambiguity I turn to phenomenology and the helpful work of a phenomenologist, Edward Casey, who works in the trajectory of Maurice Merleau-Ponty (a thinker who has been deliberate about his consideration of the body and ambiguity). Casey's work helps us to recognize the embodied features of ambiguity that motherhood "speaks" with particular clarity. More specifically, the hysteric's body functions as a framework for understanding this idiosyncratic dynamic of embodied experience.

Casey coaxes the body back from the exile of Cartesian dualism, not as a transparent, static object of examination, but as a "lived body." The body is not either/or, it is not natural or cultural, biological or socially constructed. It is an ambiguous mixture, a both/and. Casey uses schema and habitudes to trace the body as it operates as the "matrix of nature and culture." These bodily practices enact the body's skill at learning and innovation. The body learns and creates

---

1. In Patrice DiQuinzio's helpful book, *The Impossibility of Motherhood: Feminism, Individualism, and the Problem of Mothering* (New York: Routledge, 1999), she chooses to use "mothering" rather than "motherhood" because she sees "mothering" as a reference to the actual "birthing and rearing of children" and "motherhood" as an "ideological construct of essential motherhood," which she determines is an impossibility for real women (xv). I agree that mothering may point more directly to the activity of being a mother than does motherhood, and I agree with her critique of "essential motherhood" as a problematic construction of being a mother. But while DiQuinzio's critique of essential motherhood is important, I do not wish to abandon "motherhood" as a concept with which feminist thinkers should be concerned. The importance of "motherhood" rests precisely in the fact that it includes ideological construction, but is not limited to or apart from the work of mothering itself. I cannot somehow strictly separate the ideological aspects of being a mother and the actual activity of being a mother. The points of division are gray if they exist at all. My use of the term "motherhood" is not to suggest that these experiences, institutions, and practices cannot be analyzed with some precision as to how and why they develop and function as they do. The use of the term "motherhood" does, however, suggest that there is no way to point to some activity of mothering that is able to stand apart from the multilayered nature of motherhood (I do not believe, incidentally, that DiQuinzio assumes the possibility of this strict kind of separation either).

meaning on a continuum in which, on one end, the body is given to training and, on the other end, it is given to preference and value. Both skill and taste "knit together image and rule," allowing the body to be both the expression of culture and its creator and transmitter.[2] Practices like skill and taste are more or less voluntary.

These practices are complicated by the "ghosts" of how the body functions also out of what Casey calls "idiosyncratic habitus."[3] This kind of habitus is involuntary and resistant to conscious modification. Casey employs the symptoms of hysteria as a way to examine bodily practices that are not driven by conscious learning (such as swimming) or by the acceptance, however innovative, of certain standards or rules (like taste). He describes it this way:

> Unlike skill and taste, which incorporate and display cultural and social interests and norms more or less transparently, hysterical symptoms are initially opaque even if ultimately quite significant, that is to say, *telling*. They are "ghosts" of an embodiment unknown to itself in terms of first origin and final sense: shadows cast by this origin or sense that have fallen upon the hysteric's body and on the body politic with which this body is covertly continuous.[4]

The body displays its genius in hysterical symptoms because they are at once idiosyncratic and socially conditioned. The hysteric's body does not simply mimic norms, but displays what Casey calls a "style of action that is peculiar to a given hysteric's body."[5] At the same time, this idiosyncrasy reveals an internalizing of social structures that shows itself in the symptoms themselves. That is, the hysteric's body becomes a social critic in a manner (or perhaps in "mannerisms") that bypasses the ability of the conscious self to "censor" these expressions of resistance.[6] As Casey explains, "Hysterical symptoms are at once protests against the reigning social order and yet also collusions with it."[7]

The hysteric's body takes an idea or social standard that is "incompatible" (Freud's language) and "converts" it into something "somatic."[8] Resonating with the discussion of rape trauma in chapter 2 of this project, Casey describes how some trauma, in order to be survived, takes up residence (what Casey calls a "home-place") in some body part rather than in dreams or conscious memory. Hysteria, therefore, is a form of bodily memory. Freud referred to this kind of embodied expression of trauma as "somatic compliance."[9] Here a part of the

---

2. Edward Casey, "The Ghost of Embodiment: On Bodily Habitudes and Schemata," in *Body and Flesh: A Philosophical Reader*, ed. Donn Welton (Oxford: Blackwell, 1998), 214.
3. Ibid., 217.
4. Ibid.
5. Ibid.
6. Ibid., 218.
7. Ibid.
8. On Freud's description see ibid., 224 n. 51.
9. Ibid., 218.

body takes up the task of expressing what cannot be expressed in the consciousness or even in the subconscious work of dreams. This compliance, however, occurs far beyond the realm of "choice," but instead is in the ghostly regions of the body's capacity for functioning and surviving. At the same time that the "body language" of hysteria takes it to the margins of social intercourse, it nevertheless enacts its need to be heard, its need to be part of the "conversation."[10] The body does not simply hold the experience in silence, but gives it a new voice, one that demands attention and one that disrupts our ability to discern its language. It is a masterful and ambiguous rendering of relationship and survival.

Casey's discussion of the hysteric's body informs our own attentiveness to the ambiguity of motherhood. Both the hysteric and motherhood provide us with ways to think about how the body negotiates its ambiguity. The body disrupts the concepts of biology, culture, experience, "mind," and habit with the way it speaks its experience metaphorically. These metaphors are not always transparent in their meaning; it is the genius of the body that communicates this ambiguity. Motherhood invites us into how this embodied ambiguity is inescapable *and* a life-giving reality. Motherhood teaches us not to kid ourselves into thinking ambiguity is something we can avoid. What if we embrace its possibilities? What if ambiguity is the mother of our best hopes? Motherhood can teach us not to be afraid of ghosts.

The body refuses to settle neatly into a dichotomy between social construction and biological determinism. Mothers themselves live in this gray area. Mothers are partners in every life's most basic relationship—one with which we all begin and one that somehow shapes us beyond our understanding and our ability to resist its formative power. This power comes from spaces complicated in their dissonance. How mothers value themselves and how others value mothers are filled with expectations that no one can ever meet and that we fail to recognize as important.[11] In the midst of all the differing styles of mothering practices and standards, mothers are less likely to balance care of the self with the care of others. Many mothers do not have the support or the resources they need to do that. The fatigue, irritability, and resentment that result lead many mothers to mother with diminished patience and energy. This diminishment becomes another source of guilt and frustration.

10. Freud used the language of "conversation" in reference to how hysterical symptoms seek an audience in the society that helped give birth to them and that was the cause of its own estrangement from social parlance. See ibid.

11. Ann Crittenden offers a clearly argued case for how the economic system operative in the United States devalues mothers. Crittenden's final chapter has a list of interesting policy suggestions for how our economic and political systems could begin to correct this problem. Also, Sharon Hays, a sociologist, tracks how the ideals of "intensive mothering" are in direct contradiction to the assumptions and rewarded behaviors of Western individualism. See Ann Crittenden, *The Price of Motherhood: Why the Most Important Job in the World Is Still the Least Valued* (New York: Metropolitan Books, 2001); and Sharon Hays, *The Cultural Contradictions of Motherhood* (New Haven: Yale University Press, 1996).

The creativity of motherhood is often invisible in a culture that holds the productivity and profit of industry as the highest value.[12] Mothers themselves are the site of conflicting discourses on what activities are truly important in our society.[13] Ambiguity permeates the relationships a mother has with her children—how she feels about them, how they feel about her. Children give mothers something that can come from nowhere else in life. They also take from their mothers in uniquely difficult and rewarding ways. Mother-child relationships are conditioned by the many messages that come in and out of vogue for mothering practices, by the voices of other mothers, and by the way the body sometimes seems to act on indiscernible (often called "instinctual") tendencies toward certain activities and orientations.[14] These dissonant spaces feed the ambiguity of how motherhood is negotiated on all levels.

Theologically, motherhood is distorted when it is simply equated with nurture and self-sacrifice. In this equation, mothers are cast as those who "give up their lives for their children."[15] The marriage of traditional conceptions of sin and the glorification of self-sacrifice has given birth to a view of motherhood that oversimplifies the experiences that mothers encounter in raising children. Motherhood has much more to offer theological discussions than simply self-sacrifice or an ethic of care. It both points to open spaces and clears them for us. These spaces invite us to explore how indeterminacy and ambiguity are the mother of adventure and possibility. These spaces are ripe for indeterminacy to nurture a style of life awake to the potency of feeling's inheritance and novelty. These spaces create the conditions we all need to cultivate hope. The maternal

12. Bonnie Miller-McLemore argues for a closer look at "generativity" as a way to address theologically the imbalance created by a strong cultural focus on productivity. See *Also a Mother: Work and Family as Theological Dilemma* (Nashville: Abingdon, 1994).

13. The language of "conflicting discourses" describes a dynamic at work in how subjectivity is developed by Chris Weedon. For Weedon, the subject is constantly changing and being disrupted by the multiple discourses that compose everyday existence. There is no unchanging kernel of the self in the play of all of these discourses; the subject is nothing but that particular location of the conflicting discourses themselves. Seyla Benhabib discusses the self in the context of a feminist discourse ethics in a way that fills out Weedon's poststructuralism with an "interactive universalism"—Benhabib does not reduce the self only to conflicting discourses, but leaves more of a space for some perspectival coherence, although preferably this perspective is malleable enough to exercise the "reversability" of perspectives that she holds necessary for a sound moral life. Judith Butler also develops a concept of the subject as the location of shifting discourses. These feminist thinkers all occupy different places on the continuum of how thoroughly the subject is constantly shifting in its construction and in what constitutes moral agency and perspective. Benhabib holds on, albeit critically, to a stronger concept of agency than Butler does. Weedon is between them although more toward Butler in how thoroughgoing social construction is. My use of this idea of "conflicting discourses" here is somewhere between Weedon and Benhabib. See Chris Weedon, *Feminist Practice and Poststructuralist Theory* (Oxford: Blackwell, 1987); Seyla Benhabib, *Situating the Self: Gender, Community, and Postmodernism in Contemporary Ethics* (New York: Routledge, 1992); and Judith Butler, *The Psychic Life of Power* (Stanford: Stanford University Press, 1997).

14. For example, a "mother's intuition" functions strongly in some women with results like "knowing" a child is in distress or sick, being able to do the work of mothering with no prior experience, negotiating how to breast-feed, etc.

15. A quote from a sermon on Mother's Day preached at a Presbyterian church that shall remain nameless.

body's language is discordant and melodious; it is silent and it is deafening. It is our mother tongue; it is indecipherable. In motherhood we muddle through and search for opportunities to nurture life. These are the spaces for life's abundance and meaning to unfold. These are spaces available for adventure.

MUDDLING THROUGH:
MOTHERHOOD AND METAPHOR

My children cause me the most exquisite suffering of which I have any experience. It is the suffering of ambivalence: the murderous alternation between bitter resentment and raw-edged nerves, and blissful gratification and tenderness. Sometimes I seem to myself, in my feelings toward these tiny guiltless beings, a monster of selfishness and intolerance. Their voices wear away at my nerves, their constant needs, above all their need for simplicity and patience, fill me with despair at my own failures, despair too at my fate, which is to serve a function for which I was not fitted. And I am weak sometimes from held-in rage. There are times when I feel only death will free us from one another, when I envy the barren woman who has the luxury of her regrets but lives a life of privacy and freedom.

And yet at other times I am melted with the sense of their helpless, charming and quite irresistible beauty—their ability to go on loving and trusting—their staunchness and decency and unselfconsciousness. I love them. But it's in the enormity and inevitability of this love that the sufferings lie.

Andrienne Rich, Of Woman Born

When Israel was a child, I loved him,
and out of Egypt I called my son.
The more I called them,
the more they went from me;
they kept sacrificing to the Baals,
and offering incense to idols.
Yet it was I who taught Ephraim to walk,
I took them up in my arms;
but they did not know that I healed them.
I led them with cords of human kindness,
with bands of love.
I was to them like those
who lift infants to their cheeks.
I bent down to them and fed them.

Hosea 11:1–4

Motherhood embodies the utter affection of living into another and the snarl of anguish and confounding dissonance that can come with that. God mothers us with "cords of human kindness, with bands of love," and yet God tells us, "the more I called them, the more they went from me." Such utter presence and affection feeds us and nurtures us and frees us to our own particular potential, peril, and everything in between. This kind of entanglement is what it is like to be so close to life's flux, change, and power.

Ambiguity has characterized and always will characterize motherhood. This realization is the lesson of motherhood not only in the muddle of its mundane experiential layers, but also in the theoretical fruit it bears. We can notice this ambiguity in the contradictory trajectories of feminist theorizing around motherhood. Some feminists have rejected the role of motherhood and the expectations it places on women as a tool of the oppression of women (Firestone); others have embraced it as a window into an ideal that can disrupt the patriarchal order (Ruddick, Irigaray, Kristeva).[16] Still others have disturbed the feminist wrangling itself by asking questions that stem from different racial, ethnic, political, and economic positions (Collins, Williams, Glenn, Awiatka).[17] The contradictions and paradoxes of motherhood are ripe for intellectual and theoretical gymnastics.

Bonnie Miller-McLemore remains one of the few feminist theologians to have explored the "horizons and ambiguities" of motherhood in a substantial work.[18] Much of the in-depth work on motherhood has grown out of psychoanalytic orientations.[19] Feminists of the poststructuralist and postmodern tra-

16. Shulamith Firestone, *The Dialectic of Sex* (New York: Morrow, 1970).
17. Marilou Awiatka, *Selu: Seeking the Corn-Mother's Wisdom* (Golden, CO: Fulcrum, 1993). Awiatka and the other women listed (among others) have challenged the presiding assumptions and deconstruction of motherhood as those stemming largely from the white, middle-class, heterosexual context.
18. Miller-McLemore, *Also a Mother*. Also, Sallie McFague develops the metaphor of God as mother. McFague focuses on mother as the one who creates and gives birth to life, the one who can say "it is good that you exist," and the one who, because she created life, has an interest in the fulfillment and thriving of life. She uses agape, creating, and justice to develop how this metaphor communicates a particular kind of divine love. Her model is helpful ethically and she builds on it in later work. She does not, however, put herself to the task of exploring motherhood's theological import much beyond its ethical impact in the face of environmental crisis. Her ethical task is an important one, and her work uniquely pushes questions of embodiment. Also, Delores Williams uses black motherhood as a tool for theological reflection. This model of motherhood is an important and effective tool in her work, but motherhood as a more general phenomenon is not her main theological focus. In addition, Cynthia Rigby has written an article that examines motherhood theologically. This article reads more like an apologia for working mothers than a theological exploration of motherhood. Still she takes on a worthy task. Her article yields some interesting suggestions for valuing the work of women and mothers. See Sallie McFague, *Models of God: Theology for an Ecological, Nuclear Age* (Philadelphia: Fortress, 1987); McFague, *The Body of God* (Minneapolis: Fortress, 1993); Delores Williams, *Sisters in the Wilderness: The Challenge of Womanist God-Talk* (Maryknoll, NY: Orbis, 1993); and Cynthia L. Rigby, "Exploring Our Hesitation: Feminist Theologies and the Nurture of Children," *Theology Today* 56, no. 4 (2000): 540–54.
19. See Nancy Chodorow, *The Reproduction of Mothering* (Berkeley: University of California Press, 1978); Luce Irigaray, *This Sex Which Is Not One*, trans. Catherine Porter (Ithaca: Cornell

jectories have worked to theorize motherhood and to deconstruct its perceived essential meanings. I am exploring motherhood for what it embodies theologically. This style of existence is a promising space for re-membering the body. It manifests metaphors of who we all are and how we are made.

Metaphors

Sallie McFague describes metaphor as "seeing one thing *as* something else, pretending 'this' is 'that' because we do not know how to think or talk about 'this,' so we use 'that' as a way of saying something about it."[20] Metaphors are the way we "construct our world" from the time we are children; metaphor is "the way we think."[21] Metaphors represent likeness and fill out meaning. And metaphors always leave a residue of unknown meaning.

The body language of motherhood is metaphorical in both function and content. Motherhood, like a metaphor, is not the equation of itself, but always approximating, pointing toward that which it is and is not, even while functioning to create, disrupt, and reverberate the other and itself. Always negotiating another, always inhabiting that space that complicates otherness itself, always working to create life's meaning, motherhood is an embodied metaphor for ambiguity. Disruption, incompleteness, openness, and promise are the body language of motherhood. It speaks out of the amalgamation of experience with vulnerability to the "already" and "not yet" of life and assertiveness within that muddle. Motherhood constantly plays at the dynamics of living in proximity to children—the mess and stress, the tenderness and bliss, the fleeting and slow nature of it all. Motherhood's availability and vulnerability to the flux of life and to otherness make it promise-filled. Its metaphorical body language gives life meaning out of remarkable availability. Motherhood functions metaphorically in its orientation to otherness and in the productivity it finds in its alterity.

Motherhood as Metaphor

> FLASH—instant of time or of dream
> without time; inordinately swollen atoms
> of a bond, a vision, a shiver, a yet formless,
> unnameable embryo. Epiphanies. Photos
> of what is not yet visible and that language
> necessarily skims over from afar, allusively.

University Press, 1985); Shari L. Thurer, *The Myths of Motherhood: How Culture Reinvents the Good Mother* (New York: Houghton Mifflin, 1994); Michelle Boulous Walker, *Philosophy and the Maternal Body: Reading Silence* (London: Routledge, 1998); Jane Price Knowles and Ellen Cole, eds., *Motherhood: A Feminist Perspective* (New York: Hawthorn, 1990).

20. Sallie McFague, *Metaphorical Theology: Models of God in Religious Language* (Philadelphia: Fortress, 1982), 15.

21. Ibid., 16.

Words that are always too distant, too
abstract for this underground swarming of
seconds, folding in unimaginable spaces.
Writing them down is an ordeal of discourse,
like love. What is loving, for a woman, the
same thing as writing. Laugh.
Impossible. Flash on the unnameable,
weavings of abstractions to be torn. Let a
body venture at last out of its shelter, take
a chance with meaning under a veil of
words. WORD FLESH. From one to the
other, eternally, broken up visions,
metaphors of the invisible.

> Julia Kristeva, "Stabat Mater"

Motherhood mediates the "other." It connects to and differentiates from the known and unknown. It mediates what is other with what is familiar. In a patriarchal order, mother functions as the other, as the alterity, the unlike that fills out the meaning of that which is familiar. Like McFague, Eva Kittay explains that metaphors mediate between something familiar and that which is "other."[22] As that which is other, a metaphor mediates between that which is familiar and that which is (at least somewhat) unknown. In its relational function, a metaphor manipulates an understood field of meaning to fill out a "conceptual domain" that is so far undefined or "unstructured."[23] The metaphorical function is both "mediational" and "relational."[24]

Motherhood occupies unruly space where indeterminacy and unknown seek relevant and substantive expression. The play of motherhood within and outside the flux of meaning nurtures both novelty and convention. Like the hysteric's body, motherhood creates and destroys itself even as it gives birth to body language that shapes and speaks our understanding. Motherhood occupies a shifting embodied/linguistic space as metaphor's anchor of meaning, as its other, as its destroyer, and as its creator. Meaning-making comes out of this productive tension; it is a function of being available to the dissonance of experience. Motherhood's style is also the power to create meaning out of that dissonance. The ambiguity of this power to make and to be shaped by life's meaning is productive, even life-giving, and infested with pain and disorientation. This style of

22. Using the work of Nancy Chodorow, Eva Feder Kittay describes how women tend to develop a more accommodating orientation to otherness because they are parented largely by the parent of their same sex. Men develop a more oppositional orientation to the other because they are largely parented by the parent who is their opposite sex. Men must separate from the other to develop their gender identities. See Kittay, "Woman as Metaphor," in *Feminist Social Thought*, ed. Meyers, 264–85.

23. Ibid., 267. Kittay uses the example of a person's tennis game being "hot" or "lukewarm" or "sizzling" to explain the "transference of semantic relations."

24. Ibid., 266.

meaning-making is motherhood's embodied metaphorical function—it is available for meaning, and it is assertive in creating meaning.

How can we recognize and acknowledge motherhood's idiosyncratic assertiveness and malleability? We must be attuned to the subtleties and even banality of its genius. There is no clear origin or end in how the body both colludes with and critiques social standards, just as the hysteric's body "tells." Conscious assertion may or may not be operative in the way meaning is created and embodied. Consider how motherhood can sacralize the everydayness of human life. This infusion of the sacred into mundane and oftentimes invisible work is at once social critique, survival skill, burden, and blessing. Motherhood can resist value systems that only put stock in prestige, productivity, publicity, and material reward out of its own necessity. Babies must be fed and clothed; they need to be held, talked to, sung to, stimulated, read to, played with, affirmed, and given boundaries. The intensive rhythms of mothering can clarify the substance of life and provide access to human experiences that transcend materialism, consumption, and frenetic activity. Through its focus on caring for others and because its sole compensation is the satisfaction of rearing children, motherhood can create rich, thick, and even spiritual layers of meaning. This meaning-making is embedded in experience, intention, and critique—some of which may feed conscious decisions to be countercultural and/or spiritual. How these layers of meaning are embodied in practices, habits, relationships, and patterns are indeed idiosyncratically assertive and malleable.

Motherhood taps into the productivity of the margins of existence by creating and disrupting meaning in such an embodied mode. The productivity of its liminal space echoes again the genius of the hysteric's idiosyncrasy and capacity for social criticism. This capacity for resistance, even while entangled in how life is defined, is a mode of life with redemptive capacity. Its resistance and capacity to liberate have a history.[25]

> In our young minds houses belonged to women, were their special domain, not as property, but as places where all that truly mattered in life took place—the warmth and comfort of shelter, the feeding of our bodies, the nurturing of our souls. There we learned dignity, integrity of being; there we learned to have faith. . . .
> This task of making homeplace was not simply a matter of black women providing service; it was about the construction of a safe place where black people could affirm one another and by so doing heal many of the wounds inflicted by racist domination. We could not learn to love and respect ourselves in the culture of white supremacy, on the outside; it was there on the inside, in that "homeplace," most often created and kept by black women, that we had the opportunity to grow and develop, to nurture our spirits.[26]

25. For example, much of the work of womanists on motherhood reflects less on motherhood as symbolic and more on the "historical experience of nurturing." See Patricia Hill Collins, *Black Feminist Thought: Knowledge, Consciousness, and the Politics of Empowerment* (New York: Routledge, 1991).

26. bell hooks, *Yearning: race, gender, and cultural politics* (Boston: South End Press, 1990), 41–42.

The spaces of motherhood can be the tools for justice and resistance to oppression.[27] Motherhood creates spaces for overturning the standards of the broader culture. It fills out and changes meaning out of fragmentation and complexity. It creates and disrupts meaning in the way it negotiates itself.

The meaning-making that fashions the mundane into spiritual practice and into liberating space can generate what Sarah Ruddick calls "maternal thinking" (a social construct for Ruddick, not an innate tendency). She explains that maternal thinking is the "unity of reflection, judgment, and emotion," and it arises out of the activities of child rearing.[28] Maternal thinking is built on the demands of children and the practices that attempt to satisfy these demands. These demands and practices settle into three areas: preservation, growth, and acceptability.[29] For Ruddick, these goods are "frequently and unavoidably in conflict," creating in mothers the constant work of dealing with values that can directly contradict one another.[30] From these competing concerns Ruddick develops a set of virtues that are characteristic of "maternal thinking," including humility, cheerfulness, responsiveness, attention, and innovation.[31] This maternal thinking expects constant change and sees control as a liability. It is flexible and accepts what cannot be controlled. The kind of thinking that is involved in mothering is more concrete than abstract, and it is geared toward particularity, relationship, and ambiguity.

The embodied layers of feeling that feed the patterns of thinking Ruddick describes are tangled up with bliss, burden, strenuous relationships, fatigue, and all the ghosts of motherhood. Forbearance, anger, compassion, and frazzled nerves live in the cells of mothers with infinite variation. Motherhood is like the hysteric's body: toying with the genius of madness and utter sanity in any given moment. Motherhood's body language communicates the fruitful and painful intersections of all the complexities of life. It fills out meaning, not with control but by being conducive to and available to this complexity. The meaning-making is not passive, but productive, disruptive, and resourceful enough to accommodate shifting meaning. Motherhood communicates styles of existence that embody this dynamic of flexibility and indeterminacy. It has the power to give life and assert itself in the ongoing process of meaning-making.

27. Collins expresses this kind of variety of orientation as a "continuum of responses" (*Black Feminist Thought*, 118).

28. Sara Ruddick, "Maternal Thinking," in *Feminist Social Thought*, ed. Meyers, 588.

29. Ibid., 589.

30. Ibid. Ruddick uses the example of a child pushing another child out of the way to try and climb a tree. The mother is at once concerned with her child's safety, encouraging her child's curiosity and physical development, and nurturing certain social graces so that the child's interactions with others are acceptable.

31. Ibid., 590–97.

MOTHERHOOD AND FEELING

What I Learned from My Mother . . .

The cadence of a southern accent
      its melodic quirky pronunciations
      and the gentle way it can slice into you with disappointment
      or, worse yet, disapproval.

My mother taught me the tender strength of the rocking chair,
        punctuated with songs that meander between hums and lyrics
        imprinted in the soul.
        She can make anything sound like a lullaby.

Her pat, pat on the baby's back
      I re-member that kind of touch

I gestated in grief and hope in my mother.
        She taught me the cavernous wounds of dead children,
        and the hard longing of homesickness.

My mother is still my familiar
        Voices downstairs, supper almost ready,
        delight in a simple thing I did.

She always plants flowers—
      her resistance to despair.

She makes lists—a model for how to keep your head above water.
My mother knows how to be patient when making giblet gravy.
My mother knows how to use semicolons and apostrophes correctly.
My mother knows how to adore someone and how to keep living even when
it hurts.

My mother couldn't do it all, but that taught me, too. I pay attention now
and I am not afraid to ask for more sometimes, even when I know I might
not get it.
I try to breathe deeply and I don't need to draw lines in the sand or anywhere
else.

My mother taught me some of who I am—
        what I come from, where I might go.
        She made up bedtime stories to inspire me.

She got tired sometimes and needed to lie down.
She shopped for a family of six and kept a good store just in case.

My mother is enjoying her life and that doesn't really revolve around me much.

Sometimes I want to hear her downstairs or smell a roast in the oven.

I need to tell her my kids only like their roast with ketchup.

> But Zion said, "The LORD has forsaken me,
>   my Lord has forgotten me."
> Can a woman forget her nursing child,
>   or show no compassion for the child of her womb?
> Even these may forget,
>   yet I will not forget you.
> See, I have inscribed you on the palms of my hands;
>   your walls are continually before me.
>   Isaiah 49:14–16

It is not in spite of the ambiguity of motherhood, but because of it, that mother-hood is an important topic for theological consideration and construction. This ambiguous space inhabited by mothers is intimately engaged with how we are all embodied. All lived bodies deeply feel indeterminacy; it is the struggle to muddle through, and the challenge to find spaces and modes of experience that do more than muddle through. This kind of ambiguity gives enfleshed experience great promise and great peril.

Feeling points to the indeterminacy and novelty that is alive in every moment of experience. It is the holder of possibility and the limit of our particularity. Novelty and inheritance are its character. Feeling enlivens us to the openness and constraints of our past, present, and future. This common thread is providential. It has the capacity to permeate all experience down to the most cellular and primal features. God's offer of feeling comes with this providential potential for abundant life; God's uniquely powerful infusion of feeling into our lives brings the continuity of who we can become.

Three embodied metaphors are present in the body language of motherhood that in-form our re-membering. These embodied metaphors tell of the character and nature of our bodies—these are the metaphors of how we are made. They embody the sharp edges, the creative possibilities, and the concreteness of our ambiguous nature. Maternal bodies, maternal relationships, and maternal subjectivity all show forth the dynamic intersections of feeling and motherhood. These intersections create spaces for motherhood to "speak" of embodied ambiguity. These facets of motherhood create meaning even as they frustrate our ability to describe embodied truth apart from lived bodies. These metaphors

communicate the potent complex of vulnerability, interconnection, and disharmony in the lived body. They point toward the divine thread that runs though
the body's indeterminacy. Motherhood cultivates indeterminacy and God's providential activity. In motherhood, we see glimpses, fragments, shadows, ghosts of
how the ambiguity of the human condition in-forms and instructs us. Who we
are and what we need grows out of our embodied character. Most importantly,
we may be able to substantially re-member that feeling thrives on richness, zest,
complexity. It languishes in triviality and premature decision.

Our challenge is to be available and present to these character traits of ours.
Resourceful, fruitful styles of living with ambiguity find expression in maternal bodies, multiple mothers, and fragmented subjectivity. Can we live in open
spaces and thrive? Can we keep from trivializing our own complexity and not
invite existential chaos? Motherhood finds a way.

Maternal Bodies

*I never saw my mother, to know her as such more than four or
five times in my life; and each of these times was very short in
duration, and at night. She was hired by Mr. Stewart, who lived
about twelve miles from my house. She made her journeys to see
me in the night, traveling the whole distance on foot, after the
performance of her day's work. She was a field hand, and a whip-
ping is the penalty of not being in the field at sunrise. . . . I do
not recollect of ever seeing my mother by the light of day. She was
with me in the night. She would lie down with me and get me to
sleep, but long before I waked she was gone.*

Frederick Douglass

Frederick Douglass's mother negotiated her maternal body with stark complexity. Her tired feet moving toward that place that housed her sleeping child just so
she could hold him defied the space that kept her from being there for her son.
She manipulated space by holding that little body so deeply asleep in spite of
slavery's deep chasm between her desire to mother and her ability to be present.
She gave flesh to mothering by holding him in the dark. Her muscles, calluses,
cells, synapses, and yearning enfleshed her indignant maternal commitment.
Extended and entangled, this kind of embodied experience speaks volumes
where there is such quiet. And with her hard-won moments with her son come
ambiguous memories by her son as if he never knew her. Douglass later wrote
that she was like a stranger to him, that he never knew the "soothing presence"
of a mother's care. Terrible truth and interpretation conspire with and against
motherhood's best intentions.

This and other maternal negotiations of space are the subdermal play of
embodied life. How and why and when a mother holds a child is the palpable
and phantasmal playing out of how she was held, of how the baby responds to

certain positions, of how she has been told to hold, of how she is comfortable holding, of how she believes she should hold, of how circumstances shape her ability to hold, of what else there is to hold, and of the constant response and resistance of her body to all of these factors and more.

Maternal bodies are not simply biological entities. Maternal bodies are particularly and ambiguously imprinted with the expectations that come with caring for children. The maternal body is not binary, but ambiguous.[32] The binary logics of Western thinking are disrupted by the "silence" of the maternal body.[33] Maternal bodies are silent because they extend themselves in a way that language can never articulate.[34] Feeling helps us to extend this silence into the created nature of all bodies. Motherhood's complexity embodies this silence in a way that is strangely and perhaps uniquely discernible. This silence is not simply a biological phenomenon, but the workings of feeling, that cannot be reduced to the purely biological. How maternal bodies function is tied to the most immediate experiences of our bodies and to those that only rarely grow into conscious thought (Whitehead's "antecedent" experience). Maternal bodies show us this layer of how we are made with unique clarity because for maternal bodies antecedent bodily experience often entails holding other bodies. This ambiguous process of negotiating multiple bodies in space is how mothers constantly negotiate space. Children occupy spaces in common with them. The immediacy of this fact is most concrete with mothers of small children. Maternal bodies hold children, and therefore embody a sense of space that can be particularly sensitive to what surrounds it and particularly illustrative of the indeterminacy of embodied existence. The maternal body is constantly brushing up against an enfleshed determinant of its confinement and possibility. This sense of space and possibility are tied to those things that extend her body into different spaces.

Holding a child brings with it particular gestures, postures, and horizons. What exists to hold the baby other than the maternal body—from partner to car seat to crib to papoose to sling—extends the mother's embrace to expand

32. Walker makes this distinction with the help of some of the French feminists in *Philosophy and the Maternal Body*.

33. Ibid., 181. Walker describes some of the philosophical characteristics of maternal bodies by pointing to how they are silenced by binary logic. She characterizes the mother-child relationality as "an ambiguous space that refuses mother and child as either separate or fused." Kristeva calls this the "semiotic" and talks of how maternal bodies, their milk, their tears are metaphors of "nonspeech" ("Stabat Mater," 312). Irigaray uses the mother-daughter relationship to point to a similar unspeakable space for expression that is not linguistic. She uses her "labial poetics" to suggest a fluidity and ambiguity of expression that disrupts the symbolic order. See Irigaray, *This Sex Which Is Not One.*

34. I am expanding and deepening Walker's insight beyond the semiotics of biology. With the help of the French feminists, Walker does important work by pushing the ways that maternal silence "speaks" because of the way it is embodied. Her work is helpful, but I have the same questions about the way biology functions in her work as I do in the work of the French feminists. It seems, particularly for Kristeva, that biology holds the power of disruptive "semiotic" expression as somehow set apart from everything else. Her discussion is rich and subtle, but still teeters too close to biologism than I think is possible when we attend to how biology itself is elusive, not transparent, as it seems sometimes to function in the work of Kristeva and others.

her sense of space and possibility. A baby's willingness to be held by someone or something other than her mother extends the breadth and freedom of the maternal body. The desire of maternal bodies to hold children responds to how space is defined and confined; maternal bodies respond and resist with embodied palpability. Will she pick up her child or let him cry? Will she carry her child with a contraption other than her arms? How will she negotiate her body's ability to hold, to steady, and to carry? These gestures, decisions, and tendencies are not transparent in how and why they are carried out as they are; they are the result of a dizzying array of factors and features of what maternal bodies carry with them in their care of children. Holding children is not simply skill or taste or social commentary or habit but all that and more. These expressions of body language communicate the formative and amorphous grammars of relationship. Motherhood embodies presence, availability, the capacity to collapse and create space, and residues of unknown meaning that plant seeds of some new expression.

The dynamics of nursing and milk supply are metaphors of such expanding and contracting space. Nursing is extensive, proximate, entangled, and idiosyncratic; these dynamics speak of the fluidity of maternal bodies. For most new mothers, their milk comes in quickly after their babies are born when they have abundant skin-to-skin contact with their babies. The antecedent experiences of the flesh of a baby next to the flesh of his mother help create milk and connection. Many women experience milk letdown right before their children begin to stir from hunger. Babies nurse more frequently when they are entering a growth spurt. Multifarious intersections like the cry of another baby, not even one's own, can bring on milk letdown. Even months after their children are weaned some women feel milk letdown when their children are ill or when women muse about having another child.

Breast-feeding can be relaxing and joyful. Calm can wash over you as soon as your baby settles into feeding. Pleasure-inducing hormones are released into the body during breast-feeding. This hormone release, some research maintains, is connected to an increased tendency to be nurturing.[35] These hormones calm the nursing mother and help create space for her to respond to her baby's needs and be less prone to stress. These same hormones are sometimes released when a mother is exposed to "familiar sights, sounds, and activities associated with breastfeeding."[36] This kind of body language is an awe-inspiring experience for many women. For others all the voices and silences of this language translate into an insurmountable kind of stress. Distraction and stress, in turn, compromise milk production. For reasons medical science does not completely understand, some women are overcome with nausea when their babies latch on.[37] Other

35. La Leche League International, *The Womanly Art of Breastfeeding*, 6th ed. (New York: Plume, 1997), 363.
36. Ibid., 364.
37. This nausea may be connected to hormone releases during milk letdown. Many of these kinds of occurrences are documented in literature about breast-feeding; some are anecdotal from La Leche League meetings and/or from conversations with others who have and have not breast-fed.

women are unable and/or unwilling to breast-feed because of previous sexual abuse or other body issues.[38] Breast-feeding can become a physical impossibility.

The dynamics of nursing are not purely biological. They are the ambiguous (idiosyncratic) intersections of layers of connection. The body language of nursing is flesh to flesh, hormonal, spiritual, emotional, cellular, entangled, and somehow extended through open space. Maternal bodies function out of this ambiguous array of connections and experiences. Nursing mothers occupy spaces cellularly entangled with bodies of children. These spaces are negotiated in an enfleshed, albeit mysterious, mode. Initiative and surrender work with considerable force throughout the body, speaking its indeterminacy and capacity for novelty with great clarity. So much mystery and wonder is woven through the way that we are made that we cannot narrowly pinpoint the why and the how of the way we are.

Maternal bodies occupy space in this way. Boundaries are fluid; this availability for and attunement to connection nourish life. Maternal bodies surrender to and embrace and resist flesh-and-blood connection. As more spaces open up for connection and the maternal body becomes more available for entanglement, so the opportunities for life to be nurtured expand and increase. Motherhood is a lively orientation to the food of abundant life. The ambiguity of maternal bodies feeds the body's capacity for creativity and zest. It is because of, not in spite of, the vagaries and risks and indeterminacy of embodied life that there is the possibility of being fruitful, productive, and life-giving. A thread of providence occupies these places as God's sustained offer of zest and Beauty in every moment. The body lives in and operates out of this complexity in a life-giving mode. Ambiguity nurtures and feeds and invites new life. In Jesus' invitation to this vulnerability to novelty and ambiguity he promises us abundant life. Maternal bodies intuit the life-giving potential of ambiguity and find a way to be at home there.

Multiple Mothers

Whatever the known facts, it is still assumed that the mother is "with the child." It is she, finally, who is held accountable for her children's health, the clothes they wear, their behavior at school, their intelligence and general development. Even when she is the sole provider for a fatherless family, she and no one else bears the guilt for a child who must spend the day in a shoddy nursery or an abusive school system. Even when she herself is trying to cope with an environment beyond her control—malnutrition, rats, lead-paint poisoning, the drug traffic, racism—in the eyes of society

---

38. Marvin S. Eiger and Sally Wendkos Olds, *The Complete Book of Breastfeeding*, 3rd ed. (New York: Workman, 1999), 27.

the mother is the child's environment. The worker can unionize,
go out on strike; mothers are divided from each other in homes,
tied to their children by compassionate bonds; our wildcat strikes
have most often taken the form of physical or mental breakdown.
Adrienne Rich, Of Woman Born

Mothers are never alone in how we mother, and we should not be alone if we are to mother well. We are always already in the company of multiple mothers. They are the voiceless voices, the imprinting, and the bodily memories of motherhood as well as the "othermothers" that help us along the way. The ambiguity of motherhood cuts through the illusion of an inside and an outside.[39] It makes the body's geography fluid: where it stops and starts, and who is included, ebb and flow. Feeling acquaints us with this dynamic even without introducing us to all of our cloud of companions. The dynamic of multiple mothers is the ambiguous intersubjectivity at work in motherhood.

The art of mothering entails a necessary interface of webs of relationships. Multiple mothers are not just other women who are mothers, but these multiples are the complex interconnections that mothers need in order to care well for children and who in-form how we mother. These connections are crucial for the body's ambiguity to bear its best fruit. In contexts of relative isolation, feeling is forced to feed on a thin layer of connection. It ekes out its particularity from what there is with which to intersect. This triviality of isolation does not destroy feeling, but it diminishes its best possibilities. Multiple and complex embodied connections are like good food and clean water—they are necessary for abundant life. Living without a complicated web of connection has the same kind of domino effect that malnourishment does. Like eating sugar and no protein or green vegetables, we strain all of our systems to draw energy from a thin supply.

Bodies are marked by how they were mothered even before they were in this world. We are imprinted by all the generations and expectations and situations of motherhood that have played their way through time. We internalize and externalize how we are mothered. Ann Belford Ulanov describes how the hands-on parent (what she refers to as the "transformational object") marks a child in this way. "The system of care for us by this 'transformational object' becomes a major part of our own self-care system. We know these rules and styles of

---

39. Walker discusses the ambiguity symbolized in writing between mother and daughter as that which "mirrors the disruption of our sense of space in such a way as to re-figure relations between inside and out" (*Philosophy and the Maternal Body*, 176). She describes such writing as "elastic" and as resistant to spatial organization. In Walker's work the ambiguity of maternal bodies is translated into the context of philosophical writing. Her discussion is helpful to me because of the way she plays with ambiguity and the disruption of oppositions and the falsity of the perceived inside/outside dichotomy that composes the self in Western philosophical individualism. For this reason, the way that the French feminists like Irigaray (and her labial poetics) use the symbolic provides an important philosophical exercise. I believe that, in a sense, feeling accomplishes the same kind of disruption when one considers the maternal body theologically.

self-care and self-relating, but we do not rescue them into thought. We are not specifically aware of them. We do them; we do not think them."[40]

Cognition does not simply translate into action. Bodies are constantly conditioned by all else that is. This conditioning process begins from the very earliest stages of life. There is an endless regress to its inheritance of the past. On the level of consciousness, becoming a mother conjures up memories of how we were mothered. We hope we can be some of what our mothers were to us and some of what they were not. We confess not wanting to become our mothers, but we see them in us more and more.

Much deeper than our consciousness are mothering scripts we have learned from our own mothers and from many others. The scripts of our own mothers are especially prominent, although not grossly deterministic. Their effectiveness is well beneath the radar of our conscious choices, even though we can sometimes catch glimpses in how we react without deliberation to our children's needs. A flash of anger, an impulse, or a gesture that seems to come from nowhere is our inevitable inheritance surfacing. Even submerged in our cells this inheritance is constantly at work.

We thrive in connection, and we are formed in connection. The deep tissues of our formation and thriving need massage, lubrication, and nutrition. Others touch our lives, and the fibers of what can be are shored up. Patricia Hill Collins explains that in African American communities the institution of motherhood implies a "network" of "bloodmothers" and "othermothers." She asserts that "African and African-American communities have recognized that vesting one person with full responsibility for mothering a child may not be wise or possible."[41] "Othermothers" are "women who assist bloodmothers by sharing mothering responsibilities."[42] The practices of sharing mothering responsibilities were institutionalized in African and African American communities through patterns of relationship and interdependence. Child-care sharing was common between family members and neighbors, as were "informal adoptions."[43] These habits of child rearing cohere with what bodies need to live fully.[44] "Othermothers" is not simply a practice, but corporate tendencies that thrive on intimate connection.

---

40. Ann Belford Ulanov describes this dynamic psychoanalytically with the help of Christopher Bollas when she discusses how the ego models the self most closely in line with the parent who was most active in "transform[ing] our environment to adapt to us when we were infants" (*Attacked by Poison Ivy: A Psychological Understanding* [York Beach, ME: Nicholas Hays, 2001], 11).

41. Collins, *Black Feminist Thought*, 119.

42. Ibid.

43. Corporate responsibility for children was a necessity for many because of poverty and racism. These community institutions extended to all facets of child rearing—including discipline. As Collins explains, in a society in which children were seen in the dominant culture as property, this kind of community parenting was "revolutionary" (ibid., 123).

44. In contrast, Adrienne Rich's quote above gives voice to the isolation many women experienced as suburban life isolated women from one another when they were "at home."

Feeling extends Collins's concept of othermothers beyond those who share in the work of mothering to all that surrounds a mother and her work. Even when we are alone with our children, othermothers are there enacting our movements, our tendencies, our insecurities, and our confidence without our conscious acknowledgment. These are the ghosts of motherhood. Multiple mothers permeate our cells, our tissues, our muscle twitches—how we move, how we hold, how we bend, and how we define our space. They are the brushstrokes of the horizons of our possibilities and our maternal imaginations. Othermothers redeem our possibilities from the triviality of isolation and feed our potential for abundant life.

One person being solely responsible for the care of another is an embodied impossibility. Remember how important reinforcement is in the ways feeling flows and forms. A mother's influence can be unique for many reasons, but her influence is not total. Relationships and responsiveness require a network of care, as Collins's concept of "othermothers" affirms. The constant changes of motherhood mean that grandmothers, fathers, neighbors, play groups, daycare workers, nannies, coaches, teachers, aunts, uncles, siblings, and friends are "othermothers." These networks of nurture play and weave themselves into mother-child relationships and form motherhood's ambiguity.

We must be careful not to mistake this ambiguity for chaos or lack of definition. Ambiguity does not render the content of motherhood chaotic; it gives voice to the muddled and wonderful power of interdependence to feed embodied life. Interconnection is the mother of complexity, which in turn feeds zest. These connections are given flesh in how mothers need and are marked by othermothers. Motherhood is enhanced, the lives of children are enriched, and what can be is expanded. Less connection makes harmful experiences and relationships overdetermine us; more connection feeds our capacity to expand into our own best expression. Triviality defines those spaces not nourished by connection. Zest cannot abide in the uncomplicated or the unconnected. Abundant life springs from complexity and indeterminacy. Mothers witness and steward along these explosions of new life every day.

Fragmented Subjectivity

Dreams weaving, wrangling—something is pulling me away. The faint cry becomes clear as I confuse myself about where I am. The cry is clearer and clearer—the call is certain now. It is my child, he is awake and he is calling my name. I sort out the time, 2:06 am. I sort out the situation, in bed alone, my husband is out of town. I begin to converse with myself about what comes next . . . do I go in, do I wait? I want to go in, but I think I should wait. My stomach churns—unsettled by indecision. If I go in he'll never develop his own ability to calm himself down—so says my child-care book and my sister, the child psychologist. But he's only two—why should he have to have that so expertly at his disposal? I'm thirty-three and I don't. I want to bring him in bed with me. It would feel so good to fall asleep together comforted by each other—knowing we're not alone. But then what will come of it—how will I get up and work in the morning while he sleeps? If I leave the room he could fall out of bed and I'd never forgive myself. What if something is wrong—he's sick or he's cold or thirsty or afraid? He needs me; I find myself halfway across the room. The crying stops. He is so quiet now. I am restless with not knowing. I resolve to stay awake for a few minutes and creep in to check on him—just to be sure he's ok. The silence breathes relief over me along with guilt. I can't sleep. My young son's dreams exchanged for mine? My eyes adjust to the dark and I stare almost beyond it. And I wait for dreams interrupted.

Journal entry

And the one doesn't stir without the other. But we do not move together. When the one of us comes into the world, the other goes underground. When the one carries life, the other dies. And what I wanted from you, Mother, was this: that in giving me life, you still remain alive.

Luce Irigaray, "And the One Doesn't Stir without the Other"

Motherhood lives in strange textures of simultaneity. Gentle attention, lethargy, fear, hilarity, and frustration inhabit common spaces in child rearing. The needs of different children, the constantly changing needs of the same child over time, the desire for children to be able to do things for themselves, and the pangs that wish they would never grow up are held in tandem. Fragmentation is a way of life, and it informs the art of giving and encouraging life over time. Fragmented subjectivity means that there are contradictory constellations of feelings at work in our constantly developing sense of self. These contradictory constellations do not cancel one another out. Instead, there is accommodation for this multiplicity in feeling's flow. Feelings in contradiction or disharmony with one another can remain active and effective.

The self is not only its process; it is constantly conditioned by feelings that do not translate into a harmonious and unified subject. Disharmony and conflict are part of what conditions subjectivity, not by decision between the two but through the way they coexist and fluctuate in their conditioning effect. These diverse and dissonant constellations fashion our uniqueness and our ambiguity. Motherhood embodies this fragmentation and shows us how fragmentation can function creatively. Contrasts gather steam despite their contradiction and fuel a unique kind of intuition. This intuition creates space for dissonance, difference, spontaneity, and responsiveness.

Mothers get conflicting messages about what it means to be a good mother. We navigate our mothering out of these messages, even those that directly contradict one another. Children challenge and shift a mother's sense of her self and her possibilities with fluid consistency. Other voices and intersections also condition a mother's wisdom. Within these constellations are visceral reactions and impulses that we cannot always explain. Mothers experience the conflict between a gut feeling about her child and the directives of an "expert" on how she should mother. Different mothers mother with unruly variation even when they have the same information, opportunities, and resources. Fragmented subjectivity is not a cleanly coherent self, but it lives out of entangled and contorted subjectivity. Subject-craft is conflicted, strange, and always somehow clear in its incompletion.

Motherhood shines a light on the fragments of subjectivity, but it also warns us away from assuming that fragmented subjectivity is a problem to be resolved. Subjectivity is a complex embodied process that inherently encompasses disharmony, ambiguity, and indeterminacy. Motherhood styles existence in which bombardments of expectations, instructions, intuitions, situations, and institutions condition feelings, practices, and concepts. All of these feelings produce and reproduce more generalized conceptions of what a mother is and should be, some of which directly contradict others. These fragments are apparent in all the theories that ponder the dilemmas of work and family, the dance of self-sacrifice and self-discovery, and multiple approaches to child care.[45] But can we find a way to embrace this fragmented aspect of who we are and how we become? Consider the possibilities this aspect of our human condition brings with it.

Motherhood embodies fragmented subjectivity with resistance that can create the creek beds of cultural change. It is the capacity to embody these fragments with a life-giving mode that is most instructive. The fragments of oppression and resistance reveal this dynamic of existing in and giving life out of disharmony and fragmentation. In some instances, motherhood locates substantial resistance to culture's denigration of certain groups or practices. This maternal resistance provides an indeterminate space for liberating possibilities. This resistance can disrupt, for example, the powers of racism, sexism, materialism, secularism, fundamentalism, poverty, and any other system of oppression. Collins describes mothers (in the context of black mothers) as those who can mediate the identity of children who are oppressed over and against mainstream cultural norms.[46] This "culture of resistance" and its capacity for survival in racist systems translate

---

45. See Miller-McLemore and Rigby.

46. Collins, *Black Feminist Thought*, 57. Also, Delores Williams describes black mothers as those who resist and defy, those who give their children "survival and quality of life skills." Williams uses the story of Hagar to illustrate how "God-consciousness and God-dependence" for African American mothers kept racism and sexism from bringing "permanent lethargy to the community" (*Sisters in the Wilderness*, 16–22, 57).

the fragments of subjectivity into a kind of double life in which one appears to be open and forthcoming in the dominant culture in order to remain invisible to that same culture.[47]

The fragments of social roles and the assumptions that fill them with meaning and expectation mean that mothers often inhabit value systems that stand over and against American individualism. Mothers are expected to live not for themselves, but for others. In this way maternal subjectivity is encoded with societal expectations for being those who fall outside "public" values and wield influence only in the "private" realm. The resistance of mothers to individualism is simultaneously accommodation and challenge to what society values and to how Western culture has tried to "privatize" maternity. Such resistance may serve some other societal standard that in turn feeds the suppression of things maternal. Echoing the genius of the hysteric's body, maternal bodies both resist and respond to cultural messages about what is valued. They inhabit spaces both of disruption and ascent. No one trajectory of feeling may gather enough steam to offset the conditioning power of another.

Consider some other embodied fragments that motherhood lays bare for us. The amorphous "mothering instincts" mothers are so often told to trust are some of these fragments of maternal subjectivity. We cannot point to what these instincts are and how they manifest themselves apart from swatches of stories or dreams of what ideal mothers are. The desire to do work other than mothering, the resistance to being "tied down" by children, and the need to give time and energy to activities and interests that do not involve our children are often interpreted as rejection of one's "instinct" to mother. In real life these yearnings are at odds with both external and internal expectations. "Mothering instincts" are not pristinely waiting to come out—feeling fleshes out why.

Who we are is shaped by all that is, by our own experiences, by our body's level of functioning, by societal expectations and messages, by life circumstance, and by the unique personalities of every child. Feeling confirms that none of these things can be strictly parsed out. There is an ambiguity in how it is all negotiated, in why it is negotiated the way it is, and in how it is experienced. There is no way to unify exactly who we are or even who we want to be. The fragments of subjectivity are scattered within a mother's particular hopes, needs, and challenges and throughout the character of her social contexts, relationships, and experience. These fragments render an inviolable "instinct" a problematic basis for judging how we mother.

47. Collins quotes Darlene Clark Hine's apt description of this illustration of complex subjectivity: "Because of the interplay of racial animosity, class tensions, gender role differentiation, and regional economic variation, Black women, as a rule, developed and adhered to a cult of secrecy, a culture of dissemblance, to protect the sanctity of inner aspects of their lives. The dynamics of dissemblance involved creating the appearance of disclosure, an openness about themselves and their feelings, while actually remaining an enigma. Only with secrecy, thus achieving a self-imposed invisibility, could ordinary Black women accrue the psychic space and harness the resources needed to hold their own" (*Black Feminist Thought*, 96).

The fragmented subjectivity of motherhood is concrete in the midst of all of its confusion, conflict, and irreconcilable features. One's self-understanding is changing all the time, even as it lives in the embodied consistency of one's uniqueness and particularity. It is cryptic, but it is not chaotic. The fragmented subjectivity of motherhood tells us about ourselves. Who we are is open to multiple interpretations and trajectories, and informed by much more than we know. Living into that ambiguous flux clears spaces that are not overdetermined by one set of experiences. These spaces are the conditions of possibility for a unique kind of intuition that is able to live with disharmony and contradiction. This "living with" seeks abundant life. It is intuitive, flexible, and creates even when constrained. Fluctuation becomes productive with the fuel of both frustration and availability. Our allowance for disruption and dissonance tempers our need to control what we cannot contrive.

FEELING BODIES/AMBIGUOUS BODIES

Maternal bodies, multiple mothers, and fragmented subjectivity re-member the body as indeterminate, interdependent, conflicted, and full of possibility. The ambiguous body language of motherhood opens up, negotiates, and disrupts spaces. Motherhood is an icon of the life-giving possibilities held in the body's availability for and vulnerability to creating meaning. It is the cacophony of experiences that circles themselves around making and keeping life. Motherhood has not re-membered the body with a clear set of practices, inclinations, and expectations to enflesh us. It gives us embodied metaphors of ambiguity.

Ambiguity

> Could it be, I find myself wondering (and invite you to wonder
> with me), that the body's ghostly essence lies in its very capacity to
> be at once thoroughly natural and thoroughly cultural? . . . And
> I ask you to ponder, too, whether it is precisely because the body is
> such a dense matrix of nature and culture that it presents itself to
> us—indeed, must present itself—as obscure, as having a "genius
> for ambiguity" in Merleau-Ponty's altogether apt phrase.
>   Edward Casey, "Ghost of Embodiment"

Obscure, indistinct, and cryptic: ambiguity points to that which is doubtful or of uncertain meaning or intention. It refers to something being unclear, indefinite. Something is ambiguous when it is open to several possible meanings or interpretations, when it is difficult to comprehend, distinguish, or classify. Ambiguity, in the context of embodiment, is an expression of feeling. It is relational, it is risky, and it is indeterminate although not chaotic. The body's play is elusive although enfleshed. Our human condition lives into and out of this potent disharmony, vulnerability, and interconnection. The body's flesh is a curiously open space—open, yet so very deeply modified by the "already" and "not yet" of creation.

The body and culture are "never not intertwined."[48] Without one another they would both be only "ghosts" of what they are. What ambiguity means and how it plays out in embodied experience is a theological concern. And it can fill the void left by our overdependence on sin to describe human experience. One of the character traits of our sinfulness is resistance to relationship with God. This tendency to turn away from God is real and an important aspect of human experience and suffering. But we need more than a description of our short-comings to communicate our condition theologically. The balance that attention to ambiguity provides is the capacity to substantively explore how bodies hold multiple means of relationship with God. Ambiguity modifies the body's spiritual capacity with a necessary openness, indeterminacy, and fragmentation. It reclaims our bodies for theological promise by filling out how feeling is our *imago Dei*. God's image in us is feeling—the genius of our body's ability to live as spiritual and as mortal, our body's radical relationality, and our body's capacity for suffering and transformation. Indeed, ambiguity invites us into the mystery, the mystery of the Incarnation.

The body language of the Incarnation tells it all. The enfleshed body is an ambiguous mixture of internal inconsistency, flux, and blurred boundaries in a life-giving space of immense concreteness. The Incarnation tells of vulnerability to human life, of immediacy to life's movement, change, and power. And the Incarnation tells us that redemption is tangled up with bodies, with their limitations and their possibilities. Ambiguity holds the promise of the second coming as well as the plausibility of the Christ event. It is the mother of mysticism. It is the child of holy mystery. When it is embraced, it invites religious awakening as it enlivens our attunement to the Living Word, to the unfolding of the work of the Holy Spirit, to the yet-to-be-seen. Ambiguity is the condition of possibility for hope.

When ambiguity is feared, it is the root of idolatry. This fear makes us grasp for something that can stand apart from the flux of human life. This fear trivializes ritual by regarding it as superstition. It empties religious experience of its mystery. It reduces worship to an intellectual act. It legislates barriers to keep out those who blur boundaries.

Learning to live substantively in ambiguity is the corrective to dogmatism and defeatism as it nurtures humility and hopefulness. Ambiguity does not mean that there is nothing to be said with conviction. Ambiguity is not relativism, but it allows for openness to several possible meanings and interpretations. Ambiguity allows for openness to novelty and adventure. In the midst of ambiguity, authentic conviction cannot come only from examining a disassembled

---

48. Casey, "Ghost of Embodiment," 220.

collection of social mores and standards any more than it can be the result of unadulterated biologism. Conviction born out of ambiguity must be the child of lived experience. At the same time, ambiguity warns of the danger of overdetermining one set of experiences. This kind of integrity can rejuvenate the church.

Motherhood is the mediator, the connector, the giver of and the residue of meaning. It is that which orients us to otherness as it is open to the adventure and the nurturing capacity of our entanglement with otherness. Its mediating role facilitates interconnection as well as differentiation. It communicates the ingenious way that meaning is produced out of immediacy and out of interconnections. It has the power to be available to all that is, and to be assertive and malleable in its metaphorical function. Motherhood does not develop metaphor in word, but with body language. It is the unnameable at the same time that it is the meaning-filled substance of metaphor—not just word, but flesh.

Ambiguity creates spaces for self-emptying with its surrender and assertion, both features of relationality. Ambiguity also answers tragedy with a life-giving image of embodied vulnerability. Ambiguity's self-emptying, self-assertion, and vulnerability take shape and give life out of indeterminacy. We work against triviality, not against chaos. Ambiguity is not chaos; it is the fingerprint of the intricacy and genius of God's mysterious activity. Motherhood remembers that God nurtures us in our created nature as feeling bodies. In Schleiermacherian language, this feeling (*Gefühl*) is our God-consciousness, our absolute dependence on God. Ambiguity potently incorporates this providential unfolding of "God with us"—God making all things new, God redeeming human life, God indignantly suffering with us. Far from being that part of our condition that we need to conquer, tidy up, or combat, ambiguity is instead the condition necessary for our best possibilities. It invites adventure.

PART II
THE (EM)BODY(MENT)
OF CHRIST

Prologue to Part II

Dance Then

My dad was fresh out of seminary serving a church in Crossett, Arkansas, in the early 1960s when a minister friend of his told him a story. As a boy he hated going to church youth group and avoided it at all cost. But there was a girl that he had his eye on and the only way to be close to her over the weekend was to go to the church youth group. So he went. The pastor leading the youth group meeting that night spoke on the topic of dancing. According to my dad's colleague this pastor talked at length about the evils of dancing. He talked about all the bad things that happen during dancing and about all the evil things that happened after dancing. This young man listened intently to the pastor's words and was captivated by the images he spun that night. The young man approached the pastor with great earnestness after the meeting. He said, "Pastor, I listened very closely to everything you said about dancing tonight and it leads me to feel strongly that . . . I am not getting everything out of dancing that I should be!"

It strikes me that mainline Protestants could feel the same way when it comes to being and doing church. Our mission statements in many mainline Protestant churches boast inclusion and justice while our congregations are among the most homogeneous in the world. Our sermons speak of transformation and being Spirit-filled, but we are not sure how redemption relates to our flesh-and-blood bodies. Communion liturgy tells us we become the Body of Christ in the mystery of the Lord's Supper, and still we sit quietly and wonder what it all could mean for us.

Embodiment theology hits the ground in our lived existence as bodies and as the Body of Christ. The cellular truths of how we are made and how we can flourish seek resonance in our worshiping communities—not just in our words, but in our practices and in our dispositions. The next three chapters explore the implications of what we know about our bodies as tragic, relational, and ambiguous for the church.

Being uncomfortable in our own skin has consequences for the church, for how Christ's Body can flourish. We are collectively wounded by this embodied dis-ease. The marks and scars are layered into the ways we form our communities and the ways we worship. Embodied attunement intuits these wounds and the institutional bodywork that can revitalize our worshiping communities. We can cultivate the present reality of our embodied redemption, and not just defer it to some eternal by-and-by. Cultivating redemptive dispositions invites the Body of Christ to expand into our entangled cells, tissues, and coursing blood, and to seep into the dry bones of our disembodied faith.

Cultivating these dispositions in-forms and re-members who and what the church is called to be. We are the Body of Christ. We are the muscles of Christ-living. We expand and constrict with the Spirit's breath and how freely it can move in and among us. The following chapter explores how the church can cultivate the redemptive dispositions of compassion, interdependence, and adventure. Chapter 6 further explores how these dispositions can translate in the way we heal the wounds of intellectualization and fear in mainline Protestantism. Chapter 7 examines how these dispositions can find expression in the rhythms of our worship. Like a body that has been still for too long, our collective joints and fibers are stiff and sore. Slow stretching into how we are made ushers in more courageous movement toward who we are made to be. Our collective bodywork will elicit grief, connection, confusion, and healing possibilities.

An early work of Frederick Buechner, *The Final Beast*, tells the story of a minister, Theodore Nicolet. The book opens after his wife has been killed in a car accident and he is left to care for his two young children. Nicolet is working to avoid living in utter hopelessness, which for him would be hell. It is Pastor Nicolet's children who enliven him to feel and believe God's promises for him. One of his children, in her nightly recitation of the Lord's Prayer, would routinely say, "Our Father who aren't in Heaven, Harold be Thy name."[1]

In a scene early in the book Nicolet is riding in a bus and talking with the driver. The driver comments that what happened to Nicolet's wife was a real shame and that he guesses they will never really know why it all happened the way it did. Nicolet responds: "Harold's the only one who really knows." When

---

1. Frederick Buechner, *The Final Beast* (New York: Atheneum, 1965), 33.

the bus driver asks him who in the world Harold is, Nicolet responds, "He runs a dancing school."[2]

Pastor Nicolet glimpsed the promises of faith in the dreams of his children. His children dreamed of angels. When he asked them what the angels were doing in their dreams, they told him, "They were dancing." The angels are dancing, and Nicolet adds, "their feet scatter new worlds like dust." He believed it, he said, because "my kids have dreamed it."[3]

This vision that Nicolet received from his children is a vision of God's creative rhythm and poetic dance in our lives. It is the promise that the Holy Spirit will parent us and that we will be able to listen, learn, and stretch into transformation even in the wreckage of our lives, not because we are just sinners, but because we are also redeemed, because we are Spirit-filled.

Once when Nicolet was praying over a woman whose life was in shambles, he prayed to God "that she may kindle to thy dancing at the heart."[4] It was a plea that her very soul be massaged into a new liveliness, liveliness to God's incarnational promises that we are accepted. And we are more than simply accepted, we are redeemed. Even more than that, the Holy Spirit is entangled in us, in the pulsing of our blood, in the beating of our hearts, in the horizons of our imaginations.

Perhaps what our dry bones need most now is that Nicolet's prayer be uttered for us all: "O God, let us kindle to thy dancing at the heart."

2. Ibid., 35.
3. Ibid., 182.
4. Ibid., 216.

Chapter 5

Embodying Redemption

Christ-living

I long for what's between
      paradox and symmetry.
The meaning-holder,
      the sign for loss and gain.
It signals Christ-living texture.
      bursting space, life, promise and fecundity.
In that space
      there is promise
      of the way that parses itself in grey.
That shade
      casts shadows
      reflects light
      holds, creates respite
      and a steady trickle of life force.
"Force" is not adequate
      to the mode in which it operates, or "is". . . .
      It emanates, originates, pulsates, agitates, placates, gestates
      It gives birth and nurtures and lingers always.
This lingering pulse, this life giver
      is comforter, spaces of understanding, initiator.
You go there, be there,
      wander into it, seek it, find it, lose it, want it, and still . . .
        be there.

Sensation—
>color, tones, palpability, taste and you will see.

Between paradox and symmetry
>I yearn to discover the composition and hear the way it fits
>>into
>a discernible pronunciation and how it sparks recognition
>>and
>then holds its own among others

There is The Word
>Beautiful and Wonderful and Rich with possibility,
>ready, but not waiting.

Loose in the world . . .
>creating its own meaning
>and then some.

THEOLOGICAL BODY LANGUAGE

Whoever tries to gain his/her life will lose it; but whoever loses his/her life for my sake will gain it.

>Matthew 10:39

Being uncomfortable in our own skin has consequences. We are hard of hearing when it comes to body language. We are out of shape when it comes to embodied practice. And we are disabled when it comes to living with ambiguity. What we may hear of our body's language is hard for us to translate and even harder for us to trust. For many Christians, embodied life is distorted, contorted, or, worse yet, ignored.

Feeling helps us tune in, pay attention, and surrender our need to understand completely. Feeling is the translator and the teacher of a new kind of language—a language that can speak a theological word about our embodied condition at the same time that it clears a space for what words cannot articulate. Cellular stories of trauma, pregnant poetics, and muddled metaphors of motherhood tell of the tragic, relational, and ambiguous layers of embodied experience. These experiences in-form us and our communities; and our resistance to these facts of who we are also in-forms us and our communities.

In the preceding chapters we listened to body language. The pressing question now is who we are as Christians when we have heard these things about who we are and how we are made. This question is not simply an ethical one; it is a radically cellular one. Discerning how we can function, even thrive, in our bodies is a dynamic and intentional process. How do we embody the promises of embodied redemption?

THE BODY AND DISPOSITION

Redemption is both present reality and future possibility in Christianity. We feel this "already" and "not yet" in all layers of our lives; the body holds this gift and potential in its cells, muscle twitches, and habits. These redeemed and redeemable layers of embodied existence are both given and open to (re)formation. Seeing ourselves clearly is a gift of Christian witness. Our capacity to be up close to "God with us" is our good news. We are sinful, and we are children of God. We fall short, and we are accepted and embraced by God. We are distorted, and God instills wisdom and vision. But grace and conversion are not all there is to our gospel.

Jesus says, "Those who eat my flesh and drink my blood abide in me, and I them" (John 6:56). Transformation is the core promise of Christian life. And transformation is an actual change in form, not simply a new outlook on life or a welcomed assurance of an eternal reward. Our bodies change in an incarnational faith—our individual bodies and our corporate bodies. Jesus is asking to be ingested so that he can dwell in us; and we are changed in form when Deity inhabits us this way. Where sin and suffering distort us, that affliction is healed in a deep and profound way. A path is cleared for us to learn to function and feel anew. The change of the "already" and the pull of the "not yet" take hold in our thinking and doing, and in our very being. Ingesting God like food and drink means that our very cells, tissues, and sinews get nourished. We are transformed bodies, not simply transformed minds and hearts.

Living into these embodied gifts of God takes practice. Like a creek bed slowly changing course, practice is the trickling current that creates transformation in time. Practice is the wind, the push in the current. Practice nourishes our embodied competency for redemption. The body can become more and more available for redemption by nurturing itself in what I am calling "dispositions of redemption." Because of God's unique power and our divine spark, dispositions of redemption are both gifts of grace and fruits of spiritual practices. When nourished and nurtured, our *imago Dei* revives as the fuel of who we are, instead of just surviving as a flicker of who we were supposed to be. We can function as partners in the transformational promise of Jesus Christ in our lives.

I use the word "disposition" because it communicates body language. A disposition is a characteristic; it is an inclination that includes outlook, attitude, and tendencies toward certain behaviors. Dispositions have blurred distinctions among mental, physical, emotional, and spiritual characteristics of the body. They integrate all layers of embodied experience. They are not only ethical, but also existential and deeply embedded beyond the reach of conscious decision. Bodies feel and fashion inclinations, behaviors, outlooks, and character out of the constellations of feeling's flow.

Dispositions also embody that which enjoys prevalence and consistency. Over the long haul, dispositions are indications of the kind of people we are. Some say that they are our "natural" inclinations; but they also embody our intentions.

We are in-formed and con-formed by our dispositions. We also in-form them and con-form them in turn. We are not passive, but powerful players in how dispositions take hold in us. When we dispose of something, for example, we make a decision as to how something should be placed or arranged. We give it direction. We regulate it. We dispense it. Indeed, God's unique activity in the world is sometimes described with the language of disposing, dispensation, and disposition. Dispositions are creative and wise to the texture of reality. Dispositions function ethically, but they are more than that. Dispositions are both the mothers and the children of our moral decisions and actions.

Dispositions mark our particularity, our inheritances, and our hopes for who we are and for who we can be. Our habits and our decisions partner with our dispositions to condition and characterize us. Our practices are the friends of our dispositions—companionable and challenging.

Christian communities and believers are the Body of Christ in the world. We flesh out God's love for the world, the hope that defeats all despair, the healing that outlasts all suffering, and the mystery of "God with us." We flesh out this state of redemption as it already exists and as it is yet to be. Redemption helps to in-form our dispositions in this new embodied situation of grace and to work to be better than who we are. But it can be profoundly difficult to really know ourselves and our distortions, especially when they become a way of life. Fear, polarizing stances on social issues, unapologetic individualism and materialism, comfortable homogeneity, valorized guilt, stasis, rigidity, and the quest for someone to blame for our problems are just some of the distortions that find a home in mainline Christian communities. These distortions are intimately connected to the disembodied ethos that characterizes much of mainline Protestantism.

As we live into our redemption, we need intentional practices that explore how we have resisted our own embodied redemption. Confession of sin and repentance, for instance, can be more than words read on a printed page and a few seconds of silence during worship. "Because Christ shows us his wounds, we can begin to show him ours."[1] This vulnerability and trust transform us from those who bury our pain to those who embody it in our communal life together. This transformative orientation to Christ and to one another needs more open spaces than many mainline church communities have been willing to clear for it. What if we let our embodied truths find expression, healing, and promise in church? What if we began to feel our way and not just think and do our way into Christ-living? Our collective journey of faith can find its integrity in the truth about who we are.

Feeling is the conduit of God's redemptive power breathed into our bodies. God works through feeling. It is our bodies' capacity for transformation. It is the mechanism of God's redemptive power as it integrates what is hoped for

---

1. Wendy Farley, *The Wounding and Healing of Desire* (Louisville: Westminster John Knox, 2005), 112.

into what has been and what is. Feeling gives us insight into how we can dispose ourselves and cooperate in our own redemption. How we attend to bodies informs how we are able to enflesh the Body of Christ. The tragic, relational, and ambiguous attributes of our embodied existence urge us to nurture these three dispositions in particular: compassion, interdependence, and adventure. When we are awake to the tragic, the relational, and the ambiguous dimensions of embodied experience, then we can intentionally nurture practices that expand our vision of who we are and who we hope to become in God's embrace.

Dispositions of Redeemed Bodies

Present yourselves to God as those who have been brought from death to life, and present your members to God as instruments of righteousness. For sin will have no dominion over you, since you are not under the law but under grace.

Romans 6:13–14

There's nothing that does not grow light
Through habit and familiarity.
Putting up with little cares
I'll train myself to bear with great adversity.
Shāntideva, The Way of the Bodhisattva

Dispositions of Compassion: Embodying Tragedy

We all suffer. Christianity has not tried to deny that. In fact, it has attended closely to how tangled up suffering and belief can be. Suffering is part of the wages of sin; and suffering can be the price you pay for following Jesus. These and other explanations for suffering swirl around in loosely thematic ways in Christian communities. The origins and cause of suffering are not my concern here. The fact that we suffer is.

This fact of human life is most often addressed liturgically and theologically with the language of sin. But the sin-guilt-forgiveness mantra of mainline Christianity does not always have a healing effect on our suffering. Rape shows us the embodied perils of overlaying this theological formula on situations where judgment has no place. Rape shows us the dangers of offering forgiveness as the only or even best healing option for survivors. Forgiveness is not the only salve that Jesus gives us for the wounds of human life. He gives us his loving presence and his patient acknowledgment. He gives us peace and a place to be in close proximity to God in our brokenness. Jesus suffers with us and promises that he understands. Jesus embodies divine compassion, not just forgiveness.

Compassion "feels with," and it keenly tunes in to tragedy, not to blame and judgment. Tragedy feels the pain of loss as well as the strength of survival. Compassion embodies indignant suffering. It disposes this indignant suffering by pouring presence and indignation into suffering. Compassion is not afraid of grief; it inhabits shared, mournful moments of discomfort. Its consolation is in its very presence, not in its capacity to perfect. This presence is not passive; it resists destruction and despair with its indignation. Somehow suffering will not have the last word.

Shāntideva, an ancient source of wisdom in the Buddhist tradition, imparts to us a beautiful constellation of how compassion orients itself toward the suffering of the world. Compassion focuses on the human condition as such—we all suffer. Compassion does not concern itself with guilt or innocence, but it focuses on suffering itself. Shāntideva tells us that clinging to moral dichotomies in the face of suffering only increases suffering. Compassion is always, first and foremost, about the work of acknowledging and alleviating suffering.

According to Shāntideva, practices of compassion must be a part of an intricate constellation of virtues and practices. Compassion is never isolated from a broader tapestry of virtues, which includes patience and forbearance. For Shāntideva, this constellation of virtues must also always rest on the axiom of conditionality. That all things arise from conditions and causes is the foundation of compassion's ability not to rush to judgment. Conditionality grounds every being in the shared tragic structure of existence. This understanding of conditions does not absolve individuals of responsibility, but it prevents the demonization of any one person. It also prevents any simplistic understanding of guilt and blame. The complicated fabric of compassion gives us latitude of vision. All of us become who we are in a tangled, complicated web of conditions and causes.

Dispositions of compassion name and in-form the kind of people we can become as practitioners of compassion. As Christians we are called to love one another as God has loved us. God loves us with compassion—with a faithful presence, with the willingness to suffer with us, and with the refusal to let suffering have the last word. God's compassion was and is enfleshed in the life of Jesus Christ, who suffered as a body. In Christ, God suffers with us indignantly, and in every moment of our suffering God offers the unique power and promise of Beauty. This Beauty is the mysterious way that God always offers the possibility of life renewed. In God, nothing is lost; even the wreckage of life is reweaved back into who we can become.[2] God's compassion for us not only suffers with us, but it honors our capacity for redemption. God's compassion offers the efficacy of Beauty, even as our pain and suffering are truly acknowledged. God's compassion is infinitely patient and uniquely powerful.[3]

Dispositions of compassion balance out the important descriptive power of sin by creating spaces for grief apart from judgment. Compassion does not exclude sin and judgment, but it locates them within a more complicated under-

---

2. Whitehead puts it this way: "The consequent nature of God is his judgment on the world. He saves the world as it passes into the immediacy of his own life. It is the judgment of a tenderness which loses nothing that can be saved. It is also the judgment of a wisdom which uses what in the temporal world is mere wreckage" (*Process and Reality*, 346).

3. Whitehead calls "infinite patience" another characteristic of God's consequent nature rather than describing this divine virtue as compassion.

standing of the human situation. Compassion suffers with, while working to understand the conditions that gave rise to the suffering in a broader sense. But it does not try to justify suffering. Compassion does not blame the victim; and it does not condemn the perpetrator without some sense of how those who are at fault also embody the tragic nature of human embodied life. Compassion is not afraid to love others enough to hold them to its own standards, but it does not demonize. It suffers with, but that is not all. Not letting suffering have the last word means making space for what needs to be better. Compassion sits with loss, and it hopes for better. It does not rush grief as a way to hurry through the pain. Compassion pushes toward a new quality of life in which we are able to live with loss honestly at the same time that it breaks through isolation and despair.

Christian dispositions of compassion re-member the body by acknowledging, listening, and taking care of bodies who mourn. Dispositions of compassion allow for re-membering to be more than recollection. This healing work honors the body's complicated need to tell a story and to grieve. Compassion holds grieving bodies by laying on hands, anointing with oil, helping them to fall to their knees in prayer, or by simply breathing in and out (because there may be times when that is all a body can do). Compassion receives, accepts, and meanders as embodied stories ebb, flow, and even contradict themselves.

The body's ingenious capacity to hold pain means that resistance to suffering must honor the body's need to heal. Compassionate care of the body enables massage, body and walking prayers, gardening, and other bodywork to empower our brothers and sisters in Christ to heal and to live into their own bodies' resilience. Some of the church's best pastoral care for those who suffer from life's tragic blows could be a garden for survivors to tend or a safe place for them to pray with their bodies. Just as good pastors know how to refer parishioners in need of counseling to a respected therapist, we can also cultivate a circle of safe and trusted healers for our congregations. Reiki, massage, yoga, acupressure, cranial-sacral therapies, and equine therapy can be just as important as talk therapies and medications. Everyone has unique needs, but having resources that address more than minds and symptoms is a first step toward honoring the healing that bodies need.

But caring referrals does not a church make. Christianity is a healing faith, and our liturgy, music, and practices need to attend to bodies with more consistency and more depth. Redemption means we live in, and in hopes of, healing. The "already" gives way to the "not yet" when we practice what we preach. With intentional practices of compassion believers and the communities they inhabit will begin to see, feel, hear, and taste the good news in new ways. There is pain in human life; let the church be a space to express all that comes with that fact. Let the church be a space where redemption can find flesh in the power to be there and not be destroyed, in the power to suffer with indignation. Redeemed bodies accept that pain and suffering seep into the cells of our bodies.

The limits of consciousness, body loss, body function, and contorted subjectivity are the embodied stories of rape. They tell of the cellular character of tragic experience. Compassion must extend its reach into the tissues of bodies, too. This kind of care is something we all need, not just rape survivors. Dispositions of compassion intentionally address the flesh. We address self-loathing, not just self-absorption. We address brokenness, not just fallenness.

In my own experience this intention is not easy to embody around painful and destructive suffering like rape. We yearn for someone to blame, for justice to be done, and for there to be a way to get back to "normal." I have been on the receiving end of many such reactions in response to my story of rape from church members, pastors, family members, and friends. I too have found myself in pastoral situations with rape survivors tending to proceed down these paths of addressing the problem. But I have learned and I have lived the trivial nature of these approaches. They address deeply embodied problems by staying on the surface. Cultivating dispositions of compassion wears a new creek bed—and that may mean inhabiting unfamiliar territory sometimes.

Justice, for instance, has been a laudable goal of the church in response to oppressive suffering and violence. But the pursuit of justice is not first-level healing work in response to tragedy. There are paths to pursue justice for rape victims, and some survivors choose to go down those paths. Most do not. And many who do pursue justice find little healing in it, but instead experience more pain and violation in the process. Indeed, for much of life's suffering, pain, and violence there is no justice. The new creek bed that needs wearing in Christian practice is, therefore, not the pathway of justice, but that of compassion. Justice is not abandoned, but it is nuanced with the embodied reality of suffering.

Consider again (as we did in chapter 2) that the survival shift the body makes in response to trauma numbs and dulls feeling. The body does not process emotion and decisions at full throttle or full clarity. Expecting trauma victims to have their story straight and be up to fighting through the legal system, therefore, is much like asking someone with a broken leg to run a marathon. The expectation is premature, dangerous, and given to humiliation and failure. Dispositions of compassion attend to the painful and pragmatic truth that justice is not often served in these situations. Sin-guilt-forgiveness liturgies and language may not resonate. Gentle in-forming habits of health and redemption may have more to offer.

Recall the contorted subjectivity that rape shows us. All of us have these aspects of dissonance in our sense of self. But the holy habits of guilt and shame and denial that we all embody on some level take on even sharper edges with the intense self-loathing that many survivors feel. Dispositions of compassion encourage a broader landscape to who we are than guilt or innocence.

Instead of groping in the dark alone, rape survivors need a lighted room, populated with people who understand and who see them for the children of God that they are. The constricting, judging, communal tentativeness around personal brokenness and undeserved suffering that exists in many mainline churches could give way to more open, accepting spaces for those in pain. Survivors may not need to join a committee; but they may need a circle of support that is patient and receptive. Places to stretch out, to pour out emotion, to take the time that healing needs are created out of a sacred trust. What truth can churches speak to those who are broken and in pain? That truth will come in the practices themselves when we care, cradle, listen, ground, and create spaces for bodies to mourn and heal. Sacred spaces for crying, grieving, moving, and processing pain could give way . . . for the "not yet" to become "already."

Dispositions of Interdependence: Embodying Relationality

What if bodies refused to be invisible? What if they were given the space to tell the truth about our connection with all that is? What if we let models of relationship and interdependence like placentas, midwives, and bodies giving birth in-form our dispositions? The embodied embrace of this kind of truth and power could surely hasten the church's capacity to be response-able. The new creek bed in-formed by practice finds its path through the relationships and connections that intersect us all. We are tangled up with everything that is. Our connections with creation, with one another, and with God are cellular.

Even though we embody, always and already, this cellular relationality, mainline Protestant practices do very little to help us live into this fact. The church's silence on this embodied truth of life is curious considering, for instance, that the Presbyterian Church is built on the assertion of being a "connectional" church. This belief in a connectional church manifests itself in the church's polity, in its theology, and in our mission and service. Still there is a gap when it comes to understanding how our bodies are an integral layer to the connectional church. Our connections are given theoretical, intellectual, and ethical weight in a strangely disembodied mode. Surely justice and service work are cornerstones of Protestant Christianity, and these active modes of faith life involve bodies. But I am pointing toward a deeper embodied truth than a passion for mission and active service. This truth is in the cells of our bodies, in our movements, inclinations, and modes of feeling the world.

Our response-ability for interdependence is housed in us at a cellular level, not simply at an ethical one. Dispositions of interdependence do not resist this fact of life, but live into it with enlivened response-ability. These dispositions say no to the numbing effects of overintellectualized worship and belief. They have room for spiritual sensation and encounters with experiential worship forms. Such dispositions allow the consistency of God's hand in flux and difference to feed confidence, not fear. Dispositions of interdependence intuit this participation of God even in dissonance and contradiction. Dispositions of interdependence are increasingly at peace with the fluidity of how we become.

Much like the placenta, which facilitates, mediates, and nourishes, those informed by interdependence are intimately tethered to entities with differing, even competing, needs. Dispositions of interdependence grow accustomed to engaging difference and contradiction. Creativity informs these dispositions of interdependence by giving flesh to how we share in the efficacy and delicacy of creation. Dispositions of interdependence strive to read the poetics of the body for how it speaks of all creation. These dispositions integrate the fact of cellular relationality with all the activities of life. Cellular interdependence calls for response-ability that does not limit itself to human life. Environmental care becomes a spiritual practice, not simply an ethical or moral choice. Power is not imposed, but shared. In-formed by the wonder of how God self-emptied in the Christ event, human beings can empty self into relational existence. We need not fear that interdependence is the same as fusion. Our own particular uniqueness is actually more ennobled in this mode of relationship than it is in orientations that grasp for individuality or separation. In an interdependent world our uniqueness is a given, and severing ties is an impossibility.

Dispositions of interdependence adjust to the entangled nature of existence by embracing creativity with surrender and self-assertion like the birthing body. Dispositions of interdependence are receptive to how we are all conditioned by all else that is, as well as to how we impact all that is. Just as a mother giving birth needs support, affirmation of her strength, and people who see her and care for her, dispositions of interdependence practice such modes of connection within faith communities. How do we empower and affirm? How do we honor and trust? How do we surrender and assert?

The sacrament of the Lord's Supper is one of the most promising spaces for such body language. Breaking bread and drinking wine re-member our relational nature. Dispositions of interdependence strive to give that reconnection flesh. Liturgies for the Lord's Supper could allow participants to nurture responsiveness in how the meal is shared—face to face, hand to hand, voice to voice. The Lord's Supper could be emphasized for how it re-members Christ's body by putting broken relationships back together, by gathering in those who are estranged or dis-membered from the community of faith. Interdependence enables the Lord's Supper to embody what it is—a joyful feast of relationship, reconciliation, and re-membering Christ's body.

Worship experiences that allow bodies to be awake to interconnection are centrifuges for dispositions of interdependence to be practiced and to spring from lived realities. Worship can be a place where churches learn to settle in to the labor pains that usher in new ways of being church. Our entangled sense of self can find currents to follow that cohere with our *imago Dei*, our divine spark. We surrender to a power we share in. This kind of surrender brings with it expansive possibilities instead of a rigid set of standards. The power allows us to stretch out. It does not constrict. This kind of power releases us from the need to control with our consciousness or rationality; it allows us to live with contradictions and creative tension. Distortions are gently healed with relational practices that pay attention to difference, to uniqueness, to strangers who cross our paths, and to the strangers within ourselves. The idols of individualism and conformity that we tend to deify in church communities can give way to icons of active, ingenious, embodied relationship. The Spirit moves freely when the Body of Christ remains open to the interdependence of God's creative presence.

Dispositions of Adventure: Embodying Ambiguity

Perhaps the most profound error of conventional Christian belief is that our faith brings with it certainty. This grasping for certainty has a variety of faces in the Body of Christ. Biblical literalism, moral rigidity, political polarization, church splits, and the condemnation of other faiths are just a few of these faces. Another face of this grasping is the unbalanced intellectualism in worship and theology in mainline Protestantism. Many Christians fear that living in ambiguity without finding some certainty is a slippery slope to moral relativism, structural chaos, and the erosion of Christian identity. And many mainline Christians fear that living with ambiguity hastens a dumbing down of our Reformed heritage. These fears are often soothed with moral absolutes or bulletproof intellectual arguments. Motherhood models a different mode of living with ambiguity. Its proximity to the mess, muddle, stress, constant needs, wants, missteps, and steep learning curves of children steeps motherhood in ambiguity. But here indeterminacy and unknown find relevant and substantive expression not in certainty, not in relativism, but in adventure.

Maternal bodies, multiple mothers, and fragmented subjectivity are embodied metaphors for dispositions of adventure. Triviality and isolation are what we need to avoid, not ambiguity and indeterminacy. There is no way to tidy up the ambiguity of motherhood; and all of us live in that same embodied truth. Human embodied life is like that. We are deeply marked by our experiences. My body's capacity to function well is an idiosyncratic expression of relationships, experiences, feelings, resistance, surrender, and embrace. Your body's capacity is the same. The church as Body of Christ is no different. The zest and connection of embodied mothering are like the rich texture of holy mystery, spiritual awakening, sacred attunement, and tenacious hope.

The ambiguity of the body has generally been something that the church has either ignored or feared. Moral purity is often left unbalanced by substantive attention to the body's fragmentation and the promise that fragmentation holds. Ambiguity, like holy mystery, has life-giving capacity and shows traces of God's image in us. Feeling shows us that ambiguity is part of the created genius of our bodies. Dispositions of adventure do not try to erase the ambiguity, but welcome it with the confidence of faith. Dispositions of adventure embrace the capacity of the body to be a helper in our spiritual journey, not simply a distraction or, worse yet, only a liability.

The discordant and melodious metaphors of the body's language are indeed cryptic. But dispositions of adventure take their obscurity as an invitation to seek not control, but surrender, humility, and hope. Dispositions of adventure are open and indeterminate. They trust God to help us live in the gray areas of both our sinfulness and our created goodness. Dispositions of adventure are not afraid of what God's mystery makes possible. These dispositions can spot idolatry and are ready to explode the hold it has on us. Dispositions of adventure have convictions, but avoid the stagnation of unbending dogmatism.

Alfred North Whitehead asserts that without adventure civilization trivializes religion and will eventually perish from its fear of what might be.[4] He describes the nature of religion as follows:

> Religion is the vision of something which stands beyond, behind, and within, the passing flux of immediate things; something that is real, and yet waiting to be realized; something which is a remote possibility, and yet the greatest of present facts . . . something which is the ultimate ideal, and the hopeless quest. . . . The worship of God is not a rule of safety—it is an adventure of the spirit, a flight after the unattainable. The death of religion comes with the repression of the high hope of adventure.[5]

These words echo the sensitivities of some of the great mystics and negative (apophatic) theologians. Both invite this surrender and impassioned seeking of God's mystery. Religion and piety are not the quest for control or certainty, but they are the embodied trust of holy mystery. Dispositions of adventure are open to the ambiguity of God's mystery.

Dispositions of adventure do not so much feel compelled to draw lines, but seek first to clear spaces for the indwelling of God's effusive Spirit. Humility and confidence are the connective tissue of these dispositions. Such a disposition is humbled by God's elusiveness at the same time that it is emboldened by God's immanence. The body's ambiguity is not so much to be feared, but is to be accepted as part of the mystery of life. Dispositions of adventure are not afraid to welcome those who stretch the ways we have always thought and done things. These dispositions are hospitable to difference and embrace its challenges. At the same time, relativism is not the character of these dispositions. Dispositions of adventure stand firmly in the conviction of a living God who has reconciled us to that life-giving reality.

Prayer practices that open one up to the Holy Spirit's mystery can feed these dispositions of adventure. Practices like prayers of quiet, centering prayer, Julian meetings, prayer labyrinths, body prayers, and *lectio divina* not only allow for our surrender to God's mystery, but they invite the body into the practice of prayer as a partner. The body is re-membered with dispositions of adventure because it is loved for what it is, for the genius of how it was created, and for the promise of how God works through the ambiguous fibers of who we are. Dispositions of adventure can hear, even though faintly and imperfectly, the disruptive and beautiful metaphors of the body's language. These metaphors are never completely understood, but they are attended to with the passion that gives life meaning. Faith, not fear, defines this orientation toward life. Contrast, differ-

4. Whitehead describes the importance of adventure in civilization: "A race preserves its vigour so long as it harbours a real contrast between what has been and what may be; and so long as it is nerved by the vigour to adventure beyond the safeties of the past. Without adventure civilization is in full decay" (*Adventures of Ideas*, 279).

5. Whitehead, *Science in the Modern World*, 191–92.

ence, and dissonance are not simply the way things are; they are the conditions necessary for a life well-lived and for attunement to God's mysterious proximity.

Just as motherhood embodies fragmented subjectivity, dispositions of adventure give and encourage abundant life over time in the midst of contradictions. This fragmentation is not a problem to be solved but an invitation to let contradictions be part of our identity. One set of experiences is not overdetermined as the trump card of how everyone should be. What is "natural," "instinctual," or "normal" is troubled by the metaphors of motherhood. Mothers nurture, but we also must see our children for the unique creations that they are. Mothers encourage, but we cannot control. Mothers teach and form, but we cannot determine. Maintaining relationship in the midst of differences, challenges, and even insults and pain is the adventure of motherhood.

Dispositions of compassion, interdependence, and adventure wear a new creek bed in the flow of God's living water in human life. This water is God's redemptive power in our lives. We are not a passive sieve for this water, but an active ingenious partner in how it flows through us. This living water is for our bodies, for our cells, our tissue, our muscles, our minds, our organs, our veins. It gives us life, even while utterly transforming the life we know. But water is not paradox. It is instead fluid, life-giving, washing, wearing, hydrating, and flowing. How thirsty is the church for this water? Can it seep into these dry bones?

Chapter 6

In-forming the Body of Christ

Revelation

Christ light shine
    glow
    illuminate
    expose
    wash us in love and compassion
    humility and peace.

Divine spark
    Kindle us to your refining fire
    Ignite us with imagination that
    sees, feels, knows no violence,
    no harm, no hate

Spirit wind
    Scatter our idols, our fears, our grasping, our lethargy
    whisper your wisdom
    fill us with common breath
    Billow the sails of our best possibilities.

Light, spark, wind of life and work, rest and tender release,
    take brutality and terror and
    dissolve it
    in your wonderful wash of deep ocean
    its only remnant, regret that gifts memories
    and careful moments together.

INTRODUCTION

One morning a week in a vast Gothic sanctuary in northern California, we gathered for silent prayer. It was difficult for some to sit in silence for so long, but they were open to learning this new method of prayer. "Sometimes being receptive to God means simply being quiet," we told ourselves. And the quiet was thick in that sanctuary with all the stone and the years and a dense cloud of witnesses.

A woman, Barbara, not a member of the church, began coming to these gatherings a few months after we had started this new practice.[1] As a kind, generous, and friendly nurse from one of the area hospitals is how we got to know her. Not too many weeks into her participation in these prayer gatherings she started moving around in the sanctuary during the silent time. She sang, she cried, she swayed back and forth, she touched things, and she knelt at the Communion table. And she spoke in tongues. People were uncomfortable and unsettled. One church member confessed that she feared "something was wrong" with Barbara. I myself wondered if I needed to go to her and assist her the first time she was wrested in the Spirit.

Her tongues were powerful laments that were difficult for her to bear. She told us how hard it was to be there that way. "That's what comes to me in this sanctuary," she said. She kept coming and praying and speaking in tongues. Attendance dropped off considerably, but she kept coming for months and months. Many times she shared her belief that her experiences in the sanctuary were connected to things that had happened there a long time ago. I began to regard Barbara as a conduit for layers of unexpressed grief in that space. She gave us many gifts by being in the sanctuary that way. But she created problems for many people. For the most part they avoided a substantial confrontation with what her tongues meant for our church. The dis-ease and disapproval came mostly in stiffened bodies and diminished participation.

This historic urban congregation, in a very non-church-oriented community, was in the midst of learning to embrace its growing racial/ethnic diversity. The transitions in the congregation were massive and difficult. Some lifelong Presbyterians, especially those who were Caucasian Euro-American, felt adrift and disoriented, worried and unsettled about it all. For a few it was too much, and they left. Others were deeply troubled, but they stayed, some more open to the opportunities for growth than others. For others still, it felt like a whole new way to be church.

Barbara embodied many layers of the church's growth edges. She was a person of color in a congregation that had been completely white for most of its history. She was a non-Presbyterian in a church that was the flagship Presbyterian church in that area. And she inhabited her body as a religious person in a way that was "other" to most people who encountered her in this church. As if these

---

1. Barbara is not her real name, nor are any of the other names I use for parishioners.

confrontations were not enough, she came into our time of "innovative" prayer practices and she did not let it be what we intended it to be. And she was kind, generous, and impossible not to like. She was loving, compassionate, bright, and honest. Tolerating her was not enough. Welcoming her was not enough. We needed to let her in-form us.

We are in-formed when we listen to the wisdom, the pain, and the promise of body language, and we let these narratives, poetics, and metaphors enhance our embodied awareness. This dynamic forms us from the inside, out by virtue of its primal intersection with embodied experience. While we most often understand ourselves as receiving "information" cognitively, in-formation is received cellularly. The how and the why of this kind of cellular communication is the very nature of feeling itself. Feeling flows, it forms us, and it is the mode of our redemption. To in-form is to permeate, to inspire. In-formation means feeling is acknowledged, enriched, and nurtured. To in-form is to strengthen the flow of feeling. To in-form is to facilitate the integration of cellular knowing.

I use "in-form" here rather than "re-form," which would seem a logical trope given the Reformation roots of this project. "Reform," a wonderful, ongoing gift of our Reformed heritage, suggests change from something flawed to something correct. When we reform we amend what is wrong, we change to a better form, we correct. While this causation leads to change (that we always hope and pray is for the better), it carries with it a judgment of the prior behavior or action; and I want us to avoid such judgment as we stretch into our own embodied experiences. It is not that we first need to correct wrongs (although there are wrongs that can surely be healed in this process), but that primarily we need more room to know and to be who we are. Being in-formed is a tender invitation to open up to the light of Christ in you and to the embodied possibilities that we hold collectively. It is not necessarily a move from something wrong to something right; it is instead an enriching, a nurturing, a deepening, and an expansion. This in-forming dynamic also has a deconstructing nuance suggested in the word "informality." Informality softens some of the more rigid aspects of formal/accepted behavior, dress, and conversation. Informality has the capacity to clear blockages entrenched by our holy habits.

HOLY HABITS

This encounter with Barbara is an icon of our situation as mainline Protestants today. We are both settled and restless in our habituated denial of body. Our disease can sometimes be disguised as modes of being church that we feel inclined to protect. We have even created idols out of our dis-embodied mode of church; and we sometimes confuse the sacred with our particular ways of doing church. Even with the room most mainline Protestant congregations have for political and theological disagreements and differences, we expect a great deal of conformity around how we dispose ourselves as church. Mainline Protestants have always preferred a decent, orderly, even mannerly way of being church. Emotional moderation, physical control, and intellectual acumen are the unspoken expectations of those who seek church in these communities. We are heirs of a long tradition of such polished behavior.

We are also the spiritual children of religion in America, a phenomenon with the same gene pool as the nation builders who conquered First Nation Americans and brought slavery to this country. The visceral reaction so many mainline Protestants have to the impending chaos of being "uncivilized" is palpable when something like clapping in church or speaking in tongues occurs in church. Civilization is ours to lose!

> This concept [of civilization] expresses the self-consciousness of the West. One could even say: the national consciousness. It sums up everything in which Western society of the last two or three centuries believes itself superior to earlier societies or "more primitive" contemporary ones. By this term Western society seeks to describe what constitutes its special character and what it is proud of: the level of *its* technology, the nature of *its* manners, the development of *its* scientific knowledge or view of the world and much more.[2]

Mainline Protestant churches are and have been tangled up with this concept of civilization for much of our history.[3]

In the American context, Protestant Christianity was an early cooperative partner with larger cultural efforts to wipe out religious "otherness."[4] This history is ours. It should be news to no one that the church has been an instrument of this "civilizing" orientation to otherness. Institutional initiatives by mainline Protestant denominations endeavored, for instance, to "educate" and "civilize" Native Americans. In the name of Jesus, Christians attempted to dismantle First Nation languages, dances, belief systems, and practices with the "civilizing" teachings of Christianity. Many denominational entities have acknowledged this fact and reformed their practices.[5]

2. Norbert Elias, *The Civilizing Process: The Development of Manners* (New York: Urizen, 1977), 3–4.

3. Charles Long traces the term "civilization" to sometime in the 1770s. This timing places the congealed term much later than the Reformation. Long wants to be sure we understand the intimate relationship of Enlightenment thinking with the dynamics of conquest and the need to "civilize" primitive others. These ideas and trends that came together to fuel the Enlightenment period were taking shape long before the concept was "officially" articulated. See Charles Long, "Primitive/Civilized: The Locus of a Problem," in *Significations: Signs, Symbols, and Images in the Interpretation of Religion* (Minneapolis: Fortress, 1986), 79–96.

4. Obviously the Roman Catholic Church shares in this history. I am focusing on our Protestant heritage in the interest of encouraging our own ownership of this history.

5. The Menaul School in Albuquerque is an excellent example of this history and its contemporary transformation. In 1881 Sheldon Jackson began the movement toward Presbyterian education of Pueblo Indians in New Mexico with the support of the U.S. Department of the Interior. This "Pueblo Training School" later became the Menaul School founded by Reverend James Menaul in 1896. (The U.S. government had already relinquished any financial support of the school in 1891.) Today Menaul School is a day school that boasts 60 percent of its student body are of Hispanic, Native

This history of fearing and reforming religious others shows its complexity in the experiences of African American Presbyterians also. For most of the church's American existence, a white-dominated orientation toward religious experience in the Presbyterian Church created complex, sometimes even violent, spaces for African Americans. Some black Presbyterians describe constantly creating and re-creating Christian life through their own experiences while participating in the white-dominated life of the Presbyterian Church that ignored these experiences. Out of this racist dynamic came both entrenched habits of ecclesial conformity and spaces for redemption to find life.[6]

How can we attend to these wounds and these signs of resilience in the Body of Christ? These "civilizing" tendencies have formed us even as there are important constellations of resistance and resilience in who we have been. The embodied promise of more prevalent life-giving habits can in-form how we inherit this past of ours.[7] When we attend to embodied experience in a dis-embodied faith we are inviting new orientations, new wellsprings of grace and transformation. The entrenched normativity that has helped to create us can smooth itself into open spaces when we allow the contortions, entanglements, and fragments of who we are to in-form us.

We can allow ourselves to be critiqued by "otherness" in all the many ways we each encounter it. But this multilayered process is much more than an intellectual exercise. In-forming the Body of Christ embodies us with feelings that are unconscious and cellular. Some elements need to come into consciousness in order to be interrogated, healed, and disrupted. Other elements will not find new life through this process of exposure and unpacking. Instead they will gently find their future in embodied practices that wear the new creek beds of what the church will become.

Our fear and attempted erasure of otherness is not simply an external/ institutional/cultural phenomenon, it is an existential experience that estranges us from "others" and from ourselves. We are collectively uncomfortable in our own skin. This reality is embodied in each of us in particular, and in our institutions and practices. Getting to the subdermal aspects of this dis-ease first begs for intentional openness to God's mystery and contradiction. Repentance and accountability, grief and anger, woundedness and survival skills take up spaces in

---

American, or other racial ethnic minority origin, and it is a school that honors and celebrates these differences. The other 40 percent of the student body are of Anglo origin (see www.menaulschool .com). Also see Robert Laird Stewart, *Sheldon Jackson: Pathfinder and Prospector of the Missionary Vanguard in the Rocky Mountains and Alaska* (Whitefish, MT: Kessinger, 2006).

6. This redemptive capacity shines forth in Katie Cannon's description of a "double consciousness" in "Transformative Grace," in *Feminist and Womanist Essays in Reformed Dogmatics,* ed. Amy Plantinga Pauw and Serene Jones (Louisville: Westminster John Knox, 2006), 144–47. Another source of information about this complicated past of Presbyterians and race is Erskine Clarke, *Dwelling Place: A Plantation Epic* (New Haven: Yale University Press, 2005).

7. In response to the civilized/primitive metaphor that has shaped Western mentalities, Charles Long calls for the study of religion in the West to allow "proper" study of aboriginal cultures (for him this is study that does not see their otherness as a negative) in order "to demythologize . . . our own discipline, and thereby extend our understanding of religion" (*Significations,* 94).

our collective embodied experience. Communal "body" work can tell and heal the layers of our truth. This "body" work can loosen our grip on the inclinations that have formed our collective idols. These hallowed habits are embodied in how we form our worshiping communities and the role we allow for experiential dissonance in these communities.

A normative narrowing of religious experience feeds and has fed mainline Protestant practices. This narrowing has devoured much liturgical/theological space for "otherness" or nonconforming modes of religious life. Ironically this same penchant for limiting what is legitimate religious experience and expression is starting to feed on the very churches that nurtured those mentalities for so long. Mainline churches are shrinking and struggling to find our way in increasingly secular and diverse contexts. Those who yearn for religious community today are not tending toward mainline churches. The rise of nondenominational megachurches, the growing popularity of more informal worship styles, the increased embrace of contemplative practices, and new appropriations of Eastern religious sensitivities are just some traces in churches and in the broader culture of the quest for worship/practice to be more than an intellectual exercise. The biases of Western mentalities of belief and intellect leave the institutions that were formed in these orientations wondering how to adapt. We are being consumed by our own appetite for religious conformity. Churches have serious questions about who and what the church is in today's shifting religious landscape. According to Ronald Byars,

> What . . . drives these changes? In some cases, it seems to be a passion for evangelism, and particularly for reaching out to generations largely missing from traditional churches. In other cases, it seems to be an attempt to hold on to church members who are bored and reluctant worshipers. Sometimes it may be an attempt to duplicate the fabulous numerical success of single-generation congregations. But behind these various motivating factors, there is the inescapable fact of dramatic cultural change. What used to work just fine (or seemed to) doesn't work anymore.[8]

Certainly pragmatic motivations and cultural shifts that call on churches to change are a real concern. Indeed, some believe reinvigorating mainline churches is simply a matter of how we market and package ourselves. We need more technology, more stimulation, for a generation accustomed to the bells and whistles of a computer-driven life (cultural accommodation). Others think we need to pare down, center down, quiet down, and resist the urge to overstimulate. Instead we need to create a space for people to be something different (countercultural). Still others want to hold on to "the way we have always done things" and not give in to accommodating temptations to change what we do.

---

8. Ronald P. Byars, *The Future of Protestant Worship: Beyond the Worship Wars* (Louisville: Westminster John Knox, 2002), 2.

The church needs to remember who it is and stand fast in why we are what we are (historical consciousness).

The pragmatic pull to change is only a superficial indication of deep wounds and imbalances in the subdermal Body of Christ. Pragmatic approaches may change the packaging and may even invite some new kinds of practice, but by and large they do not deeply explore how our limitations might be rooted in who we are. Perhaps we hope that our need to change is only because of external shifts, not because of something internal to us. Indeed, it is a frightening prospect to think we need to change from the inside out. So much is concealed in our dis-embodied contexts. Still more is obscured. We protect, we avoid.

Overlay what we know about ourselves as bodies (tragedy, relationality, and ambiguity) onto the ways we "do church" and we begin to acknowledge some of our wounds, ruptures, and fears and some of our possibilities. Just as we hold in our own bodies the ruptures that result from denial of relationship and the woundedness of unattended pain, the gathered body of the church also holds these dynamics within itself. Our collective body can live into enlivened embodied experience with much the same dynamic as we do in our particular bodies. The more we tune into our embodied nature, the more at home we are in our own bodies. The more we are at home in our own bodies, the more we can be at home as the gathered Body of Christ. Being in-formed by the healing, liberating, and truth-telling capacity of embodied experience is a lifeline for mainline churches. New habits of healing, new modes of relationship, and new ways to live with ambiguity can reinvigorate the Body of Christ. The church reinvigorated extends the church's capacity to be a source of healing, connection, and adventure in the wider world.

The church is the Body of Christ—his hands, feet, heart, face, mind, imagination, fingers, feelings, cells, and sinews in the world. The Body of Christ needs more than heads and hands, it needs attention to how it is disabled by unconscious fears about people who do not look like us, talk like us, experience God like us, read the Bible like us, or love the same people we do. The Body of Christ can be in-formed by how we are made and how we can thrive when we attend to bodies with more intention. Traumatized bodies, pregnant bodies, and mothering bodies urge us to wake up to these layers of our human condition. We embody our inheritances, our relatedness, and our ambiguity when we gather as church. We are contorted by harm, entangled in relatedness, and fragmented by the dissonance of differences within and outside of ourselves.

Our sacred spaces and communities hold more than what we think we know. They hold mystery, contradiction, grief, and bodies that are awake to God's movement through them. Cultivating dispositions of compassion, interdependence, and adventure nourishes the sacred purposes of the Body of Christ. These sacred purposes have been diminished in the disembodied ethos that has helped to form us. Our estrangement from our own bodies makes welcoming the stranger who is external to us a bone-chilling prospect; confronting our own dis-ease and unfamiliarity with ourselves is painful and disorienting. Confronting the "other" can leave us feeling incompetent, out of kilter, and afraid. Our disembodied dis-ease, our discomfort in our own skin, often sends mainline believers to the assurance of our intellect and/or our moral codes. These respected coping skills may also be mechanisms of avoidance. Will an encounter with the stranger open the door to an encounter with our own contradictions and gray areas?

SACRED WOUNDS

Aaron and all the people looked at Moses and saw that his face was shining and they were afraid to come near him.

Exodus 34:30

And the disciples kept silent and in those days told no one of any of these things they had seen.

Luke 9:36

God's sacred nature is poured into human life when God comes close enough to change a tribe of people in the Exodus account. God is not untouchable, but radically close, close enough to see who they could really be at their best. God seeks relationship, and the sacred is born out of this brush of humanity with the Divine. God's proximity makes Moses shine not just in his own countenance; but this glow shines a light on who humanity is and who we can be at our best: communities built on trust and respect and truth. This best-case scenario that the Law communicates is the founding vision of sacred community in our Judeo-Christian heritage.

God is trying to carve out a relationship with this group of humans so that they can live to their best potential, so they can live in a world in which life is respected (thou shall not kill), so they can trust each other (thou shall not lie or steal). God urges humanity to know how to work and how to rest and how to live with each other so that everyone's humanity is affirmed. This sacred purpose makes the Law itself sacred.

This vision of sacred community founds us even as we struggle to find our own expression of it. Our time is no different than any other that acutely experiences cultural transitions. We ask ourselves: Is nothing sacred? We usually ask this question out of bewilderment when "the way things were" no longer lines up with "the ways things are." Is nothing sacred? Is there nothing that stands apart, nothing that is protected from the vagaries of time? Is there nothing that can preserve treasured traditions and hallowed values?

This question has a complicated history. It has sounded off the lips of those who sought to protect systems of segregation, of those who wanted their own privileges to be untouchable, of those who wanted to be entitled to reverence because of their station in life. We can mistake the sacred quality of something for our own grasping, for our own privilege, for our own comfort. So, when we hear this question in our churches, and in our cultures: "Is nothing sacred?" we need to be clear on what we are asking. Something is sacred when it is set apart for the purpose of serving and/or worshiping the Divine. It is dedicated to that purpose and therefore entitled to special regard. It is allowed to hold sacred content, and it is saved for certain kinds of activities and modes of experience that are, themselves, sacred or consecrated. This sacredness (in content and mode) is handled with care by protecting it from the profane.

The profane violates, abuses, or vulgarizes with intense irreverence for the purpose for which something has been set apart. To profane is to do violence through an utter disregard for the very nature of that which is sacred. Often this word is used, however, to label those who are rejected or marginalized. This word, "profane," has been used to degrade and diminish everyone from lepers and prostitutes to women who speak in church and those who love people of their same gender. A more accurate example of the profane is when a bomb goes off in the middle of a mosque in Iraq or Pakistan during a time of prayer for Muslims. This act desecrates with a profanity that we can all recognize as a violation of the sacred intention of that space.

As we deepen our embodied understanding, we ask questions with a more finely tuned ear for the sacred and the profane. How does the church embody its sacred character? Are we fulfilling a sacred purpose in what happens in church? What is sacred about our spaces, practices, and expressions of church? Opening ourselves up to new practices, new music, and new movement can feel like a desecration, an abomination of what is sacred. I have heard in numerous churches the sentiment that the sanctuary is "desecrated" when people clap or when we use a different kind of music in worship. Our attempts to recognize the sacred in our midst and in our modes of church is dangerous work in a disembodied faith.

Our spiritual instincts may be dulled when embodied feeling is not encouraged to stretch in our religious sensitivities. Our habits can obscure the sacred quality of the unconventional. Being in-formed by dissonant experiences and practices may not be aesthetically pleasing to many. The experience can feel like an untuned piano sounds to an ear accustomed to a finely tuned instrument. Institutional bodywork takes time to settle into us with harmonies we have the ears to hear. Institutional bodywork invites us to feel our way into God's unpredictable movements among us.

God seeks closer relationship with humanity. This yearning for relationship not only shines a light on the one who reveals God's nature to us; it shines on us, on our human nature, that we might see ourselves more clearly in relationship to God.

This intimacy with God often may not feel like a cool breeze or a toasty campfire. This interdependence is awe-inspiring, confusing, even terrifying. Like the disciples who witness Jesus' transfiguration, we are not sure what to say or do. We grope for the sacred. The most bone-chilling layer of this entanglement with Divinity may just be that God's revelations tell who we are too. Jesus shows us who we are with utter clarity. He bears the sins of the world; he shines a light on our humanity. He shows us our shadows, our best face, and the divine capacity in each of us.

Sacred ground is created not where God is revealed as untouchable, but where God becomes touchable. The sacred is filled up with this purpose. In sacred communities we come close to God. We are touched by God. We are empowered to embody God in the way we live as bodies and as Christ's Body. This proximity to God comes with a distinct character: sacred spaces invite us into a divinely inspired way of being together and of being human. Fear and avoidance in sacred communities keeps us from the depths of God's redemptive promises for us. What if telling the truth really does set us free? What if living a lie really does afflict us?

Triage for the Church

Sacred communities cannot rest in triviality; their very nature is to flourish in the infinite resources of proximity to God. Church is gathered for a sacred purpose: to cultivate conditions that enable our lives to be tangled up more and more with God. Sacred communities can be bold in this divine gift of purpose. And sacred communities can find humility in our constant need to interrogate just how robustly we embody this purpose. Sacred communities embody feeling and its mode of operation with the same impulse toward zest that our particular bodies do. Our bodies hold the wounds inflicted by triviality. So does the Body of Christ. When we cut off layers of our relationship with God in order to protect the ways we have always done things, we harm this Body. When we deny our deep connection to everything that is, this Body suffers from ruptures of relationality. The Body of Christ is diminished when feeling is thwarted.

When we habituate a need for certainty and/or conformity this Body is informed by fear of otherness and avoidance of ourselves. Can we have vibrant, robust, zestful churches when we are comfortable with homogeneity? Can we embody God's redemptive promise if we still live in fear? Can we imagine that God empowers us to embody contradictions? Just as a laboring woman rides waves of delight and devastation, self-assertion and surrender, so too can the church collectively give birth to new life. We cannot do this, however, without embracing the support and wisdom of God's diverse kingdom. And we cannot do it out of fear. We can listen, respond, create, and nourish this new embodied life when we attend to our wounds, resist triviality, and surrender to the divine imagination that sees who we can be.

I will examine two collective wounds of our dis-embodied faith: the wound of intellectualization and the wound of fear. Both of these wounds carry the stories and poetics of our pain and our redemptive possibilities. Our wounds need healing wind and light and care. Institutional bodywork begins with acknowledging where movement feels painful, maybe even dangerous. Where does it hurt? Where is it hard to stretch? Where are nerve endings dulled? Where are anxieties held?

The Wound of Intellectualization

During one pastoral hospital visit I asked (as I always do) if I could pray with the parishioner before I left. The parishioner I was visiting that day, Sarah, said, "Oh, I don't believe in intercessory prayer, but you can if you want to." It struck me while quietly collecting myself to pray for this wounded skeptic how completely she had given herself over to the formation she had gotten in mainline Protestantism. For Sarah prayer was an irrational thing that pastors did in hospitals, far from any kind of connective tissue of the Body of Christ. Her strong commitment to justice was her spiritual calling card; prayer was meaningless in a world where rational thinking informs doing. Sarah put her faith into action. Hers was a faith embodied on the ethical layer of her being and doing. And, to be sure, all the work of great saints like Sarah is embodied and deeply important to how the Body of Christ is alive in the world. But her dismissal of prayer trivialized how her faith could be transformative in her life, not to mention the lives of those for whom she could be in prayer. Prayer was intellectually embarrassing and pragmatically useless to her religious sensitivity. Sarah's faith had integrity, but the mysterious power of prayer made no sense in her well-ordered system.

It is perilous to keep our faith above the neck. In psychoanalysis, "intellectualization" is a defense mechanism that protects us from stress, anxiety, and discomfort associated with confronting painful problems or fears.[9] We intellectualize when we use excessive reasoning to respond to confrontations with difficult emotions, painful problems, or unconscious conflicts. It is a defense against anxiety. In therapeutic situations patients intellectualize when they should instead trust the process of free association and allow all thoughts feelings, memories, images, and sensations to be voiced as they come to mind so as not to censor the unconscious.

In mainline religion this intellectualization is a collective defense against an embodied surrender to the mysterious and idiosyncratic nature of religious experience. It keeps us from acknowledging and expressing embodied pain, confusion, delight, and ambiguity. These are the marks of how we are created, yet we awkwardly conceal ourselves from such disclosures in church. The habituated nature of this collective defense has entrenched our dis-embodied dis-ease. We instead tend to reason our way through divine mystery with theology, through human pain with theodicy, through religious experience with orderly liturgy, and through diversity with mission statements about inclusion. This arsenal of intellectualization leaves us feeling cut off, denied, and blocked from embodied expression by our holy habits of operation.

9. The term "intellectualization" was coined by Anna Freud in her 1937 book, *Das Ich und die Abwehrmechanismen,* which was translated as *The Ego and the Mechanisms of Defence* (trans. Cecil Baines; New York: International Universities Press, 1946), e.g., 172ff. Anna was the eldest daughter of Sigmund Freud, and the mother of psychoanalysis as an ego-focused therapeutic method. She was also a major contributor to developmental theories in modern psychology.

How do we drink in divine mystery? How do we make room for wonder? How can we stretch into affirming deeply embodied brushes with Divinity? The wound of intellectualization keeps us from feeling our way through many of the gifts of Christian life. This is not a superficial wound, but one that has deeply affected our approach to things. We can even mistake it for a virtue. One of the most treasured character traits of mainline Protestantism is intellectualism. Higher education is one of our greatest accomplishments and offerings to the larger society. This examination of our unbalanced intellectualism is not a rejection of education. Our problem is not that we value the intellect; the problem is how this valuing has fed our disembodied ethos. This commitment to education and learning becomes problematic when it is tangled up with a rejection of embodied ways of knowing, being, and feeling. This problem gets back to our denial and rejection of the body itself. Feeling is trivialized, cut off, mistrusted when intellect or even consciousness are privileged as the only reliable sources of knowledge. This trivialization of feeling has radically in-formed mainline Protestantism.[10]

Modernity's assault on religious belief entrenched the unbalanced intellectualism of mainline churches. Religion was made appropriate for the learned with the rise of historical biblical criticism even as Protestant churches in America struggled with our relationship to the academic study of the Bible.[11] The mystery of religious experience, the visceral aspects of belief, and the embodied capacity to idiosyncratically express and respond to brushes with Divinity were often seen as intellectually embarrassing. This experiential layer of faith found no place in orderly worship.[12] As is characteristic of religious life in America, when dissonant religious experience surfaces in religious communities and people want space to express it, we show them the door. We seldom create room for such embodied testimony. The Body of Christ fractures into pieces estranged from itself and insulated from "the other."

10. I see a window into how this unbalanced intellectualism has harmed us in the development of fundamentalism in American religion. Karen Armstrong argues that the scientific rationalism of modernity backed religious belief into a corner, forcing it to prove its own legitimacy with scientific proof and rational argument. Fundamentalism is a child of this dynamic. Certainty was assured in biblical literalism when the biblical witness became literal history and science as well as moral code. I see a similar dynamic in the way mainline Protestantism found its legitimacy in modernity in the academic study of the Bible and of ethics. See Karen Armstrong, *The Battle for God: A History of Fundamentalism* (New York: Ballantine, 2000).

11. For more on the internal struggle of Presbyterians over the deeply connected question of the authority of Scripture see Eugene March, "'Biblical Theology,' Authority, and the Presbyterians," *Journal of Presbyterian History* 59, no. 2 (1981): 113–30. The academic robe worn by the preacher in much Protestant worship is also a sign of intellectual legitimacy.

12. The birth of Pentecostal communities in America is a direct reaction to this narrowed view of religious experience. The birth of the Church of God in Christ unfolded around the importance of ecstatic experiences, namely speaking in tongues. When the pioneers of this movement broke away from the Baptist Church they were seeking a practice of holiness that embraced the importance of the Holy Spirit's activity in "spiritual baptism." See Elsie Mason, "Bishop C. H. Mason, Church of God in Christ," in *Afro-American Religious History: A Documentary Witness,* ed. Milton C. Sernett (Durham: Duke University Press, 1987), 285–95.

The wound of intellectualization cuts our faith experience off from the neck down. This wound keeps us from feeling our way into dissonant and idiosyncratic religious experience both for ourselves and others. This wound makes it hard for us to imagine what an embodied faith could look like beyond the work of mission and service. This wound alienates us from our own bodies and the feelings that we ignore at our peril. It also alienates us from those religious "others" who might enrich our worshiping communities with deeply embodied practices that have the integrity of deep devotion and connection to God. Intellectualization keeps these "others" at arm's length and keeps our own confusion and dissonance under the guise of a settled ethic and view of the world. It also keeps our own religious experience tethered to a small palate of acceptable modes of encounter with the Divinity.

When words, doctrines, and ideas take up all the space in our religious imagination, we run the risk of making our ideas and images gods themselves. Our resistance to such institutional idolatry has been the lifeblood of our protest against the church abusing its power. Perhaps our rallying cry has made it even harder to recognize when we have succumbed to the same human tendency to make ultimate our own ideas. In our case it may be that we have made ultimate our own intellectual prowess. Divinity penetrates the very stuff we are made of and finds its way into all of who we are. Living into this transformative promise does not bring with it bulletproof intellectual arguments and rational explanations of all the faith is.

In-forming Mystery

We are asked to "be there" close to God's mystery even if we cannot completely understand. In Isaiah's call narrative he glimpses the Holy; he gets close enough even to overhear God's conversation (Isa. 6). There are heavenly creatures, six-winged seraphs, and the immensity of God is palpable. The hem alone of the robe of the Holy filled the temple—just the hem! Isaiah knows without hesitation that he has a language problem. He does not, he cannot, speak their language. He has unclean lips and he lives and talks among others who have unclean lips. His new prophetic vocation is made possible by the fire of hot coals pressed to his lips. Isaiah's brush with Divinity not only entitled him to speak in God's name, but it compelled him to do so. Isaiah's proximity to God changes what he can do and say and hear and be. He simultaneously runs up on both the limits of his language and the horizons of God's mysterious power to transform.

Nicodemus's encounter with Jesus in the Gospel of John (chap. 3) also pushes our understanding to go beyond accepted categories of thinking. Nicodemus was a faithful man seeking understanding. He comes to Jesus in the dark of night, perhaps a little sheepish about seeking out this man whom the Jewish establishment was trying to understand, perhaps afraid of being seen, but yearning still to talk to him and to know him. A linguistic dance ensues. Jesus wants Nicodemus to learn a new vocabulary. The limits of language are coaxed into new territory by the experience of being close to Jesus. This dialogue between

Nicodemus and Jesus becomes a conversation about language, about words and their meaning and how Jesus was to be understood. But it is also a conversation about mystery and being up close to Divinity.

Nicodemus tries to make sense of something he is not up close enough to to truly understand. Jesus uses Nicodemus's mistaken acknowledgment as a teaching moment, a language lesson. He says no one can see the kingdom of God without being born *anothen*. The Greek cannot be adequately translated into English as in the Greek this word holds within it simultaneous meanings: "from above" and "again."[13] It is hard for us to hear both meanings simultaneously, but the writer of this Gospel has Jesus challenging Nicodemus in this exchange to hear the deeper meaning of his teaching. There is a temporal and spatial aspect to the kingdom of God. This new birth clears a space for expanded access to God in an immediate sense. Nicodemus's imagination cannot go there.

Jesus tries another set of metaphors to move Nicodemus into a new space of understanding when he says that one must be "born of water and Spirit." The waters of physical birth and spiritual birth do not negate each other, but instead they require each other for a full immersion into divine relationship. Again, the Scripture uses the subtlety of a word that carries within it layers of meaning—"the wind blows where it chooses and you hear the sound of it, but you do not know where it comes from or where it goes. So it is with everyone who is born of the Spirit" (John 3:8). This Greek word for "wind," *pneuma*, is the same word that is used for "Spirit." We cannot pick and choose our meaning, but we must somehow abide in its inherent complexity. Like the wind, the Spirit can be perceived as present, but as human beings we cannot track its exact movement. This new birth is like that; it is a mystery we can sense, but not completely understand or control.

Nicodemus's last words of this story are: "How can these things be?" Jesus was moving between heaven and earth; he was clearing a space for a new intimacy with God, for new proximity, a new horizon of being in God's presence. The Incarnation was and is an invitation for us to come closer, to listen and feel and see and receive, and to be there in God's presence. We are invited into palpable proximity, a space where our words and ideas and categories run out of steam, a space where the filing systems in our brains cannot find a place to put what is happening. Intimacy with God challenges us to "be there" even as we grope for words to describe, understand, and express divine mystery.

Christian rhetoric about religious identity is frequently wrapped up in the guise of certainty, and if not certainty then ethical integrity. Mainline Protestants do not tend to find language for the fact that our entanglement with God is a body-penetrating mystery. Mystery is a footnote to who we are; sometimes it is a dumping ground for how so many awful things can happen when a loving God is supposed to be in charge. Mystery can also be a way to describe the faith aspect

---

13. The NRSV translates this word as "from above," and in a footnote says that it can also mean "again." The NIV translation does the reverse.

of religious belief—that we do not have to figure everything out, we just believe because we have faith.

Embodying divine mystery is much more concrete than the celestial mysteries we can never explain. Religious experience is not simply an intellectual assent to a great set of moral/ethical standards. It is also not simply a need for a community that has someone bigger than itself at the helm. Embodying divine mystery means we seek out ways to be available to God's capacity to find a home in us. This promise of sanctification is often left to the marginalized traditions of mysticism and negative theology. But far from being on the margins, mystery is at the very heart of religious devotion and experience. Intimacy with God is the heart of Christian identity, and such proximity requires being able to abide in the quiet, ethereal, concrete moments of God incarnate in and among us. We can be close to God and close to the world's pain, including our own. It is what Jesus did, and he told us we could too. Eternal life is a brushstroke of this intimacy with God that allows us to be in the world and not be destroyed by it.

What takes us into Christ's light is more about surrender than it is about semantics. Pseudo-Dionysius wrote his mystical theology out of this recognition. He used the negation of words and concepts and metaphors to point us toward Divinity.

> O Trinity
> beyond essence and
> beyond divinity and
> beyond goodness
> guide of Christians in divine wisdom,
> direct us towards mysticism's heights
> beyond unknowing
> beyond light
> beyond limit,
> there where the
> unmixed and
> unfettered and
> unchangeable
> mysteries of theology
> in the dazzling dark of the welcoming silence
> lie hidden, in the intensity of their darkness
> all brilliance outshining,
> our intellects, blinded—overwhelming,
> . . . .
> released from all,
> aloft to the flashing forth,
> beyond all being, of the divine dark.[14]

14. Pseudo-Dionysius, *Mystical Theology*, in Harvey Egan, ed., *An Anthology of Christian Mysticism* (Collegeville, MN: Liturgical Press, 1991), 96–97.

The "divine dark" invites us into mystery's expansiveness. As Christians, we are not just able to be there, we are, like Isaiah, compelled to be there, to be up close to God's mystery. It is there that we rest in God's massiveness and mercy. It is there that we abide in God's compassion and communication. We are close enough to overhear and drink in what we cannot fully understand.

In *The Secret Life of Bees*, by Sue Monk Kidd, a young woman named Lily finds home among a group of women who tend the bees on their South Carolina farm. Lily's slow walk into this world of effusive love is one that brings her into more and more immediate contact with love and its complex capacity to hold violence and healing and promise and pain. She describes her first encounter with a cluster of beehives in the morning like this:

> According to August, if you've never seen a cluster of beehives first thing in the morning, you've missed the eighth wonder of the world. Picture these white boxes tucked under pine trees. The sun will slant through the branches, shining in the sprinkles of dew drying on the lids. There will be a few hundred bees doing laps around the hive boxes, just warming up, but mostly taking their bathroom break, as bees are so clean they will not soil the inside of their hives. From a distance it will look like a big painting you might see in a museum, but museums can't capture the sound. Fifty feet away you will hear it, a humming that sounds like it came from another planet. At thirty feet your skin will start to vibrate. The hair will lift on your neck. Your head will say, don't go any farther, but your heart will send you straight into the hum, where you will be swallowed by it. You will stand there and think, I am in the center of the universe, where everything is sung to life.[15]

As Christians, we dare to abide in the buzz and vibration of such life. We can surrender to it because we have been up close and felt the warm glow of God's unique transforming power. It is the mysterious dialogue we have been invited to overhear. Your head may say, "Don't go any further," but your heart will send you straight into the hum—into the divine dark, "where everything is sung to life."

The Wound of Fear

One Sunday morning some members of a Holiness church that used a room in our church building decided to come to our worship service to support one of their church members who was singing in our service. These visitors were warm to everyone around them and followed along in the format of our service with great ease. During the sermon they were respectful listeners by letting me, the preacher, know that they were listening. They said "Amen!" and "Yes!" and "Preach!" at points in the sermon to indicate they were coming along with the message. During the anthem they clapped and moved. One person even had his

---

15. Sue Monk Kidd, *The Secret Life of Bees* (New York: Penguin, 2001).

tambourine and played it from the pews. Many people in the congregation that day commented on what a great service it had been and how good it felt to move during the music and to feel like people were being affected by the message.

But others had not been touched this way; rather, they were deeply offended and angry about how worship had gone. One church member, Sue, approached me afterward and said, "I don't have a problem if 'they' want to come to our church, but they have to learn how to be respectful." When I asked her if she wanted our church to be a place that welcomes all kinds of people, she said that she most certainly did. I asked Sue if she felt it was welcoming to ask everyone who shows up to act just like us. She said she would need to think about that. In this particular case, Sue did think about it, and it led her into a deeper exploration of her feelings about race and fear of people who were not like her. For others, this worship service was their reason for leaving the church for good.

Jesus tells us not to be afraid, especially of those who are "other"—like the Samaritan woman at the well (John 4:1–42) and our brothers and sisters in Christ who play the tambourine to worship God. So why are we still so afraid? And what are we afraid of? Our unspoken expectations of conformity reveal themselves in the homogeneity of most mainline congregations. Only 8 percent of all congregations are of mixed ethnicity and race.[16] Historically, Protestant churches have the most unsuccessful record on diversity of any group.[17] Among these mainline churches only 2 to 3 percent are of mixed ethnicity and/ or racial makeup. One of the more interesting statistics is that 11 percent of whites say they worship in an integrated church, but when survey teams visited those congregations they found in most cases that the diversity had been greatly exaggerated.[18]

The homogeneity of most mainline churches is both clearly revealed and strangely concealed. We know this about ourselves, but we are not sure how to admit it. I have heard it said many times in all or mostly white churches that we "tried everything" to no avail to invite diversity. We have set out the welcome mat, but those who are different from us just do not seem to show up. When they do, they are looking for something else so they leave. Homogeneous congregations tend to accept the segregation of church life as part of the way things are that we really cannot change. "They" do not want to come to "our" churches. It is hard to imagine how we could do anything about that. Mary McClintock Fulkerson asserts that many white, able-bodied churchgoers are oblivious to

---

16. The data are from the Multicultural Congregations Project, directed by Michael Emerson, Department of Sociology, Rice University; referenced in John Dart, "Hues in the Pews: Racially Mixed Churches an Elusive Goal," *Christian Century* 108, no. 7 (2001): 6–8. The study defines a mixed congregation as one that has 20 percent or more of its membership who are racially/ethnically diverse.

17. The study finds that Catholic churches are three times more likely than Protestant churches to be multiracial. Also, 25 percent of independent nondenominational churches have a racial mix in which the dominant group was no more than 60 percent of the congregation.

18. See Dart, "Hues in the Pews," and Emerson's Multicultural Congregations Project for a description of this tendency to exaggerate.

their own aversion to those who are different from them or outside their view of "normal."[19] And this obliviousness can and does coexist with clearly articulated mission statements of inclusiveness.[20]

I assert that this aversion and obliviousness are intimately linked to our dis-ease with our own skin, our own bodies. Even when our doctrines, our sacred stories, and our mission statements describe our hope for and commitment to inclusion, our embodied practices and gathered communities speak of our fear of moral chaos and loss of identity. We camouflage our lack of trust in God with who we say that we are. We may unconsciously reject those who are outside the range of our comfort zones even when we believe ourselves to be hospitable to difference. When encounters with "others" stir up subdermal fears of not being who or what we think we are, we repel them without having to say a word. Hav-ing to face the fragments of our own bodies is a deeply repulsive prospect for many of us. When someone intersects with us who embodies the jarring truth that there is contradiction, complexity, and ambiguity in human embodied exis-tence, we fear the chaos they may bring with them. Fear wounds us as the Body of Christ. It trivializes who we are and how the future becomes.

Faith should be the antidote to fear, but fear still grips the church. Lynn Jap-inga writes, "Perhaps 'Fear not' is such an excellent speech because most human beings are afraid of something."[21] She asks: "Why is a church that claims to be confident about the grace of God so fearful about its future?" In our Reformed faith our fears are all encompassed in three categories: fear of the other, fear of being wrong, and fear of being irrelevant.[22] Indeed, our fear of otherness has given rise to fractures, schisms, and splits. Our fear of being wrong stifles conver-sation and keeps us from taking risks with one another. Our fear of irrelevance has weighed the church down with anxiety about its own survival.

Institutional fear has the same antidote as embodied, personal fear. Remem-ber the birthing body and the ruptures caused by fear. Support, affirmation, embodied knowing, and trust are all enfleshed antidotes to the paralyzing effects of fear. When we surrender out of power and not out of fear then we are more response-able. When a woman gives in to the power of her own body, then her body is freed up to do the work it knows how to do. "Fear not!" is not a sugges-tion. It is the cornerstone of Christian life.

19. Mary McClintock Fulkerson, *Places of Redemption: Theology for a Worldly Church* (New York: Oxford University Press, 2007), 20.

20. She traces this bodily habituation and its role particularly through white people in response to people of color and/or differently abled people in a church setting. She calls this obliviousness a wound for white, able bodied people.

21. Lynn Japinga, "Fear in the Reformed Tradition," in *Feminist and Womanist Essays*, ed. Pauw and Jones, 1.

22. Ibid., 4.

In-forming Surrender

What if churches spent more time practicing how to surrender to divine power, to the Christ-living power that vivifies who we are? Isaiah and Paul are two of our forebears who had their fingers on a pulse categorically different from fear. These men were immersed in the world, but not overcome by its cruelty and disappointment. And their visions are not naive. They reflect and refract a strong intention to live toward God. Isaiah invites believers to respond to God's work in the world with thanksgiving: "Surely God is my salvation. I will trust in God; I will not be afraid; God is my strength and my might; with joy I will draw from the well of salvation. . . . I will sing to the Lord" (Isaiah 12:2, 5). Thanksgiving is an act of trust and it is a rejection of fear. It is even the audacity to be joyful in the midst of hardship and peril.

Paul bears this out for us in his letter to the church in Philippi, especially in 4:4–7. Like Isaiah's, Paul's vision of the world is not born out of naiveté or lack of contact with the shadow side of human life. Paul wrote this letter from prison. And Paul was someone who had known fear and loathing. He had at one time built his life around hate. Paul was a man transformed by the compassion and love of Christ. In this letter to a church he loved he wants to extend this disposition of "gentleness," which is how the NRSV and NIV translate *epieikes* (4:5). It is really much more than gentleness; the term suggests generosity toward others. Other translations use words like "forbearance" or "moderation." This gentleness is intimately entwined with compassion. This mode of operation does not just tolerate other people; it is intentional in its generosity toward others. This disposition is not a "live and let live" libertarianism; it is a committed involvement with people. It is the willingness to bear the differences or limitations of another.[23] This disposition is patient and merciful; it is not anxious or harsh. This, according to Paul, is that for which followers of Christ should be known.

In this practice of compassion and gentleness, Christ's mind and heart can become ours. This gentle, generous, thankful heart is not timid. Its boldness comes not from fulfillment or from certainty; it comes from the deeply informed surrender to the way God's unique power works. If we are thankful in all things, then we can even be thankful when God's Spirit intersects our lives with those "others" who scare us so much. We can encounter differences as providential. We can embrace the mystery of this gift in our lives without fear.

In God's plentitude we can also let go of our fear that there is not enough of God's grace to go around. Trusting that means living as if it is true. The church can model how to live in a world of fear with revolutionary embodied compassion and surrender. Hospitality to the stranger can become more than nice welcome packets to give visitors when they walk in the door. This kind of trust

---

23. For instance, giving someone who owes you money more time to pay is one understanding of forbearance. Another example is deliberately not responding to provocation.

in God means that we embrace the strangers who walk in and embody the "otherness" that we fear the most because they are there for us. The church cannot be church without them. Theological, racial, economic, and other expressions of differences are not just a nice idea. They are an embodied necessity for the Body of Christ to thrive. Our interdependence is linked into all of these "others." Our embodied interdependence means that ruptured relationships with those we "otherize" diminish our lives in Christ. Like a good midwife, the saints of the church can support and attend to difference and the new life it can birth.

Christian community is no place for fear. When we cast out fear, we expect and we embody great things: an end to racism, an end to homophobia, and an end to violence. We expect and embody the day when justice flows and promises are fulfilled. We look for it, we anticipate it, and we dispose ourselves accordingly. Being informed by surrender is not easy for mainline Protestants. We are accustomed to being in control. This act of trust means that Caucasian Protestants, in particular, may need to reflect on their fears and the privileges whites in particular have secured by letting fear dictate how our communities are formed and function. Such vulnerability is only palatable when we re-member ourselves in God's hands.

IN-FORMATION

When Barbara came into the venerable sanctuary and spoke in tongues, she embodied a gift of God's imagination for us. She gifted this congregation that had been completely white for most of its history and intensely Presbyterian in all of its practice with a new way to see ourselves. She inhabited her body as a religious person in a way that was "other" to most people who encountered her in this church. And mysteriously, she was what we needed to awaken our own sleeping hopes that we are truly open to God's effusive presence in our lives. The gift of Barbara's presence was more than our minds could explain. Most members of the congregation never even knew she was there. And yet she in-formed us even so.

Chapter 7

Re-membering the Body of Christ

God's Eye

Green pulses of
    life giving wind
     wafting and smiling
      me into myself—
       God's child, daughter of Divinity's goad to create.

Fresh air traveled
    and was sure of its freedom—
    shifting and drifting
    through the pillows of something alive.

Blue sky or expanse—
    Blue eternity there
    close and stretching all around itself,
    surrounding me with clean open hands.

There is movement and rhythm,
    dancing motion that sways
     and leans me into
      solid ground

An ethereal countenance re-members where I have been
    and sips on the peaceful nectar of now.
    Sing, move, gestate, gyrate, and be still.

INTRODUCTION

Barbara was not the only one who showed up at that church in California who brought her body along with her. Many others embodied their deep-tissue devotion to God in the way they moved around in that place. They stretched the church to grow into itself. They acquainted us with estranged layers of ourselves. Decades of changes in the inner city had left this beautiful Gothic cathedral, which could seat more than three thousand people, with a sprinkling of less than one hundred people for worship on Sundays. At some point they had put barbed wire along part of the property to protect this sacred architecture from the tough world that surrounded it. When a new pastor arrived, shortly before I began my ministry there, they took the barbed wire down.

As the barbed wire came down, we caught more and more glimpses of what zestful ministry could look like in that neighborhood. Embodied tragedy, relationality, and ambiguity were immediate to the Christ-living in that place. The work was rich and excruciating. The more we acknowledged the truth of who we were, the more deeply we were disposed toward God's unlikely movements among us. We began to see these seeming interruptions and differences as support for a new way to be church. It was the most blessed and most difficult experience I have had in ministry. Life in the Body of Christ should be nothing less.

RE-MEMBERING THE BODY OF CHRIST

What if we brought our bodies with us to church? What if church was a place that healed our bodies, helped us wake up to our bodies, and gave us a way to embrace our bodies? The wounds of intellectualization and fear need us to attend to the unconscious layers of our collective lives. These wounds have hindered who the church is and even our vision of what the church can be.

In the midst of all the institutional limitations of the church, we still expect God to show up in what and how we do, say, and feel things there. Our expectation for proximity with the Divine is particularly palpable in how we worship. The yearning to be close to God, to please God, to do right by God, and to thank God draw us into worship. This yearning comes from a place deep inside us where a spark of divine purpose and affection flickers. From that flicker we recognize sparks of God's unique power around us and within us. This visceral intuition of Divinity burns within us, and worship embodies this glowing truth about us.

So, why do we come to worship with such a thin layer of ourselves? And why does our worship enforce such controlled, dis-membered encounters with the One who feeds our desire in such deep, embodied places? What if we brought our bodies with us to church? Perhaps what we fear most is being vulnerable to the chaos of something like ecstatic speech or other strange, uncomfortable brushes with divine whimsy. Or maybe we do not know our bodies well enough to believe they could be so moved. This estrangement from our bodies runs deep into subdermal layers of our disembodied faith; we are estranged from our-selves and from the One who created us. These deep blockages, just like those in our own bodies, are profoundly formative but beneath our awareness. They are obscured by well-worn habits, traditions, and "best" practices. When we rest too comfortably in our accepted ways of doing things, we trivialize the encounter with Divinity that worship embodies.

God's-Eye View

Worship is the intentional expression of thanksgiving to God. It helps shape our lives into a seamless expression of thanksgiving. Worship directs us toward God's vision for us. It forms and in-forms us. In this formational sense, worship meets us where we are.[1] Even while we honor and acknowledge this important layer of worship's efficacy for us, we are deeply shaped by our Reformed heritage's empha-sis on the objective nature of worship. Worship is about God, not about us. This important theological foundation, however, somehow in many mainline contexts became confused with a condemnation of embodied expressions of emotion in worship, whether they are elicited by grief or delight or anything in between.

There are the foils to this moratorium on emotion in more emotionally charged expressions of Protestantism.[2] But many mainline churches place their practices over and against such "feeling-based" worship. Both a disembodied objective view of worship and an intensely subjective orientation to worship truncate the space that bodies take up in how we worship. After all, feeling as we have explored it in this project is not emotion, but interdependent, embodied experience. When we are intentional in our collective encounter with Divinity we are more than each of our emotional twinges or even the sum of all of them. We are bodies tangled up into this promise of being something more—the Body of Christ in the world.

This re-membered embodied Body that we are empowered to become fills us with possibilities of ennobling ways of being together, of a generous ethic of sharing, and of a confessional knowledge of eternity. But this tangle of re-membered limbs and tissues is more than a sanction for behaviors, lifestyles, belief sets, and moral codes. This re-membering transforms us down deep in the caverns of our cells and our hearts, our hands and feet, and our intuitions and dispositions. What would it look like for us to bring our bodies with us to church and drink in the God-centered nature of what worship is?

---

1. John Calvin suggests this formational/pedagogical layer of worship in his writing. And the Presbyterian commitment to the pedagogical aspects of worship became even more apparent in the Scottish Presbyterian focus on moral formation. The rhythms of Reformed worship call us to give thanks, hear the Word proclaimed, and respond to this Word with our lives.

2. As discussed briefly in chapter 6, in the American context the birth of Pentecostalism is a later reaction to even the absence of "spiritual baptism" in Baptist churches. See Elsie Mason, "Bishop C. H. Mason, Church of God in Christ," in *Afro-American Religious History: A Documentary Witness,* ed. Milton C. Sernett (Durham: Duke University Press, 1987), 285–95.

Who Do We Say That We Are?

Reformed worship blesses Christians all over the world with attention to Scripture, substantive proclamation, expansive prayers of the people, corporate confession, and rich musical heritage. The rhythms of Reformed worship invite believers to respond to God's Word with the way we live our lives. Closer attention to embodiment does not mean abandoning any of the church's important commitments to how worship forms us ethically and morally. This attentiveness to bodies does bring a few theological and practical questions to the surface: How can we believe in redeemed and resurrected bodies and diminish the body's role in our sanctification and formation to the degree that we do in mainline Protestantism? How can we be an incarnational faith and worship in ways that give our bodies such minimal room? Where are the sacred spaces for embodied responsiveness, participation, and joy? How much do we harm our own bodies and the Body of Christ when the need for order, for a certain genre of music, or for particular kinds of prayer become the sole determining factors in how we worship? Implicit in all these questions is the quandary of how to make room for the mystery of religious experience in all of its variety and unruliness. In mainline Protestant practice these unruly aspects of faith are often seen as irrational, overly emotional, and intellectually embarrassing.[3]

We grope for ways to feel our way in the embodied layers of religious life. The constant residue of mystery does not delegitimize religious devotion; it is the very condition of possibility for the existence of religion. There is no shame in the fact that we have palpable experiences that nourish our capacity to believe in miracles or at least to pique our awareness of a poetic hand at work in life's tapestry. Worship expresses our gratitude for the ways God's goodness weaves itself through us and through our common life. It expresses our deep yearning for God to stay close by and to inhabit every part of who we are—including our flesh-and-blood bodies.

This chapter invites mainline churches to consider some of our tendencies in worship in light of what we know about the tragic, relational, and ambiguous natures of our bodies. This invitation does not radically shift our worship orientation from God to our own experiences. On the contrary, this invitation ushers us into the deep intentionality of living an embodied life ordered toward God, filled with God's Spirit, and transformed by Jesus Christ. The objective nature of worship in Reformed theology correctly protects the transcendent nature of this liminal moment in human life. Bringing our bodies to church says we believe that God wants all of us, every part of who we are and how we are made. Bringing our bodies to church honors the blessed fact that Christianity is an incarnational faith. Embodied redemption is not simply an idea for some day in eternity; it is a cellular reality today. Worship can re-member this gift.

---

3. A related dynamic is the fact that theology remains on shaky ground in the landscape of the academic study of religion—for some it outthinks itself, for others it cannot escape the illegitimacy of confession.

RE-MEMBERING WORSHIP

Three movements in the rhythms of Reformed worship have the capacity to awaken and stretch our bodies into worshipful encounter with God. Confession, the Lord's Supper, and music each have this potential for bodies to take up more space in how we lean into God's sacred promise to be with us. There is no script for embodying these practices more deeply. We cannot think our way into this rhythm of being present to God. Letting God's presence seep into us and letting our awareness intuit this blessed truth takes practice and space for idiosyncrasy. Confession provides space for embodied healing. The Lord's Supper can deepen our experience of connection. And music can kindle in us a revitalized sensation of devotion, healing, interpretation, and thanksgiving. Embodied healing, connecting, and revitalizing re-member how we are made and how we can flourish.

Tragedy, Compassion, and Confession

When Jesus saw him lying there and knew that he had been there
a long time, he said to him, "Do you want to be made well?"
John 5:6

Thirty-eight years he survived, this man with the mat in John's Gospel. He learned how to live with an illness, he learned how to keep going, and he apparently also learned how to accept his own helplessness. There were concrete reasons why this man had never made it to the pool. We can picture him there, lost in the shuffle of all the invalids. Yes, survival is a skill. The longer we are at it, the better we get at it and the more entrenched our strategies for survival become. Some of those strategies are good for us, others we need to learn to let go of, and still others become something we cease to recognize. They become unconscious, second nature.

Jesus says, "Do you want to be made well?" That is a tough question for us. How ready are we to get up and take our mat and walk into new well-being? Churches are full of people like you and me who are not sure if we are really ready to be well. We find comfort in the familiar even in our brokenness. We do not want to be honest in church about who we really are or the pain we really have. And we really do not feel like we can trust some unreliable, chaotic, disorderly Holy Spirit that blows in and out at will without so much as a little warning that we have to let go of so much.

And why should we let go? Do we really believe this healing promise, this promise of whatever kind of healing it is that God tells us we can have? Do we really drink in the forgiveness, the peace that passes understanding, the deep assurances of God's unique power? If we do, it will change us. If it sinks in, it will transform us. It will change the way we live and breathe. It will change the way we feel and the way we want to be. Can we look ourselves in the eye and feel the integrity of an embodied yes to Jesus?

The first step to being made well is telling the truth. Confession is our moment of truth; it is our time to be honest about who we are. This moment of truth in worship has traditionally circled solely around our sin.[4] Confession is our time to fess up about all of our shortcomings, all of our missteps, all of our failures, and to our prideful refusal to be who God calls us to be. This kind of truth telling is important and should not be abandoned. But it acknowledges only a fraction of who we are and the truth we need to tell. Limiting the practice of confession only to the sin-guilt-forgiveness cycle in Christian piety blocks deep layers of healing that this moment of truth has to offer us.

Sin, indeed, is more than messing up. Sin is an orientation toward the world that misses the truth. But it is a bitter irony that our most pious moment of self-understanding in worship offers only the category of sin as our way of understanding and expressing ourselves. The irony is that when sin is the only way we see ourselves, we allow it to rule us with a tenacious power. We entrench the power of that from which we are seeking freedom. We are silent about the suffering we experience that is no fault of our own. We are silent about how much it hurts to live in a world as tragic as ours is. We are oblivious to our own redemptive capacity.

Our truth is not just that we are disobedient, misguided, estranged, and willful. Our truth is also that we are broken and tired and in need of more love than we seem to get sometimes. Our truth is also that we were created good and made to flourish. Our truth is also that God is at work in us sanctifying and redeeming whatever those raw places of pain might be. When we do not tell the whole truth, we in effect continue to live a lie.

We are sinful, yes, but we are also redeemed—and therefore our lives are fertile ground for the gifts of the Holy Spirit to take hold in us. The Christian life has always been about more than just repentance. This life embodies the gift of transformation, this gift that gives us the power to live toward God. It is a gift that reaches those most secret places in our hearts. It empowers us to let God be there in the shadows of our lives.

Do you want to be well? We can be wise to the complicated texture of our inheritance. Re-membering intertwines souls and institutions, hearts and systems. Re-membering empowers the Body of Christ to be courageous in its embrace of indeterminacy, audacious in its quest to be available to God's mysterious activity. Re-membering brings believers to rest not in the familiar, but in

---

4. William A. Dyrness describes this theological system clearly. "Confession is necessary, quite simply, because we are sinners. . . . Our problem is that we do not ordinarily connect our feelings of inadequacy or loneliness with God, or with our estrangement from God. We often do not even connect them with any failure or mistake on our part . . . in various ways we seek to avoid facing our failures" ("Confession and Assurance/Sin and Grace," in *A More Profound Alleluia: Theology and Worship in Harmony*, ed. Leanne Van Dyk [Grand Rapids: Eerdmans, 2005], 33–34). So, according to Dyrness, when these feelings of our human experience do not intuitively match up with the theological category of sin, that too is a failure on our part to understand the depth of our sin. He leaves no room for the possibility that these kinds of human experiences may actually spring from other conditions of our existence.

the ongoing renewal of God's redemptive work. Confession is not just a survival skill, it is an embodied practice that re-members the truth of our redemption.

This moment of truth in our worship cannot be just words; we need practices that wear the new creek beds of our compassion in the face of all suffering. We center ourselves in God's mercy with humility and a sense of support, safety, and assurance. We trust God enough to tell the truth. We move into a sacred space where we can be who we are. We can tell the truth, we can see ourselves and be seen. Centering music can invite worshipers to be more fully present to this sacred space. Expanded silence with permission to move, kneel, weep, lay down a burden, or be still can stretch this practice into our bodies.[5] Confession could include healing liturgies, anointing with oil, laying on hands, and movement forward for prayer. God will surely inhabit our embodied intuitions about the kinds of truth than can set us free.

Relationality, Interdependence, and Eucharist

"How can this man give us his flesh to eat?" So Jesus said to them, "Very truly, I tell you, unless you eat the flesh of the Son of Man and drink his blood, you have no life in you. . . . for my flesh is true food and my blood is true drink."

John 6:52–53, 55

What if Jesus' words are not just food for thought? Life in Christ includes our whole bodies, even the rawest places inside us. Jesus wants to nourish us there. But this passage in John has a strange ring to our ears. "Eat my flesh and drink my blood" sounds bizarre, even inappropriate, to our refined ears. Making Jesus' words metaphorical tempers their jarring sound. Surely Jesus is not really talking about his flesh and blood, but about some kind of spiritualized assent to who he was and is. That sounds more like something we can hear. The metaphor lets us keep our distance from the words themselves. And this metaphorical interpretation authorizes our perceptions of embodied distance from each other, from our own bodies, and from everything that lives and breathes.[6]

---

5. As it currently stands in most traditional Reformed worship the balance tips in favor of more corporate spoken prayer and a brief silent time. If the balance shifted the other way and we let our bodies participate more fully in our corporate truth telling, this practice could cultivate more deeply embedded dispositions of compassion. Silence does not necessarily make confession a private affair. Silence in a corporate context is profoundly connective and collective. Our shared sin and suffering could find expression in ways other than words.

6. It strikes me as no coincidence that the tiny individual cups so typical in eucharistic practice were the creation of American Presbyterians in the nineteenth century because of fears about germs. This distancing and fear of too much embodied entanglement has added to the disembodied way we experience the Lord's Supper. James F. White puts it this way: "Whatever else they believe, Americans believe devoutly in germs. In 1894, members of Central Presbyterian Church in Rochester, New York, became convinced that only by using small individual communion glasses could people come to the eucharist without fear" (*The Sacraments in Protestant Practice and Faith* [Nashville: Abingdon, 1999], 95).

In our Reformed context we also distance ourselves from this language of ingesting Jesus because of the biases of our theological heritage. We have a deep communal distrust of any whiff of the Roman Catholic concept of the bread and wine really turning into the actual body and blood of Jesus Christ. Much of the scholarly wrangling on this passage tends to correlate with whether the scholar is part of the Catholic tradition or the Reformed tradition.[7] Reformed scholars tend to say that any sacramental meaning here is probably put in by a later editor who wanted to correct this Gospel writer's antisacramental tendencies. Much of this sacramental theologizing got tangled up long ago with Enlightenment thinking about substance.[8] Understanding Jesus' words got bogged down in rational philosophy, church politics, and liturgical practices built around maintaining theological turf about how flesh turns into bread, and blood into wine. The rich theological discussion that defined the Reformation era around the Eucharist has mostly been lost on us, so much so that experience of the true body and blood of Christ in the Lord's Supper is perhaps not even an expectation of ours.

In order to avoid all of this strange talk of metamorphosis and eating flesh, Reformed thinking has conventionally tended toward making the sacrament more of a memorial meal. This swing toward memorial trivializes the theological struggle of even Ulrich Zwingli himself, to whom this view is often attributed.[9] The triviality of only remembering is especially palpable when we consider John Calvin's strong dependence on the Holy Spirit's intervention in the Communion meal. In Calvin's thinking we are clearly not to leave the sacrament at a memorial moment. We encounter the actual body and blood of Christ somehow, in the mystery of the Holy Spirit, through the communal Eucharist.[10] Yet our trivialized view of the sacrament keeps the Lord's Supper at arm's length and is a deeply formative layer of our disembodied inheritance.

There are theological reasons and historical reasons to explore the sacrament more deeply than a simply metaphorical interpretation allows. There are also important existential reasons why we come up short if we reduce it down to just a metaphor or memory. While these orientations toward Eucharist may be on grammatically firm ground and even on exegetically firm ground, where do these interpretations leave our bodies?[11] We keep our distance from Jesus, just like those who questioned the rationality of his pronouncement at the time. "How can this man give us his flesh to eat?" How can this be? How can Jesus want to

---

7. Gail O'Day, "Excursus: John 6:51c–58 in Critical Scholarship," in *New Interpreter's Bible*, ed. Leander E. Keck (Nashville: Abingdon, 1995), 9:606–7.

8. White has a solid discussion of this use of philosophy to describe and justify theological concepts about the Eucharist in *Sacraments*, 75–84.

9. See White on Zwingli and the Wesleys, ibid., 81.

10. The Scots Confession of 1560 says of the sacrament of the Lord's Supper: "this union and conjunction which we have with the body and blood of Christ Jesus in the right use of the sacraments is wrought by means of the Holy Ghost, who by true faith carries us above all things that are visible, carnal, and earthly, and makes us feed upon the body and blood of Christ Jesus."

11. Herman Waetjen spends a fascinating few pages debunking "cannibalism" in these verses: *The Gospel of the Beloved Disciple: A Work in Two Editions* (New York: T&T Clark, 2005), 214ff.

get so close to us? Why would Jesus want to be inside us? This intimate prospect invades and offends us. We are afraid to get that close. It is too personal, too strange, too undignified for us.

But Jesus does not stop. "Those who eat my flesh and drink my blood abide in me, and I in them" (John 6:56). Jesus wants to be inside you and me. He manifests the metaphor; he embodies the cellular poetics. He does not want to just be outside as a great man who did great things and a good example of how to live. Jesus wants to be inside you and me, inside us that we might share the same body and blood, that we might be his body in this world. This is not simply an ethical argument—it is an ontological argument. It is about our essential selves, the rawest places of the soul. It is about our created nature, our proper nature. That is where Jesus wants to be, not just in your head, but in your heart and soul, even in your flesh and blood, in your bones.

The Lord's Supper does not just remember who Jesus was and what he did for us. The Lord's Supper re-members Jesus Christ, the promises he made to be with us, to guide us, to in-form us, to dwell in us, and to transform us. We put this Body back together when we gather around this bread and cup.[12] We are reconciled with who Jesus Christ was and is; we are reconciled with ourselves and the way we were made and the way we can flourish. We are reconciled with one another and with all the entanglements of being alive—with wind, wheat, fruit, sensation, soil, rain, and labor. Re-membering rejoins body parts that have been harmed, severed, maimed, mutilated, or displaced. Re-membering reconnects, reintegrates, and rejoins body parts that have been dis-membered. Re-membering puts the body back together in line with its redeemed state, in line with God's offer of life abundant. There is an ethical model and mandate, and much more to this practice of chewing, swallowing, sharing, serving, and being fed.

Remembering the Body of Christ means re-membering our bodies as redeemed by the Body of Christ, by the promise of God embodied. Re-membered bodies are bodies "heard" and honored for their spiritual capacity, even as they are known in their limitation. Liturgies could expand our intuitions of these reconnections embodied in the meal by giving language, spoken and figurative (body) language, to the relationships that made the bread and the wine, how they were made, how they got to that place, where they came from, and how their making impacted the created world with the kind of soil and care that served its growth. Dispositions of interdependence seek practices that speak a poetics of embodied intercession. Eucharistic practice could more explicitly welcome those who are disconnected to come and share the meal—a practice that could joyfully stand in direct opposition to past practices that fenced off the Communion table to those who were "unworthy."

12. Paul Galbreath describes an "active form of remembering" that came alive for him in Don Saliers's words at the table, "Do this for the re-membering of me" (*Leading from the Table* [Herndon, VA: Alban Institute, 2008], 40). I am suggesting moving this "activity" even deeper into the cells of our flesh and blood. I would add that the re-membering I am suggesting is also not just cellular or muscle memory. This re-membering is the expression of cellular interdependence.

The ethical mandate of this feast that glimpses God's kingdom can go even deeper. The sacrament is not a metaphor or simply a sign for sharing, for abundance, for generosity, and for justice. The sacrament embodies these blessed ways we are tangled up with everything that is. And the mystery of God inhabiting our flesh and blood sinks in as we chew and sip.

Ambiguity, Adventure, and Music

Be careful then how you live . . . do not be foolish, but under-
stand what the will of the Lord is. Do not get drunk with wine,
for that is debauchery; but be filled with the Spirit, as you sing
psalms and hymns and spiritual songs among yourselves, singing
and making melody to the Lord in your hearts, giving thanks to
God the Father at all times and for everything in the name of our
Lord Jesus Christ.

Ephesians 5:15, 17–20

In the middle of a government housing development in a city in North Carolina sat a humble church building that could not have been further from the Gothic architecture of that church in California. Simple, spare, and rough along the edges, this church was a healing ministry for many layers of life in its community. This church offered job training programs, parenting classes, after-school programs, a preschool, and a prison ministry. Worship on Sundays was a remarkable blend of solid, prophetic preaching and rousing gospel music all placed in the orderly movement of Reformed worship. I loved this church at first because of the good work it did in the community. The music was another story.

I was raised in the typical Presbyterian church with a commitment to excellence in its music program. The music was beautiful and intensely well crafted. Like many Presbyterian churches we had a wonderful organ and gifted music directors who could make the most of the instrument. Many highly trained musicians graced our worship. I still love that music and the hymns that I learned from the beginning of my life. The worship was formal and the music conformed to what many of us can recognize as "typical" Presbyterian standards.[13] So the improvisational, responsive music at this little North Carolina church took some getting used to for me. Honestly, at first it did not measure up to my theological or musical standards.

---

13. Dean Chapman's *How to Worship as a Presbyterian* (Louisville: Geneva, 2001) describes what I refer to as "typical" in his effort to prescribe the appropriate use of music in worship. Music is "offering not entertainment," and therefore "certain behaviors are more appropriate for choir members." He lists them: "(a) keep your eyes on the director; (b) wear robes (or similar simple dress . . .); (c) move only in concert with the rest of the choir; (d) be seated quietly following the anthem; and (e) trust God to accept your offering, and let it go!" (60).

I was startled when these new melodies got inside me and I learned a few by heart. "I Am Coming Up on the Rough Side of the Mountain" was the song the choir was singing when I really woke up to what it could mean to bring my body to church. I was sitting in the third pew on the right side as one faces the pulpit singing along with the choir.[14]

> I'm coming up on the rough side of the mountain,
> and I will hold to God and his powerful hand . . .
> and I'm doing my best to make it in.

I looked into the eyes of the women and men in the choir and they looked at me. And I saw their stories of pain and strength: drug addiction, affliction, illness, loneliness, poverty, betrayal and exclusion, divorce and disappointment. They stood up there and sang out loud about the Jesus I had known only privately in the shadows of my life. The Jesus I always heard about at church was the Jesus who expected a lot of me and who died for the horrible things I had done. But here, in full view of everyone, they were not afraid to tell about the same Jesus who held me in the dark in my secret shame, the Jesus who had whispered to me that all would be well, the Jesus who stayed with me in the shadows when no one else did.

As we sang and sang that morning I started to feel a flood of grief come rushing from way down inside. Tears flowed out like an underground spring that had just found earth that would give way. I could not stand up. I had to sit down and just cry because I had been coming up on the rough side of the mountain for so long, and I had lived in absolute fear that someone might find out. Church had never been where I could tell the truth that my life did not fit together the way it was supposed to. But here they understood with more than words. They understood with gestures, swaying, tears, and joy. They understood with the countenance of embodied knowing. They knew, and they were wise people, not foolish. They knew that the will of God was for us to do more than just survive. They knew Jesus wanted better for us; Jesus wants us to thrive and be filled with the Spirit.

There are lots of ways to be filled with the Spirit as music kindles our hearts to God. What I woke up to that day was how profoundly church is diminished when worship denies us room for feeling bodies—for tragic, entangled, ambiguous bodies. We cannot help but come to church with our bodies that feel, with the fragments of who we are that do not make sense. But church should not be a place that further disconnects us from how God inhabits these complicated bodies of ours.

Music has the capacity to embody our worship in a way nothing else in human life can. Music is not just words, but rhythms, tones, deep poetic

---

14. At this church every song the choir sang eventually became congregational singing, too.

expression, complicated harmonies, and minor keys. It elicits and expresses more than just our taste for what sounds nice, but our taste for the Divine. The so-called worship wars in mainline Protestantism staged mostly as a standoff between "traditional" and "contemporary" music is really a false argument.[15] How music graces our worship is not a matter of style. It is a matter of sacred encounter. The problem in mainline Protestantism is that too many churches have mistaken their preferred genre of music as the best way to preserve the sacred purpose of worship.

I have worked with some remarkably talented musicians. They have amazed me with their skill and hard work and ethereal touch in the music they love. The steep learning curve for many music directors is not about being able to do something different. The place that demands careful work, prayer, and conversation for them is about whether doing something different compromises the sacred purpose of worship. In other words, the fear of many fine church musicians is that if we are simply catering to taste, then we have lost our way. If we are changing our music to entertain, then we have lost our way. If we are simply trying to wake up sleeping congregations, then we have lost our way. In all of these concerns they are absolutely correct to take great care with why we, as mainline Protestants who pride ourselves on excellence in our music, would stretch into territory that seems dangerous or at least dubious.

Tuning in to our bodies expands this conversation about music in the church into a richer, thicker space than one about taste, style, pragmatics, or even fears of compromising our principles. Calvin himself said, "Hence it is perfectly clear that neither words nor singing (if used in prayer) are of the least consequence, or avail one iota with God, unless they proceed from deep feeling in the heart. Nay, rather they provoke his anger against us, if they come from the lips and throat only, since this is to abuse his sacred name, and hold his majesty in derision."[16] Tuning in to our bodies invites us to stretch into expanded musical expression in worship so that we might better honor what we know about our bodies. Expecting the Body of Christ to find one mode of musical expression disembodies believers. Welcoming new musical forms into worship disposes us toward the adventuresome layers of life in Christ.

Habitual denial of embodied feeling harms us all. Bach, gospel, praise music, Handel, and Taizé can help feeling to flow toward God's best hopes for us. Harpsichord, dulcimer, guitar, drum, and banjo can inflame our hearts for God just as organ and piano can. Both rich hymnody and simple call and response can give voice to our thanksgiving, grief, and hope. The integrity of worship rests in our intention, not in stubborn tradition. Our heritage is to resist the idols of insti-

---

15. Thomas G. Long describes this battle well in *Beyond the Worship Wars: Building Vital and Faithful Worship* ([Bethesda, MD]: Alban Institute, 2001).

16. John Calvin, *The Institutes of the Christian Religion*, 3.20.31, trans. Henry Beveridge, 2 vols. (repr. Grand Rapids: Eerdmans, 1995), 2:180.

tutions entrenched in their own habituated practice. That spirit of protest that gave birth to mainline churches came from a subdermal troubling in the souls of devoted believers. These Reformers resisted the well-worn habits of tradition and dogmatic certainty, and they began the slow work of wearing new creek beds of how to do and be church. This is our heritage, this legacy of trusting God's flame in each of us to guide us in a new song.

"MAY WE KINDLE TO THY DANCING"

One Sunday at the church in California where Barbara spoke in tongues and barbed wire became a thing of the past, we gathered for worship. Like every Sunday we told the truth about ourselves, we heard the Word proclaimed, we sang together, and we left the doors wide open. We were slowly adding some new songs to our worship repertoire. While we were singing "Order My Steps," a song we were trying to learn by heart, a man walked in from the back of the church. He walked down the long aisle in that cathedral space, all the way to right in front of the chancel. He had tattered clothes and shoes that did not match. He had all his belongings with him in plastic Safeway grocery bags. He had on lab goggles and surgical gloves.

The look of wonder on his face while he made his way down that long aisle was beautiful, ethereal almost. As he walked in everyone took note. A few people looked perplexed. But we kept singing and the piano kept playing.

> Order my steps in your word, Dear Lord,
> Lead me, guide me, every day.
> Send your anointing, Father, I pray.
> Order my steps in your word.

> [We kept singing. He kept coming forward.]

> I want to walk worthy,
> Thy calling to fulfill,
> Please order my steps, Lord,
> And I'll do your blessed will.

The man put his things down in the very front of the church. And he started to dance right in front of the Communion table. He danced like ancient ones around a sacred fire.

> When I need a brand new song to sing,
> Show me how to let your praises ring.
> In your word, in your word.
> Order my steps in your word.

We kept singing and he kept dancing. I am not sure how long we went on. It was sacred time.

When the singing and dancing faded, I went up to him and said I was glad he was there and showed him where he could sit down on the front pew. He pulled out a telephone. It was not a cell phone, but one of those phones with the push buttons and all the cords. He held the receiver up to me and said, "I've got a call for you. God told me to come here."

The service ended with a laying on of hands to send me off because it was my last day in ministry there. The whole congregation came forward to bless me on my journey and he, that man who came in and danced, quietly stood right next to me with his hand on my shoulder during the whole thing.

One of the church's elders came up to me afterward. She was a white member of the congregation who had been working hard to trust what God was doing in our changing church. She had been in the middle of much of the church's transition from a bunker mentality to an open door. She said, "When I saw that man walk in today, I thought to myself. . . ." And I held my breath, because I was not sure where she was going with her comment. She said, ". . . I thought to myself, we must be doing something right."

God is amazingly resourceful. God knows what we need and works wonders to get it to us. God knows full well how much you and I can do, and God knows, too, how much you and I stand to gain if we embrace these promises with all of who we are. But we have to be willing to see and accept support from places we have not expected to before, and we have to be willing to be vulnerable, not sometimes, but all the time. By vulnerable I mean open to the fact that God is doing something all the time in your life to persuade you to be who you were made to be. Embodied wisdom can come from unlikely places, like from a man with lab goggles with his possessions in three Safeway bags. For God, such startling experience is fair play, and it just may be what saves us.

Scripture tells us again and again that this is the way God works: Jesus asks a Samaritan woman for a drink, a man gets up and walks after thirty-eight years of sickness, a Canaanite woman changes Jesus' mind, God entrusts a man with a speech impediment with the most important road trip in history. Jesus tells us to eat his body and drink his blood. God lives and breathes and dies and rises. What kind of God is this, who would do such unlikely things to give us what we need? The kind of God who emptied God's self to get closer to us, to tell us what we need to hear, to show us how we need to live, and to hold us close enough that we can breathe in divine winds of change.

This is the God who made us with nerve endings, synapses, marrow, and dividing cells. God made us this way. And God takes the write-offs, the castoffs, the invalids, the despised and puts them at the center of our salvation story. And God says, "Trust me." We can be broken and strong. We can be a source of healing and in need of compassion. We can be a light in someone's shadows and the one who needs a hand to lead us out of a painful place. We can be God's children, called out to change the world, and we can be God's children, confused and lonely, just needing to be held for a while. What a blessed space God has cleared for us to be well.

We can be part of a healing revolution by bringing our bodies with us to worship on Sundays. We can sing and dance and feel our way to a renewal and revival of the Body of Christ. We can embody new zest by feeling God's vibrating music of redemption. This music yearns to course through our veins and strengthen the heartbeat of our gatherings. It longs to in-form us, to transform us, and to teach us how to dance. Surely it is the adventure of God's beautiful mystery that breathes life into dry bones, that allows dead bodies to rise, and heals the Body of Christ with bodies chewing on bread and swallowing wine.

God has laid sinews on the dry bones and has caused flesh to come on them. God has put breath in these bones so that they will live. This is the work of hope that never breathes its last. And the bones dance!

Selected Bibliography

American Psychiatric Association. *Diagnostic and Statistical Manual of Mental Disorders.* 4th ed. Washington, DC: American Psychiatric Association, 1994.

Anderson, Kenneth N., ed. *Mosby's Medical, Nursing, & Allied Health Dictionary.* 5th ed. St. Louis: Mosby, 1998.

Arms, Suzanne. *Immaculate Deception II: Myth, Magic, and Birth.* Berkeley: Celestial Arts, 1994.

Armstrong, Karen. *The Battle for God: A History of Fundamentalism.* New York: Ballantine, 2000.

Awiatka, Marilou. *Selu: Seeking the Corn-Mother's Wisdom.* Golden, CO: Fulcrum, 1993.

Bass, Ellen, and Laura Davis. *The Courage to Heal: A Guide for Women Survivors of Child Sexual Abuse.* Rev. ed. London: Vermilion, 1990.

Benhabib, Seyla. *Situating the Self: Gender, Community, and Postmodernism in Contemporary Ethics.* New York: Routledge, 1992.

Bordo, Susan. *Unbearable Weight: Feminism, Western Culture, and the Body.* Berkeley: University of California Press, 1993.

Buchwald, Emilie, Pamela Fletcher, and Martha Roth, eds. *Transforming a Rape Culture.* Minneapolis: Milkweed, 1993.

Buechner, Frederick. *The Final Beast.* New York: Atheneum, 1965.

Butler, Judith. *Bodies That Matter.* New York: Routledge, 1993.

_____. *Gender Trouble: Feminism and the Subversion of Identity.* New York: Routledge, 1990.

_____. *The Psychic Life of Power: Theories in Subjection.* Stanford: Stanford University Press, 1997.

Byars, Ronald P. *The Future of Protestant Worship: Beyond the Worship Wars.* Louisville: Westminster John Knox, 2002.

Calvin, John. *The Institutes of the Christian Religion.* Translated by Henry Beveridge. 2 vols. Repr. Grand Rapids: Eerdmans, 1995.

Capacchione, Lucia, and Sandra Bardsley. *Creating a Joyful Birth Experience.* New York: Simon & Schuster, 1994.

Caruth, Cathy, ed. *Trauma: Explorations in Memory.* Baltimore: Johns Hopkins University Press, 1995.

Chapman, Dean. *How to Worship as a Presbyterian.* Louisville: Geneva, 2001.

Chodorow, Nancy. *The Reproduction of Mothering*. Berkeley: University of California Press, 1978.

Chopp, Rebecca. *The Power to Speak: Feminism, Language, God*. New York: Crossroad, 1992.

Christian, William A. *An Interpretation of Whitehead's Metaphysics*. New Haven: Yale University Press, 1959.

Clarke, Erskine. *Dwelling Place: A Plantation Epic*. New Haven: Yale University Press, 2005.

Cobb, John B., Jr., and David Ray Griffin. *Process Theology: An Introductory Exposition*. Philadelphia: Westminster, 1976.

Collins, Patricia Hill. *Black Feminist Thought: Knowledge, Consciousness, and the Politics of Empowerment*. New York: Routledge, 1991.

Cooper-White, Pamela. *The Cry of Tamar: Violence against Women and the Church's Response*. Minneapolis: Fortress, 1995.

Crittenden, Ann. *The Price of Motherhood: Why the Most Important Job in the World Is Still the Least Valued*. New York: Metropolitan Books, 2001.

Dart, John. "Hues in the Pews: Racially Mixed Churches an Elusive Goal." *Christian Century* 118, no. 7 (2001): 6–8.

Derricotte, Toi. *Natural Birth: Poems by Toi Derricotte*. Trumansburg, NY: Crossing Press, 1983.

Diamond, Susan L. *Hard Labor*. New York: Tom Doherty Associates, 1996.

DiQuinzio, Patrice. *The Impossibility of Motherhood: Feminism, Individualism, and the Problem of Mothering*. New York: Routledge, 1999.

Eiger, Marvin S., and Sally Wendkos Olds. *The Complete Book of Breastfeeding*. 3rd ed. New York: Workman, 1999.

Elias, Norbert. *The Civilizing Process: The Development of Manners*. New York: Urizen, 1977.

Eugene, Toinette M. "'Swing Low, Sweet Chariot': A Womanist Response to Sexual Violence and Abuse." *Daughters of Sarah* 20 (Summer 1994): 10–14.

Farley, Wendy. *Tragic Vision and Divine Compassion: A Contemporary Theodicy*. Louisville: Westminster/John Knox, 1990.

_____. *The Wounding and Healing of Desire*. Louisville: Westminster John Knox, 2005.

Firestone, Shulamith. *The Dialectic of Sex: The Case for Feminist Revolution*. New York: Morrow, 1970.

Fortune, Marie. *Sexual Violence: The Unmentionable Sin*. New York: Pilgrim, 1983.

Fulkerson, Mary McClintock. *Places of Redemption: Theology for a Worldly Church*. New York: Oxford University Press, 2007.

Galbreath, Paul. *Leading from the Table*. Herndon, VA: Alban Institute, 2008.

Gatens, Moira. *Imaginary Bodies: Ethics, Power, and Corporeality*. London: Routledge, 1996.

Glenn, Evelyn Nakano, Grace Chang, and Linda Rennie Forcey, eds. *Mothering: Ideology, Experience, and Agency*. New York: Routledge, 1994.

Grosz, Elizabeth. *Volatile Bodies: Toward a Corporeal Feminism*. Bloomington: Indiana University Press, 1994.

Hays, Sharon. *The Cultural Contradictions of Motherhood*. New Haven: Yale University Press, 1996.

hooks, bell. *Yearning: race, gender, and cultural politics*. Boston: South End Press, 1990.

Irigaray, Luce. *Je, tu, nous: Toward a Culture of Difference*. Translated by Alison Martin. New York: Routledge, 1993.

_____. *The Sex Which Is Not One*. Translated by Catherine Porter with Carolyn Burke. Ithaca: Cornell University Press, 1985.

_____. *Speculum of the Other Woman*. Translated by Gillian C. Gill. Ithaca: Cornell University Press, 1985.

Jacobs, Sandra, and the American College of Nurse-Midwives. *Having Your Baby with a Nurse-Midwife*. New York: Hyperion, 1993.

Kidd, Sue Monk. *The Secret Life of Bees*. New York: Penguin, 2001.

Kitzinger, Sheila. *Rediscovering Birth*. New York: Pocket, 2000.

Knaster, Miraka. *Discovering the Body's Wisdom: A Comprehensive Guide to More Than Fifty Mind-Body Practices that Can Relieve Pain, Reduce Stress, and Foster Health, Spiritual Growth, and Inner Peace*. New York: Bantam, 1996.

Knowles, Jane Price, and Ellen Cole, eds. *Motherhood: A Feminist Perspective*. New York: Hawthorn, 1990.

La Leche League International. *The Womanly Art of Breastfeeding*. 6th ed. New York: Plume, 1997.

Leslie, Kristin J. *When Violence Is No Stranger: Pastoral Counseling with Survivors of Acquaintance Rape*. Minneapolis: Fortress, 2003.

Levitt, Laura. "Becoming an American Jewish Feminist." Pages 154–64 in *Horizons in Feminist Theology: Identity, Tradition, and Norms*. Edited by Rebecca Chopp and Sheila Greeve Davaney. Minneapolis: Fortress, 1997.

_____. "Speaking Out of the Silence around Rape: A Personal Account." *Fireweed* 41 (Fall 1993), 20–31.

Lewis, Abigail. *An Interesting Condition: The Diary of a Pregnant Woman*. Garden City, NY: Doubleday, 1950.

Long, Charles. *Significations: Signs, Symbols, and Images in the Interpretation of Religion*. Minneapolis: Fortress, 1986.

Long, Thomas G. *Beyond the Worship Wars: Building Vital and Faithful Worship*. [Bethesda, MD]: Alban Institute, 2001.

Lowe, Victor. *Understanding Whitehead*. Baltimore: Johns Hopkins University Press, 1962.

Madigan, Lee, and Nancy C. Gamble. *Society's Continued Betrayal of the Victim*. New York: Lexington Books, 1991.

March, Eugene. "'Biblical Theology,' Authority, and the Presbyterians." *Journal of Presbyterian History* 59, no. 2 (1981): 113–30.

McFague, Sallie. *The Body of God*. Minneapolis: Fortress, 1993.

_____. *Metaphorical Theology: Models of God in Religious Language*. Philadelphia: Fortress, 1982.

_____. *Models of God: Theology for an Ecological, Nuclear Age*. Philadelphia: Fortress, 1987.

Meyers, Diane Tietjens, ed. *Feminist Social Thought: A Reader*. New York: Routledge, 1997.

Miller-McLemore, Bonnie J. *Also a Mother: Work and Family as Theological Dilemma*. Nashville: Abingdon, 1994.

Mosby's Medical Dictionary. 3rd ed. St. Louis: Mosby, 1990.

Nordenberg, Tamar. "Escaping the Prison of a Past Trauma: New Treatment for Post-Traumatic Stress Disorder." *FDA Consumer* 34 (May 2000): 21–26.

Northrup, Christiane. *Women's Bodies, Women's Wisdom: Creating Physical and Emotional Health and Healing*. Rev. ed. New York: Bantam, 1998.

O'Day, Gail. "Excursus: John 6:51c–58 in Critical Scholarship." Pages 605–7 in vol. 9 of *The New Interpreter's Bible*. Edited by Leander E. Keck. 13 vols. Nashville: Abingdon, 1994–2004.

Parrot, Andrea. *Coping with Date Rape and Acquaintance Rape*. New York: Rosen, 1999.

Pauw, Amy Plantinga, and Serene Jones, eds. *Feminist and Womanist Essays in Reformed Dogmatics*. Louisville: Westminster John Knox, 2006.

Poole, Catherine M., and Elizabeth A. Parr. *Choosing a Nurse-Midwife*. New York: John Wiley & Sons, 1994.

Profet, Margie. *Protecting Your Baby-to-Be: A Revolutionary New Look at Pregnancy Sickness*. Reading, MA: Addison-Wesley, 1995.

Presbyterian Hymnal. Louisville: Westminster/John Knox, 1990.

Pseudo-Dionysius. *Mystical Theology*. Pages 96–104 in Harvey Egan, *An Anthology of Christian Mysticism*. Collegeville, MN: Liturgical Press, 1991.

Rich, Adrienne. *Leaflets*. New York: Norton, 1969.

————. *Of Woman Born: Motherhood as Experience and Institution*. New York: Norton, 1976.

————. *Your Native Land, Your Life*. New York: Norton, 1986.

Rigby, Cynthia L. "Exploring Our Hesitation: Feminist Theologies and the Nurture of Children." *Theology Today* 56, no. 4 (2000): 540–54.

Ruddick, Sara. *Maternal Thinking: Toward a Politics of Peace*. Boston: Beacon, 1989.

Schleiermacher, Friedrich. *The Christian Faith*. Edited by H. R. Mackintosh and J. S. Stewart. 2 vols. Repr. New York: Harper & Row, 1963.

Schmidt, Ruth. "After the Fact: To Speak of Rape." *Christian Century* 110, no. 1 (1993): 14–17.

Sernett, Milton C., ed. *Afro-American Religious History: A Documentary Witness*. Durham: Duke University Press, 1987.

Shāntideva. *The Way of the Bodhisattva: A Translation of the Bodhicharyāvatāra*. Translated by the Padmakara Translation Group. Boston: Shambhala, 1997.

Steingraber, Sandra. *Having Faith: An Ecologist's Journey to Motherhood*. Cambridge, MA: Perseus, 2001.

Stewart, Robert Laird. *Sheldon Jackson: Pathfinder and Prospector of the Missionary Vanguard in the Rocky Mountains and Alaska*. Whitefish, MT: Kessinger, 2006.

Suchocki, Marjorie Hewitt. *God, Christ, Church: A Practical Guide to Process Theology*. Rev. ed. New York: Crossroad, 1995.

Thurer, Shari L. *The Myths of Motherhood: How Culture Reinvents the Good Mother*. New York: Houghton Mifflin, 1994.

Tripp, David. "The Image of the Body in the Formative Phases of the Protestant Reformation." Pages 131–52 in *Religion and the Body*. Edited by Sarah Coakley. Cambridge: Cambridge University Press, 1997.

Ulanov, Ann Belford. *Attacked by Poison Ivy: A Psychological Understanding*. York Beach, ME: Nicholas Hays, 2001.

Van Dyk, Leanne, ed. *A More Profound Alleluia: Theology and Worship in Harmony*. Grand Rapids: Eerdmans, 2005.

Waetjen, Herman. *The Gospel of the Beloved Disciple: A Work in Two Editions*. New York: T&T Clark, 2005.

Walker, Michelle Boulous. *Philosophy and the Maternal Body: Reading Silence*. London: Routledge, 1998.

Weedon, Chris. *Feminist Practice and Poststructuralist Theory*. Oxford: Blackwell, 1987.

Welton, Donn, ed. *Body and Flesh: A Philosophical Reader*. Oxford: Blackwell, 1998.

White, James F. *The Sacraments in Protestant Practice and Faith*. Nashville: Abingdon, 1999.

Whitehead, Alfred North. *Adventures of Ideas*. New York: Macmillan, 1933.

————. *The Function of Reason*. Boston: Beacon, 1929.

————. *Modes of Thought*. New York: Free Press, 1938.

————. *Process and Reality: An Essay in Cosmology*. Edited by David Ray Griffin and Donald W. Sherburne. Corrected ed. New York: Free Press, 1978.

————. *Religion in the Making*. Cleveland: World, 1960.

_____. *Science and the Modern World*. New York: Free Press, 1925.

_____. *Symbolism: Its Meaning and Effect*. New York: Fordham University Press, 1927.

Williams, Delores. *Sisters in the Wilderness: The Challenge of Womanist God-Talk*. Maryknoll, NY: Orbis, 1993.

Young, Iris Marion. *On Female Body Experience: "Throwing Like a Girl" and Other Essays*. New York: Oxford University Press, 2005.

Index